THERE SHALL BE NO POOR AMONG YOU

Poverty in the Bible

LESLIE J. HOPPE, O.F.M.

D1430521

Abingdon Press
Nashville

THERE SHALL BE NO POOR AMONG YOU
POVERTY IN THE BIBLE

Copyright © 2004 by Abingdon Press

This book is printed on acid-free paper.

Library of Congress Cataloging-in-Publication Data

Hoppe, Leslie J.
   There shall be no poor among you : poverty in the Bible / Leslie J. Hoppe.
      p. cm.
   Includes bibliographical references.
   ISBN 0-687-00059-9 (perfect binding : adhesive : alk. paper)
   1. Poverty—Biblical teaching. 2. Poor—Biblical teaching. I. Title.

BS680.P47H67   2004
261.8′325—dc22   2004007853

04 05 06 07 08 09 10 11 12 13—10 9 8 7 6 5 4 3 2 1

MANUFACTURED IN THE UNITED STATES OF AMERICA

CONTENTS

ABBREVIATIONS

AB	Anchor Bible
ABD	*Anchor Bible Dictionary*
ANET	*Ancient Near Eastern Texts Relating to the Old Testament,* ed. James B. Pritchard (3rd ed.; Princeton, N.J.: Princeton University Press, 1969)
ATR	*Australasian Theological Review*
b.	Babylonian Talmud
BA	*Biblical Archeologist*
Bib	*Biblica*
CBQ	*Catholic Biblical Quarterly*
DJD	Discoveries in the Judaean Desert
DSSE	G. Vermes, *The Dead Sea Scrolls in English* (Baltimore, Md.: Penguin Books, 1969)
ET	English translation
EvT	*Evangelische Theologie*
ExpTim	*Expository Times*
IDBSup	*Interpreter's Dictionary of the Bible: Supplementary Volume,* ed. K. Crim (Nashville: Abingdon Press, 1976)
IEJ	*Israel Exploration Journal*
Int	*Interpretation*
JBL	*Journal of Biblical Literature*
JNES	*Journal of Near Eastern Studies*
JQR	*Jewish Quarterly Review*
JSOT	*Journal for the Study of the Old Testament*
JSOTSup	Journal for the Study of the Old Testament: Supplement Series
JTS	*Journal of Theological Studies*
JW	Josephus, *The Jewish War*
m.	Mishnah
NAB	New American Bible
NCB	New Century Bible

NEAEHL	*The New Encyclopedia of Archaeological Excavations in the Holy Land*, ed. E. Stern (4 vols.; Jerusalem: Simon & Schuster, 1993)
NJBC	*The New Jerome Biblical Commentary*, ed. R.E. Brown et al. (Englewood Cliffs, N.J.: Prentice-Hall, 1990)
OBT	Overtures to Biblical Theology
OTL	Old Testament Library
OTP	*The Old Testament Pseudepigrapha*, ed. James H. Charlesworth (2 vols.; Garden City, N.Y.: Doubleday, 1983, 1985)
RQ	*Römische Quartalschrift für christliche Altertumskunde und Kirchengeschichte*
RSV	Revised Standard Version
SBL	Society of Biblical Literature
SBLDS	Society of Biblical Literature Dissertation Series
ScrHier	Scripta hierosolymitana
TDNT	*Theological Dictionary of the New Testament*, ed. G. Kittel and G. Friedrich (trans. G. W. Bromiley; 10 vols.; Grand Rapids, Mich.: Eerdmans, 1964–1976)
VTSup	Supplements to Vetus Testamentum
WBC	Word Biblical Commentary
ZAW	*Zeitschrift für die alttestamentliche Wissenschaft*
ZNW	*Zeitschrift für die neutestamentliche Wissenschaft und die Kunde der älteren Kirche*

PRONUNCIATION OF HEBREW WORDS

This book represents Hebrew words with an academic system that may be unfamiliar to some readers. Vowels in this system can be long (e.g., *ā*), short (e.g., *a*), and half (e.g., *ŏ* and *ᵉ*). Hebrew has two gutteral consonants (ʿ and ʾ), for which there are no English equivalents. Other Hebrew consonants you will encounter are *ṣ* (pronounced ts or tz), *ś* (pronounced s), *š* (pronounced sh), *ḥ* (pronounced like the ch in Bach), and *w* (pronounced v).

INTRODUCTION

This book deals with motifs that occur throughout the Bible: the poor and poverty. Its purpose is to determine how the Bible can help individual believers and communities of faith shape their response to the poor and poverty today. One assumption behind this study is that the Bible can indeed tell us something important not only about spiritual concerns but material concerns as well. But anyone who begins to study what the Bible says about these motifs will notice that there is a wide variety of affirmations made about poverty in the Bible. For example, sometimes the Bible speaks of poverty as a curse: "My child, do not lead the life of a beggar; it is better to die than to beg. When one looks to the table of another, one's way of life cannot be considered a life" (Sir 40:28-29). Other texts assert that it is a blessing: "Blessed are you who are poor, for yours is the kingdom of God" (Luke 6:20). Sometimes the text is concerned exclusively about material poverty; other times poverty becomes a metaphor for another reality. The approach taken here is to describe the variety of ways the books that make up the Bible deal with the poor.

Obviously the biblical texts that speak about the poor cannot be detached from their historical, political, and economic backgrounds without the very real danger of misunderstanding. For example, it makes quite a bit of difference whether the poor are spoken of by the wealthy or by the poor themselves. It matters very much whether "Blessed are you who are poor" was said by someone who was poor himself. In other words, it is important to know what was being said to whom and by whom. Before a study of the motif of poverty in the Bible can begin, it is also necessary to set this discussion in the context of the economy of ancient Israel and Roman Palestine. Without a grounding in socioeconomic reality, the poor of the Bible become nothing more than literary symbols of an attitude of dependence upon God and the Bible's concern for them becomes detached from the existential situation of economic need and social injustice. While spiritualizing the texts that deal with poverty may be a legitimate way of appropriating such texts by believers today, the Bible must not become a caricature of itself so that its concern for the poor and for justice becomes muted by a narrow focus on "spiritual poverty." It is necessary, then, to begin a study of the poor and poverty in the Bible by examining the economic structures of ancient Israel and Roman Palestine.

The Economy of Ancient Israel

Ancient Israel's economy was based on agriculture. Ideally each Israelite family was to have a plot of land on which to grow crops and raise livestock that would provide that family with food and clothing. Most Israelites were subsistence farmers who were able to grow just enough crops to feed their families and livestock, to provide seed grain for the next growing season, and to offer tithes and sacrifices, which were intended to secure the blessing of fertility from God. Farming in Israel, however, was not a simple matter. The land was fertile enough, though rocky. Villagers who lived in the central highlands had to terrace the hills to make the land serviceable for the growing of crops. This, of course, was very labor intensive. The coastal plain was much more desirable, but for most of Israel's history most of that land—especially in the south—was controlled by Philistine city-states. The more serious challenge for Israelite farmers was the availability of water. Israel was not blessed with a river system like Egypt and Mesopotamia. The Nile in Egypt and the Tigris and Euphrates in Mesopotamia made large-scale irrigation possible. But this was not the case in Israel. The moisture that made its land fertile had to come as rain. In years when rainfall was not sufficient, the Israelite farmer faced the real danger of famine, for subsistence farming did not produce surpluses that could see a farmer through a difficult year. Lack of sufficient rain put the Israelite farmer in great peril. Other threats to productivity included injury or sickness that prevented farmers from working their fields and poor planning or lack of industry that kept the land from yielding its full potential. To minimize the effects of such misfortunes, the Israelites worked the land in extended families. Despite these efforts, agricultural yields were generally low.

The challenges to the Israelite farmer came not only from the land and climate but more so from the social and economic structures of Canaan. The early Israelites withdrew their allegiance from the political and economic system of Late Bronze Age Canaan. The governments of the Canaanite city-states supported themselves by taxing the peasants. These taxes took the form of payment in kind and conscripted labor. When peasants were forced to work on the projects of the state or serve in the military, they were unable to work their land. Requiring peasants to hand over a portion of their harvest to the state also was a severe burden since, as subsistence farmers, they did not produce the type of surpluses that made the payment of taxes possible without causing severe hardships. Circumstances sometimes made it impossible for some peasants to pay their taxes. They became debtors who had to sell their children into slavery and, in some cases, sell their land to satisfy their creditors. Without land, the peasants had no access to the means of production and were reduced to poverty. The city-states of Canaan, then, were responsible for the creation of poverty among their citizens.

The religion of ancient Canaan supplied a theological support for the political and social system that deprived the peasants of a portion of their produce and, at times, drove them into poverty. The gods of Canaan sustained the political, social, and economic status quo, while the God of ancient Israel took the side of the peasants against the rulers who oppressed them. The Israelite peasants considered the land that they worked to be a gift of this God. It was to be a perpetual inheritance passed on to one's descendants to ensure their well-being. It was not the property of the king that the peasant worked for the benefit of the state. The Israelites offered their allegiance and their tithes to a nonhuman Lord who freed them from state-sponsored oppression.

The Israelite tribes that emerged in the central highlands of Canaan during the thirteenth and twelfth centuries BCE were free to keep the fruits of their labor because there was no imperial power demanding tribute and the Israelite national states had not yet developed. Of course, Israelite farmers did have to contend with raids. The book of Judges, for example, describes raids by the Midianites (Judg 6:1-6). The effects of these raids were so serious that they threatened Israel's continued existence in the central highlands. To provide for defense against such raids, the ancient Israelites developed associations such as clans and tribes. While these associations did provide an adequate response to raids, they did not undermine the freedom of the Israelite peasants.

In early Israelite society, it was the community—the extended family and clan—that protected the rights of individual Israelite peasants to work their land for the benefit of their families. The elders of the extended families and clans provided the leadership that made possible the efficient use of available resources, the allocation of land, and the settling of disputes. This political system allowed Israelite peasants to keep the products of their labor and to work together cooperatively for the benefit of the entire community.

The social, political, and economic system of early Israel was possible because Egypt, which had controlled the economy of Canaan for three hundred years, was experiencing a decline that made continued domination of Canaan impossible. The Canaanite city-states that were simply satellites in the Egyptian system wore themselves out in internecine conflicts. The early Israelites then benefited from these circumstances and had a flourishing, decentralized economic system that was able to maintain itself without a state structure for about two hundred years. It was during these two hundred years that Israel developed the systems to maintain its decentralized economy. Among these was a political structure that made possible cooperation among the extended families and clans without requiring a centralized state system, which the early Israelites experienced as oppressive. Another one of these structures was a religious identity that flowed from the early Israelite political and economic system. Early Israel worshiped a God who opposed oppressive political structures, who gave the peasants the land necessary for their survival, and who blessed that land with fertility.

Of course, early Israel was not without its problems. There were conflicts among the Israelites tribes, some of them very serious (see Judg 19–21). Also, there were some Israelites who did not see the worship of Baal as incompatible with the worship of Yahweh. While the latter was responsible for freeing the Israelites from their oppressive masters and giving them the land that was their support, many believed that it was Baal who provided the rain that made the land fertile. Still, despite these problems, early Israel developed social mechanisms, a political system, and a religious identity that made it possible to have a flourishing society in the central highlands of Canaan.

External and internal pressures in the middle of the eleventh century BCE brought about dramatic changes in ancient Israel's political and economic system. Canaan in the thirteenth to the eleventh centuries BCE witnessed its share of social unrest. The Israelite presence in the sparsely populated and agriculturally unattractive central highlands was relatively secure. But the situation changed dramatically in the middle of the eleventh century. At that time the Philistines, who had gained a foothold along the southern coastal plain, began to expand toward the north and east into areas settled by the Israelites. The Philistines constituted a serious and sustained threat to the Israelite tribes. Some Israelites believed that a king with a standing army was necessary to successfully stand up to the threat posed by the Philistines.

Another source of pressure for the establishment of an Israelite monarchy and the social and political structures that would accompany it came from those Israelite families whose prosperity was greater than those of other families. These more prosperous families supported a social structure that would preserve their economic gains. A monarchy with its hierarchical social structure provided just what they were looking for. The monarchy taxed its subjects and those who could least afford to pay these taxes were at the mercy of the more successful. This led to the development of creditor-debtor relationships and the growth of a permanent debtor class: the poor. This is reflected in Samuel's warning about the economic disadvantages of the monarchy for the Israelite peasant (see 1 Sam 8:10-18) and the description of Solomon's taxation districts (1 Kgs 4:7-19).

With the establishment of the monarchy, the earlier notions of every Israelite's access to the means of production changed. The land was not seen as God's gift to Israel but as the king's possession. The peasants were able to live on the land as long as they were able to pay their taxes. Creditors offered assistance to those who were unable to pay. Very often, however, debtors lost their land to their creditors because of high taxes, exorbitant interest rates, and a corrupt political and judicial system. There were no controls—no safety nets—on borrowing and lending. Lenders could charge any interest rate they chose and could call in debts whenever they liked. Borrowers were at a distinct disadvantage. Circumstances such as war, drought, and illness could send families into a cycle of debt from which they could not escape. Because lending was unregulated, the system tended to favor the exploitation of the poor.

The prophets decried this system because of its blatant, state-administered injustice. For example, Isaiah aimed his words of judgment against those "who join house to house, who add field to field, until there is room for no one but you" (Isa 5:8). The small family holdings characteristic of early Israel were replaced by the large estates of the wealthy. The effect of this was not only to deprive Israelite peasants of their land but also to drive them deeper into poverty. The main crops grown on family plots were grains. Bread, supplemented by vegetables in season, was the staple of the peasants' diet. The estates of the wealthy, however, devoted much of their land to the cultivation of grapes and olives. Wine and olive oil were export crops that brought a good price. With less land devoted to the production of cereals, grain prices rose. This put added pressure on those without land, driving them deeper into debt, which helped create a permanent debtor class in Israel. Poverty, then, was a deliberate creation of the people of means who wished to preserve and, if possible, enhance their economic power by increasing their holdings. But the cost of their prosperity was paid for by the peasants.

The ideology of the monarchy in the ancient Near East presented the king as the protector of the poor and the promoter of justice. Of course, the realities of maintaining a monarchy made attaining this ideal impossible since the economic support needed to preserve the monarchy is precisely what engendered social inequities that created poverty. Eliminating poverty and ensuring social justice would be tantamount to suicide for the monarchic system. While there were some attempts at reform, they were too limited in scope and duration to have any appreciable effect at altering an economic system that the monarchy needed to survive.

There was a very serious deterioration of the peasants' economic situation when the kingdom of Judah became a vassal state of the Assyrian, Egyptian, and Babylonian empires in succession beginning in the eighth century BCE. It was Judah's peasantry that had to bear the economic burdens of vassalage. They supplied the goods and the labor that were required to pay the indemnity owed to the empires by the Judahite state. The peasants had to support two monarchies. The result was that even more were driven into the permanent underclass that the Bible terms the "poor" and the "oppressed." The increased levels of taxation naturally led to increased levels of indebtedness.

Judah's political system underwent a striking change following an unsuccessful attempt to end Babylonian hegemony. After a two-year siege, Jerusalem fell to the Babylonians in 587 BCE. The Judahite state ceased to exist and its territory was absorbed into the Babylonian provincial system. The king and the elite of Judah were taken as exiles to Babylon while the peasants, for the most part, remained on the land. The conditions under which the Judahite peasants lived are not known for certain. Though they were no longer responsible for maintaining Judah's monarchic economy and though they were free from the debts owed to Judah's elite, the peasants' economic status probably did not improve appreciably. One by-product of the uprisings against the Babylonians was severe damage to Judah's agricultural infrastructure, preventing any improvement of the peasants' lot.

With the fall of Babylon to the Persians, the exiles from Judah were allowed to return. The Judahite native dynasty and national state, however, were not restored. Judah was a small subprovince of the Persian Empire, and was required to pay tribute to the empire. The economy of Judah eventually was controlled by the elites who returned from exile. Taxes and loans were reintroduced. Debtors and creditors reappeared, with the gap between the two growing so wide that elements of Jewish society gave up on this world as a place where justice would eventually triumph. They began looking toward another world. There would be a reversal of fortunes in this new world so that those at the bottom of the economic ladder would find themselves on the top.

A Jewish monarchy was established following the successful revolt of the Maccabees against the Greeks (167–164 BCE), who replaced the Persians as the masters of the Levant. The first effect of the Maccabees' success was freeing the people of Judah from the requirement of paying tribute to the Greeks. Unfortunately, the kings of the Hasmonean dynasty soon put into place a taxation system that was every bit as burdensome as that of the Greeks. In addition, the wealth created by the Hasmonean control of commerce in the region enriched the elites while the peasants remained as poor as they were under foreign domination. When the Romans ended the independence of the Hasmonean kingdom, the burden of taxation and debt grew enormously, helping to spark two unsuccessful revolts against Roman rule.

The Economy of Roman Palestine

The Roman economic system benefited from the production of goods and services by slaves. While Roman slavery was not widespread in the territory of the former Israelite kingdoms, which the Romans called "Palestine," the formidable power of the Roman Empire was sustained by the productivity of its slaves. Rome burdened the people of Palestine with heavy taxes. Jewish peasants had to pay between 30 and 40 percent of their income as taxes. A sizeable portion of this tax burden was collected through agents whose livelihood depended on meeting quotas set by Roman authorities. Still, the major portion of Palestine's wealth was channeled through the temple, whose priests collected taxes for themselves and for the Romans. The Jews of Palestine hated the Romans because they saw their wealth going to the empire, though the intensity of the opposition to Rome varied. The priests were coopted by the Romans and were the least likely to support a revolution. Shopkeepers and artisans formed the core of the Pharisaic movement. They were not overburdened by Roman taxation. It was the peasant farmers and laborers who suffered most under Roman occupation. They saw their meager earnings disappear into the Roman coffers and were, therefore, among the most eager to rise up against the empire.

Both the Roman authorities and their priestly collaborators saw in Jesus someone who could ignite the anger of the Jewish peasants into open revolution. Apparently the bulk of those who resonated with Jesus' message were those Jews who were being taxed into poverty. The priests identified Jesus as a threat to their temple-based economy. They and the Romans did not hesitate to eliminate Jesus, whom they regarded as posing a serious challenge to the economic and political status quo. Eventually the Jews of Palestine did revolt against Rome, and among the revolutionaries were those who wanted to return to an economy similar to that of the Israelite tribes of the thirteenth to the eleventh centuries BCE. But they were unable to dislodge the Romans and were forced to survive as best they could after the fall of Jerusalem in 70 CE.

The first Christian communities lived in a money economy. One characteristic of such an economy is the huge difference between the rich and the poor. The rich seek to maximize their profits to amass greater wealth. This makes poverty inevitable since the supply of money is, of course, limited. Some of the poor—farmers, artisans, merchants—were able to eke out an existence that allowed them to survive, but without the kind of surpluses that make it possible to amass wealth. But there were other poor who could survive only by begging. The apostle Paul, more than any other New Testament author, addressed the problems created by the money economy as he asserted that greater gains should not be the goal of the Christian in such an economy. The authentic Christian will not amass wealth but share it. Rather than treating money as a commodity that they need to gather for themselves, Christians were to consider money something they ought to give to their brothers and sisters in need.

Jerusalem in the first century CE was a city of people dependent on charity. Legislation regarding the second tithe, which had to be spent in that city, provided for the needs of its Jewish inhabitants.[1] Well-off Jewish Christians provided for members of their community who were poor (Acts 4:34-35), but their resources eventually were not sufficient, so Paul began collecting for the poor of Jerusalem from other Christian communities (e.g., Acts 11:29-30). Many of the city's poor were deeply in debt, so that when the First Revolt against Rome began in Jerusalem, records of debts were burned to free the poor from their burdens (JW 2.426-27).

The Bible was produced by people for whom the struggle over the economy of the ancient world was a matter of their very survival. The Bible, then, will reflect this struggle not only in its content but also in its very formation. The process of canonizing a group of ancient texts and regarding them as authoritative when Judah did not enjoy political independence was an act of resistance that rejected foreign political and economic domination. It held up the ideal of a community-based economic system based on mutual support and equal access to the means of production. It demanded that social interaction be based on justice and equity and condemned all economic exploitation as an affront to the divine will.

But those responsible for assembling the ancient texts and committing ancient tradition to writing did not all come from the same social and economic group. The leadership of the Jewish community did not want to imperil their privileged position in the community by seeming to support rebellion. There were others who wanted to eliminate the privileges of the priests and reestablish a community of equals. The Torah affirmed the special status of the priests within the community while the words of judgment found in the prophetic books were preserved as a warning to the leadership of the community. The canon reflects not only the theological diversity of the early Jewish community but also the conflicting social and economic ideologies of the groups that made up this community. The Bible, then, offers different perspectives on social and economic questions. It is not a charter for social revolution nor is it simply a theological justification for the status quo.

The Jewish community of Palestine had little choice but to accept the social and economic system imposed by the Persian, Greek, and Roman empires. Still, the Bible preserves the ideals of a community that gave all equal access to the means of production. It condemns economic exploitation and social injustice. But because the empires continued their domination, those who preserved the religious traditions of ancient Israel concluded that this world would not witness the inevitable triumph of justice. At the same time, however, the Bible served to move people to struggle against all forms of injustice while waiting for God to establish that new world of justice.

While it is important to understand the basic contours of the economy in the biblical period, for the Bible the term "poor" embraces not merely the economic but also social and political orders. The ownership of land, political influence, and social status all made a person rich, while the poor were those who lacked these. This lack made the poor vulnerable to exploitation by people of means and placed them on the margins of their society. In the Hebrew Bible, the word *'ebyôn* refers to people who were destitute. The Greek word *ptōchos* serves the same purpose. But Hebrew also uses words for "poor" such as *'ānî* and *'ānāw* that imply vulnerability to oppression more than destitution. The biblical view of the poor, of course, centers on their economic deprivation but it embraces much more. For this reason, the biblical response to poverty is not merely charity but justice.

The Vocabulary of Poverty

The Hebrew Bible has an unusually extensive vocabulary to speak about the poor. Its various books use at least nine terms, each with a specific connotation, while the New Testament has a less extensive vocabulary.[2] One aim of this study is to look at every text in the Bible in which a word having "the poor" in its semantic field appears; however, this book does not follow the classic "word-study" approach. Focusing only on texts in which the word "poor" appears can lead to shortsighted conclusions. For example, the vocabulary of the poor is notably absent from the Former Prophets (Joshua to 2 Kings). This has led some to conclude that the issue of poverty was relatively unimportant in these books.[3] But social conflict is one of the engines that drives the story of Israel in the land as found in the Former Prophets, and certainly one by-product of social conflict is poverty.

The bulk of this study focuses on texts from the Hebrew Bible. That should not be surprising since the bulk of the Christian Bible is concerned with these scriptures. In addition to canonical texts, the book contains references to the apocryphal or deuterocanonical books, and to intertestamental and rabbinic texts. The intertestamental literature has been included to give a fuller picture of the religious and social situation that was characteristic of the time of Jesus' ministry and the emergence of the church. The rabbinic material gives an idea of how a community of faith that was another heir to traditions found in the Hebrew Bible appropriated and reinterpreted those traditions.

Hearing the Scriptures

A basic assumption that colors this study is that "the poor" belong on the agenda of the community of faith. It is clear enough that ancient Israel, early Judaism, Jesus, the first Christians, and the rabbis did not forget the poor. If believers today wish to be faithful to their biblical heritage, neither can they. Of course, readers should have no illusions about the "objectivity" of this study. No method is objective. The interpreter's experience and perspectives will color the analysis of the biblical material. Readers ought to become actively engaged in direct conversation with the texts under study here. Sometimes biblical texts are quoted in full but most often they are simply cited with the appropriate reference. Readers ought to look up these references and study these texts, using this book as a way to enter into dialogue with the Bible on their own. The readers' experience may lead them to a different understanding of a particular text than the one presented by the author. One "objective" standard for authentic interpretation is to ask questions like the following: Has my understanding of this text given new direction to my conversion? Has it contributed to the vitality of the community of faith? Has it reshaped not only my attitudes but also my actions? Has it led to a deepening of my life of prayer?

CHAPTER ONE

THE TORAH

If one confines the study of how the Torah deals with the poor by focusing only on the words for "poor" mentioned in its five books, the results will give an incomplete picture. Various Hebrew words that can be translated as "poor" or "needy" occur only fifteen times in the Torah, yet the poor are much more of a central concern to "the books of Moses" than that statistic indicates. First, the narratives of the Torah include stories of how people of means often use their status as an advantage in their dealings with those whose economic situation is precarious. The effect of these stories is to demonstrate that poverty and oppression do not just happen. They are the result of deliberate decisions that the people of means make. Poverty and oppression, then, are not impersonal forces that are endemic to economic structures. They are human creations. Second, the legal traditions not only serve to delineate the rights of the poor, but they also regulate how the more successful Israelites are to deal with those on the margins of the ancient Israelite economy. The laws attempt to prevent a permanent economic and social underclass in ancient Israelite society.

The Deuteronomic Credo (Deut 26:5-10)

Gerhard von Rad suggested that the origins of the first six books of the Bible (Genesis to Joshua) in their present form were to be found in the confession of faith that an Israelite farmer was to make as he presented the firstfruits of his harvest in the temple (Deut 26:5-10). According to von Rad's hypothesis this prayer was composed in the early period of the judges and served as the form-critical nucleus of the books from Genesis to Joshua.[1] The narratives that begin in Genesis and extend through the book of Joshua are the result of an extraordinarily complex expansion of the credo of Deut 26. Though von Rad's thesis has proven to be untenable, it is important for this study to recognize that the

Deuteronomic confession of faith focuses on the poverty of the Hebrew slaves in Egypt. Verse 6 may be translated as "The Egyptians treated us harshly, made us *poor*, and imposed hard labor upon us" and the following verse asserts that "the LORD heard our voice, and saw our *poverty*."

The Deuteronomic text is similar to another "historical" summary found in Num 20:14-21. The text from Numbers tells the story of the Israelites and the king of Edom, from whom Moses asked safe passage. The summary from Numbers, which is earlier than that of Deuteronomy, does not explicitly mention the impoverishment of the Hebrew slaves. The liberation of the Hebrew slaves from bondage in Egypt, then, came to be understood as deliverance from poverty by the Deuteronomic tradition. The gift of the land was the means to make this deliverance permanent. The Deuteronomic confession acknowledges the God of Israel to be the liberator who led the poor to freedom and prosperity in "a land flowing with milk and honey" (Deut 26:9).

In presenting the story of the Hebrew slaves as a deliverance from poverty, the Deuteronomic confession makes three important assertions. First, it presents the poverty of the Hebrews in Egypt as a consequence of a decision by the Egyptians to enslave the Hebrews. Poverty, then, was not some "natural" condition; it was the result of conscious decisions that the Egyptians made. Second, God does not tolerate the oppression of the poor. God heard the cries of the oppressed Hebrew slaves. Poverty ought not to be understood as a condition that places one in a closer relationship with God but as a condition that God will not tolerate. God takes the side of the poor against their oppressors because God did not intend people to be poor. Third, God gives the impoverished Hebrew slaves a fertile land to ensure that their impoverishment will not be a permanent state. Without this gift, the liberation of the Hebrew slaves would have been only a temporary measure. Eventually they would have been forced back into slavery in order to survive. The gift of the land makes it possible to break the cycle of poverty by enabling the Hebrew slaves to support themselves through their work. These three assertions form the core of the biblical approach to poverty and the poor.

The Narratives

The Patriarchal Narratives

While the bulk of the Torah is the result of codifying ancient Israel's legal traditions, the Torah also contains stories about ancient Israel's ancestors.

These stories reflect the values of those who composed and transmitted them and helped shape the values of those who first heard or read them. The narratives in the Torah, then, provide valuable insight into ancient Israel's attitudes toward the poor.

The stories of the patriarchs (Gen 12–50) portray ancient Israel's ancestors as people of means. Abraham was a wealthy man, "very rich in livestock, in silver, and in gold" (Gen 13:2), with a retinue of slaves to serve him (see Gen 17:23). He had the resources to engage in a war with four kings (see Gen 14:1-24). But stories about Abraham's family life illustrated the challenges faced by those who, like the poor, found themselves on the margins of ancient Israelite society.

As much as Jewish tradition came to revere Abraham, the Torah candidly tells the story of how Abraham ignored his responsibilities to those who were economically dependent on him. When Sarah, Abraham's wife, was unable to conceive, she suggested that he take Hagar, her Egyptian slave, as a secondary wife. Abraham could then have children with her. When Hagar became pregnant, tension developed between her and Sarah. Abraham allowed Sarah to settle the matter. She so mistreated Hagar that the slave ran away even though she was pregnant. But God heard Hagar's lament and assured her that she was to bear a son and that her descendants would be too numerous to count (Gen 16:1-12). With this assurance, Hagar returned to Abraham's camp and bore Abraham a son whom he named Ishmael. Some years later, after Sarah herself gave Abraham a son named Isaac, the tensions between Sarah and Hagar resurfaced. Sarah wanted her son to be Abraham's sole heir so she engineered a second expulsion. Abraham acceded to Sarah's wishes and sent Hagar and her son off into the desert with a little bread and water. Again, God heard Hagar's cries as she and her child were dying of thirst. God showed Hagar a well, and she and the boy survived (Gen 21:1-19). Twice the mother of the Ishmaelites cried out because of the oppression that she experienced at the hands of the mother of the Israelites. Each time God heard and responded. Oppression, no matter who the perpetrator and who the victim, is never ignored by God.

Abraham's son Isaac was a very wealthy man like his father (Gen 26:13), but circumstances in the early adult life of Jacob, Isaac's son, made Jacob an economically dependent person. After managing to secure the birthright and blessing that belonged to his elder brother Esau, Jacob became a refugee, fleeing from Esau's anger. Their mother and Jacob's coconspirator, Rebecca, sent him off to her brother Laban in Haran (Gen 27:43). Jacob worked as a shepherd for Laban for seven years. At the end of that time, Laban was to allow his daughter Rachel to marry Jacob. Instead of fulfilling this agreement, Laban gave Jacob his elder daughter Leah. Jacob was forced to work another seven years for Rachel as well. When Jacob decided to end his stay with his father-in-law, Rachel took the images of her family's household gods.[2] When Laban confronted Jacob with the theft, Jacob justified Rachel's actions. He complained that Laban gave him nothing for all his work, but that God had seen his plight (Gen 31:17-42).

The story illustrates how people of means like Laban had to be compelled to give what was justly due to those who were economically dependent on them. If Laban had had his way, Jacob would have received no compensation for his years in Laban's service. A great injustice perpetrated by the wealthy is depriving the poor of what is rightfully theirs. Laban represents the people whose wealth is created for them by their servants and their tenants, who enjoy nothing of the wealth that their work produced. Despite Laban's miserliness and injustice, Jacob eventually became a wealthy man (see Gen 32:14-16).

Another narrative illustrating how some people have to be compelled to give justice is the story of Tamar and Judah. Tamar was married to Er, one of Judah's sons. After his death, she married Onan, Er's brother. Children of that union would be considered as though they were Er's. But Onan's untimely death was considered a judgment on his unwillingness to fulfill his duty to his deceased brother. Judah refused to allow a third son to marry Tamar and he sent her back to her father. But she had no claim on her father for support. Judah's family was obligated to support her. Tamar concocted a scheme to force Judah to give her justice and Judah fell into her trap. In the end, Judah recognized his fault and received Tamar into his household (Gen 38).

Among the most well-developed narratives in the Bible illustrating God's vindication of the oppressed is the Joseph story (Gen 37; 39–50). Pride, jealousy, and mistrust all contributed to the animosity that Jacob's ten sons had for their brother Joseph, the son of Rachel, Jacob's favorite wife. The brothers succeeded in convincing Jacob that Joseph had been killed by a wild animal. Actually they had sold him into slavery. The scion of a family that had been wealthy for generations had to face life as a slave. Without his family's wealth to protect him, Joseph experienced the life that the poor were forced to live. Eventually Joseph was sent to prison by his master because of trumped-up charges brought by his master's wife after Joseph spurned her sexual advances (Gen 39:6-20). The wealthy can lie with impunity, for who would take the word of a slave against his master? However, by a marvelous series of events, Joseph was not only freed from prison, but also rose to a position in Egypt second only to that of the pharaoh. Joseph acknowledged God's hand in these events when he named his son Ephraim: "God has made me fruitful in the land of my misfortunes" (Gen 41:52).[3] Again, God took the side of one who was treated unjustly. The Joseph story paints a positive picture of a wealthy and powerful man using that power for the sake of those in need. Without prejudice, he provides food for all those who come to him in their need. His experience as a slave and a prisoner made Joseph especially attuned to the voice of the poor.

A common thread in the patriarchal narratives is that people of means and people with power create "poverty." They will expel an unwanted slave, defraud, withhold wages, enslave the free, falsely accuse, and otherwise fail to meet their obligations to give justice. Poverty, then, does not just happen. It is a creation of the wealthy who, for a variety of reasons, choose to oppress those in their power. What is most surprising is that the guilty parties in most of these stories are the revered ancestors of the Israelites. Not surprising, however, is that God takes the side of the oppressed and poor, ensuring that they have justice done to them despite the intentions of their wealthy and powerful oppressors. While von Rad may have been mistaken about the date of the Deuteronomic credo, he was right in regarding this text as expressing the essence of the ancient Israelite understanding of God's actions on Israel's behalf.

Moses and the Exodus

Of course, the most important of the Torah's narratives are those about Moses and the Exodus. The descendants of the free and wealthy patriarchs are reduced to slavery and poverty by the Egyptians. The story of the liberation of the Hebrew slaves should have taught the people of ancient Israel that God takes the side of the poor against those who cause their oppression.[4] That story begins, of course, with the accession of a "new king . . . who did not know Joseph" (Exod 1:8). The new pharaoh decided to enslave the Hebrews because they posed a threat to the Egyptians. The impoverishment of the Israelites, then, was the result of the fear of the Egyptian upper classes. The Israelites were vulnerable because they were aliens in Egyptian society. Those with political and economic power in Egypt wished to preserve their position of dominance by diluting the strength of those below, so they forced the Israelites into slavery and carefully controlled their birth rate by having male children thrown into the Nile (Exod 1:8-21). Of course, the Egyptians did not react to the threat they perceived from the Israelites in an unprecedented way. This is precisely how members of the upper class in societies act when they see their position threatened by those whom they consider their inferiors. They use their economic, social, political, and sometimes military power to maintain their position. Poverty and oppression, then, are human inventions.

Every oppressed and impoverished group can identify with the story of the Hebrew slaves. Their oppression was the result of a conscious decision of the upper classes to preserve their position of power in society. This was the purpose of Jim Crow laws in the South and the anti-union practices of industrialists in the North. It is the reason for the conflict between the government and the indigenous population of Chiapas, Mexico. One important difference between the biblical story and current situations is that today the conflict between the rich and the poor takes place on a global stage between the northern and southern hemispheres. The people of the United States and the European Union can maintain their lifestyles only because of the economic and political power they wield over the still developing nations in the southern hemisphere. The wealth of the North is maintained by the poverty of the South.

That poverty is the result of decisions made by human beings is underscored as the story of the Hebrew slaves continues. Exodus 5 describes the initial negotiations by means of which Moses sought to give the Israelites some measure of freedom. When confronted by the just demands of the Hebrews for their freedom, Pharaoh refused to listen. He made the oppression even worse (vv. 7-9). The Exodus story, then, does not regard the poverty of the Israelites as deserved. It is not their fate nor is it the will of God. The social and political system, represented by Pharaoh, decreed and maintained the wretched state of the Hebrew slaves.

The heart of the Exodus story is God's liberation of the Hebrew slaves. It is important to note, however, the radical nature of the solution to the problems caused by the Egyptian oppression of the Israelites. The solution is not merely to ameliorate their situation. God's solution is not simply to lead the Egyptians to be more benevolent to their Hebrew slaves in order to ease the pressure from the slaves for their liberation. God effects a complete breakdown of the Egyptian economic system built on slave labor by leading the Israelites out of Egypt. In other words, God does not come to the aid of the Israelites *in* Egypt; rather, God removes the Israelites *from* Egypt. There is no attempt to "reform the system." A political and economic system that so impoverishes people is beyond reform. There is really no possibility of successful negotiations with the Egyptians who, of course, want to maintain the status quo. The only alternative is to remove the Israelites from the Egyptian economic system entirely.

Acts of kindness by individual Egyptians would not solve the problem created by Pharaoh's impoverishment and enslavement of the Israelites, since the Egyptian economic system had become accustomed to being supported by the labor of the Israelites. While the action of Pharaoh's daughter in adopting the infant Moses is commendable, this single benevolence can have no real effect on the fate of the many thousands of Hebrews living in poverty and slavery (Exod 2:1-7). Given the enormity of the problem, isolated, individual acts of kindness were not even a good palliative. Similarly, acts of resistance by individual Israelites also proved to be inadequate to the task of ending the oppression of the Hebrew slaves. For example, when Moses saw an Egyptian abusing a slave, he killed the oppressor. The reaction of the Israelites to Moses' act was predictable. They had become so terrified of the Egyptians that they regarded Moses' action as dangerous. Moses had to flee Egypt (Exod 2:11-15) and nothing changed for the Israelites. As noted above, the negotiations with Pharaoh to improve the lot of the Israelites were futile (Exod 5:1-9). It was obvious that the system was beyond reform since the system was based on the maintenance of injustice.

The episode of the plagues (Exod 7:8–11:10) shows how irredeemable the system that kept the Israelites impoverished and enslaved really was. As one disaster after another befalls the Egyptians, Pharaoh is adamant in his refusal to free the Israelites. Though the Egyptian economy and society suffer, Pharaoh's "heart was hardened." He was so attached to a system that exploited and oppressed the Hebrew slaves that he could not conceive of the Egyptian economy without them. The disasters that befell the Egyptian economy because of the plagues did not move Pharaoh to free the Hebrew slaves. The system was beyond reform; it had to be destroyed. Ironically, Pharaoh was the instrument of that destruction. In the end, Pharaoh was compelled to let the Hebrew slaves go. God brought the oppressive Egyptian system to an end.

This solution was so novel, so radical, that the Israelites themselves were unable to grasp its significance. An important motif in the Exodus story is the murmuring in the wilderness (e.g., Exod 14:10-12). Despite their suffering under the Egyptian economic system, the Israelites wanted to go back almost immediately after they began their uncharted trek to the "promised land." The slaves had become so accustomed to their oppression that they could not cope with freedom. The former Hebrew slaves found it difficult to accept their freedom and wanted to return to Egypt and to slavery. This is a dramatic demonstration of the system's power. Not only was Pharaoh unable to imagine Egypt without the Hebrew slaves, the Hebrew slaves were unable to imagine life outside of Egypt in spite of the misery that life there brought them.

It is little wonder, then, that the Bible presents the liberation of the Israelites from slavery and poverty in Egypt as a miracle. God accomplishes that liberation "with a mighty hand and an outstretched arm, with a terrifying display of power, and with signs and wonders" (Deut 26:8a). To complete this act of liberation, God led the Israelites through the wilderness and gave them "a land flowing with milk and honey" (Deut 26:9). God leads the Israelites into a new place—a place of unparalleled prosperity—in order to create a new economic and social order. In this new order there was to be no poor among the Israelites (Deut 15:4). God's acts to save the Israelites do not merely result in the amelioration of their condition nor in a reformation of the Egyptian economic system. God's actions lead to the creation of a new society in which poverty and slavery were not to exist. The liberated slaves were to constitute a new society. The precise contours of that new society are given in the legislation that makes up the bulk of the Torah.

Moses, as an individual, became the paradigm for the oppressed. He was raised by Pharaoh's daughter, but his concern for the Hebrew slaves aroused the anger of Pharaoh and Moses had to flee to Midian, where he became a simple shepherd (Exod 2:5-22). Later, after leading the Hebrews from Egypt, Moses was confronted by members of his own family because he married a woman from Ethiopia (Num 12:1-9). Moses did not respond to the criticism. God defended him. The text comments that Moses was "humble" (v. 3). The Hebrew word that is translated as "humble" is *ʿānāw*, which is derived from the verb *ʿānâ* ("to be afflicted, oppressed"). The story about dispute occasioned by Moses' marriage to a non-Israelite does not portray Moses as a model of humility, but as a paradigm of those who depend upon God to defend them—in other words, the poor.

The Legislation

The Torah in its present form is a product of the Persian Period (sixth to fourth centuries BCE). The Persians did not attempt to provide a single law code for their vast empire. The imperial authorities charged priests from the diverse regions of the empire to assemble local legal traditions that became the basis of the imperial law in that region. The Persians provided an administrative structure that allowed the priests of Jerusalem to codify ancient Israel's traditional legal practices. Artaxerxes I sent Ezra, a Jew serving in the Persian bureaucracy, to the province of *Yehud* (Judah) to enforce the "the law of God," which was the "king's law" for the Jews (Ezra 7:1-26). Nehemiah 8 describes a ceremony in which Ezra read the "law of Moses" to the people. This book of the law in all likelihood was the Torah in some form.[5]

The Widow, Orphan, and Alien

The culture of the ancient Near East is marked by a concern for the poor.[6] The peoples of the region believed that widows, orphans, and others without economic power were under special divine protection. Kings proudly claimed to be protectors of the poor and widows and orphans—all those who depended on others for their survival because they had no economic resources of their own.[7] The legislation in the Torah reflects this concern for the poor, which was a value common to the ancient Near East. But in the biblical tradition, all people—not just kings—are responsible for the well-being of the poor. Exodus 22:21-22 is particularly harsh on those who mistreat widows, orphans, and aliens. Widows and orphans had no right of inheritance and were particularly vulnerable in the economies of the ancient Near East. Men, of course, dominated these economies. Aliens could not own land and, therefore, had no access to the means of production in ancient Israel's agricultural society. The Exodus text warns any potential abusers that their own families will experience the same kind of exploitation that they inflict on the defenseless. Deuteronomy places those who exploit the defenseless under a curse (27:19).

Deuteronomy not only forbids exploitation of the people who find themselves outside of the economic mainstream, it also calls for the Israelites to take specific actions to prevent the precarious position of those on society's margins from degenerating. The purpose of Deuteronomy's legislation is to give these dependent people more economic security. To accomplish this, Deuteronomy calls on the generosity and concern of the wealthy. The basis of Deuteronomy's legislation regarding economically dependent people is a statement about how God acts: "[God] executes justice for the orphan and the widow, and . . . loves the strangers, providing them food and clothing" (Deut 10:18). This statement about the character of God was to have implications for Israel's behavior. God's particular concern for those in the community whose social status was low and whose economic prospects were dismal ought to move others to ensure that these people receive justice. Deuteronomy then widens the circle of responsibility for the welfare of Israel's dependent classes from God and the king to all people of means. Deuteronomy wishes to protect the widow, orphan, and alien from the kind of exploitation that was so easily accomplished and so difficult to undo because they were outside the economic and sometimes the judicial mainstream. Deuteronomy commends dependent classes to the care of their more well-off neighbors. The generosity of the wealthy can prevent the cycle of poverty from becoming a downward spiral. Finally, Deuteronomy consistently seeks to motivate Israel to obedience. In the case of its laws regarding the treatment of the economically dependent, Deuteronomy associates God's blessings upon Israel with Israel's care for the widow, orphan, and alien (10:14-19; 24:17-22).

Deuteronomy adds another group to the traditional list of economically dependent: the Levites (see Deut 14:29; 16:11, 14). The book has a special concern for those who served in the local sanctuaries that its laws of centralization rendered illegitimate as sites of worship (Deut 12:2-6). Because Deuteronomy declared all sacrificial worship outside the central sanctuary illegitimate, it effectively deprived the priests of these sanctuaries of their liturgical role and the related benefices. Deuteronomy, then, created another group of economically dependent people: the Levites. To ensure that the Levites would have some economic support, Deuteronomy commends them to the charity of their fellow Israelites (Deut 12:12, 17-18; 14:27). Deuteronomy does make a provision for the Levites to serve at the central sanctuary and thereby derive some support from exercising their liturgical functions (Deut 18:6-8). But Deuteronomy's provision that the Levites could serve at the central sanctuary when present there was not a very practical solution to the problems that the priests from the local sanctuaries faced. There were, after all, many local shrines. The one legitimate place for sacrificial worship that Deuteronomy allows could never support all of Israel's Levites. Josiah's short-lived attempt at centralizing Israel's sacrificial worship illustrates the problems that centralization brought on "the priests of the high places" (2 Kgs 23:9). Josiah allowed these dispossessed priests no liturgical function at the central sanctuary, though they were permitted to receive some support from the temple. Eventually the Levites came to serve as a type of second-rank clergy, but Deuteronomy was not responsible for this arrangement (see Ezek 44:9-14). The best Deuteronomy was able to do was to commend the Levites to the charity of their fellow Israelites.

Loans to the Poor

The widow, orphan, and alien were at the margins of the ancient Israelite economic system and needed the help of their fellow Israelites to survive, but unfavorable circumstances could lead even those in the mainstream of the economy to find themselves in need. A poor harvest, illness, theft, drought—any one of these could seriously threaten the well-being of subsistence farmers and push them to the brink of economic disaster. The Torah insists that those in need are to be helped by their fellow Israelites with interest-free loans (Exod 22:25; Lev 25:35-38; Deut 23:19-20). The loans envisioned by the Bible's legal tradition have no resemblance to those central to today's capitalist economy. The interest-free loans to those in critical need were not given in order to raise capital for expanding holdings or operations. The biblical legislation envisions loans of food to prevent hunger or starvation and of seed to raise the next year's crop.

While Exod 22:25 does not elaborate on its prohibition of interest-taking, both Lev 25:35 and Deut 23:19 refer to the Israelite facing economic difficulties as "your brother" and assert that no one should profit from a brother's need for financial help. Also, Lev 25:36-38 suggests that devotion to God ought to motivate Israelites who are successful to be compassionate and generous toward those who have experienced setbacks that threaten them with poverty. The inclusion of the self-identification formula ("I am the LORD your God") in verse 38 explicitly grounds the prohibition of interest in God's authority. The text goes on to remind Israel of its deliverance from slavery and of the gift of the land, implying that God expects those who have freely received the land from God to freely give of its fruits to those in need. It is "the fear of the Lord" that is to motivate people's generosity toward those in need (Lev 25:36). Devotion to God must lead to compassion for others. In a similar fashion, Deut 23:20 asserts that God will give more than adequate provision to all Israel if the community is faithful. There should be no need to supplement God's gracious bounty with interest earned on loans to fellow Israelites in need.

Another aspect of lending and borrowing is the matter of collateral. Both Exod 22:26 and Deut 24:10-13 forbid keeping overnight a person's outer garment taken as surety for a loan. Exodus reminds borrowers of the hardship that would follow were a person to be deprived of this garment necessary to ward off the night's chill. Deuteronomy follows the lead of Exodus in the case of a debtor's garment taken as collateral (Deut 24:12-13). Creditors must return such garments before nightfall. When a debtor had to offer his outer garment as a pledge of repayment, he must be very poor and unable to offer anything else of value. Both Exodus and Deuteronomy call creditors to be compassionate. While Exodus implies that divine retribution will come on those who fail to be understanding (Exod 22:27b), Deuteronomy takes a more positive approach by asserting that compassion toward those in need will bring with it God's approval (Deut 24:13). Deuteronomy consistently shows that it understands the relationship of God and Israel to be contingent on good relationships among the members of the Israelite community. Sensitivity and compassion toward the poor effect the kind of righteousness that God honors.

Deuteronomy adds another specification that serves to make borrowing less of an embarrassment. The book forbids creditors from entering debtors' homes to secure collateral (24:10-11). Deuteronomy's concern is to maintain the dignity of the poor by avoiding unnecessary public humiliation. The practice of some creditors rummaging about inside the homes of their debtors for some suitable item to take as collateral was demeaning to families that found themselves in severe economic need. Keeping creditors outside the homes of their debtors preserves at least a modicum of dignity and self-respect for the poor. Another limitation that Deuteronomy puts on creditors seeking collateral is that they are forbidden from taking a family's millstone as surety (Deut 24:6). Without a millstone, grain could not be ground to prepare bread, the staple of the ancient Israelite diet. Demanding such collateral would involve a hardship for any family, especially a poor one.

Debt-Slavery

A person could go so deeply in debt that he could negotiate no more loans because he had no possibility of repaying his outstanding debts. In such circumstances, Israelite debtors resorted to selling themselves and their families into bond slavery. This allowed them to work off their debts. One of the main sources of slave labor in ancient Israel was the debtor class and so it was necessary to regulate this institution to ensure that people of means would not take advantage of the poor who had no other way of handling economic setbacks. The Torah deals with debt-slavery three times: Exod 21:2-11; Lev 25:39-43; and Deut 15:12-18. Debt-slavery was not to be a permanent condition since those who were forced by circumstances to sell themselves could not be kept in slavery for more than six years (Exod 21:2; Deut 15:12). The unfortunate person who had to resort to such a remedy was to be treated as though he were a hired workman rather than a slave (Lev 25:39-40). The work that the debt-slave is required to do should not be such that crushes the body and thereby destroys the spirit. Leviticus suggests that gentleness toward the bond servant was a practical expression of the master's devotion to God (Lev 25:43).

If a person had become landless because of economic adversity, the law that limited the length of his service to six years probably did not change his social status but allowed him to seek service with a more sympathetic master. If a landless person is satisfied with the landowner for whom he works, the law makes it possible for the landless peasant to become permanently attached to his master (Exod 21:6). Deuteronomy, however, does not wish the master-slave relationship to become permanent and so encourages the slave to take the option of reclaiming his or her freedom. In addition, Deuteronomy explicitly mentions female slaves in 15:12—something the law in Exodus fails to do. Leviticus 25:41 also makes it clear that the children of the bond slave are free as well. Masters cannot use a person's children as pawns to coerce the debt-slave into additional service. The motivation for freeing the debt-slave and his family is the remembrance of the Exodus, when God "purchased" all Israel and made them God's servants. No Israelite then can be sold as a permanent slave to another Israelite. This would constitute theft from God.

Deuteronomy ensures that debt-slaves can rejoin the ranks of the free by requiring their former masters to make a generous provision for them as they leave:

> And when you send a male slave out from you a free person, you shall not send him out empty-handed. Provide liberally out of your flock, your threshing floor, and your wine press, thus giving to him some of the bounty with which the LORD your God has blessed you. (Deut 15:13-14)

Without such help from their former masters to make a smooth transition to freedom, the former slaves would eventually find that their newly reacquired freedom brought them to the same kind of destitution that led them into bond slavery in the first place. The Deuteronomic law, then, sought to break the cycle of poverty that kept the poor in economic dependency.

Unique to Deuteronomy is the law regarding slaves fleeing from their masters (Deut 23:15-16). Unfortunately, the law is stated in an unusually succinct manner. One consequence of this terseness is a question regarding the scope of this law. Does it apply only to slaves who flee to Israel from other countries? Does it apply only to Israelite bond slaves and not to foreigners who become slaves in Israel? Does it forbid cooperation in extradition proceedings against escaped slaves? Does this law apply only to the situation in which a slave flees from an Israelite master and seeks refuge among other Israelites? First Kings 2:39-40 describes Shimei pursuing two slaves who fled from his house in Jerusalem to Gath, a Philistine city. Another possibility is that it applies to slaves from foreign countries who flee to Israel. The Code of Hammurabi (ca. eighteenth century BCE) forbids aiding runaway slaves and some ancient Near Eastern treaties made provision for the return of runaways (*ANET*, 166-67, 200-3). But the Deuteronomic law does not specify its scope.

It may be that Deuteronomy considered slavery to be an embarrassment because the existence of this institution was in tension with a basic datum of Israelite religious tradition: the God of Israel frees slaves. Perhaps Deuteronomy forbids returning a runaway slave in order to weaken slavery's position in the Israelite economic system. Not only is bond slavery limited to no more than six years (15:12), but also runaway slaves are not to be returned to their masters. These two provisions effectively undermined the foundations of bond slavery, an institution that hardly corresponds to the Deuteronomic image of Israel as a community of brothers and sisters. Likewise, Deuteronomy, as Moses' final testament to Israel, is set precisely when Israel is making the transition from slavery to freedom. What is surprising is Deuteronomy's failure to reject slavery explicitly as incompatible with Israel's divinely ordered pattern of life. Of course, ancient Israel's legal traditions sanctioned slavery, so the best Deuteronomy could do was to undermine this institution in its own legislation.

The Year of Release (The Sabbatical Year)

Another tack that Deuteronomy took in trying to prevent a permanent debtor class from arising in Israel was its provision that debts were to be forgiven at the end of every seven years (Deut 15:1-11). This law probably had its origin in the practice of allowing the land to lie fallow at regular seven-year intervals (see Exod 23:10-11 and Lev 25:2-7). In fact, Deuteronomy's law requires the Israelites to "make a release" (*š^emittâ*), using a noun derived from the verb used in Exod 23:11: "you will let it [the land] rest and lie fallow" (*tišm^etennâ*). The version of this law in Exodus is not explicit about the way it was to be implemented, and some interpreters suggest that the observance of a fallow year was staggered throughout Israel; however, Leviticus clearly expects there to be a single year in which all the land in Israel goes unworked. Still, either individual or universal observance of this law would be difficult for people in an economy as dependent upon agriculture as was that of ancient Israel. Both Exodus and Leviticus suggest a humanitarian dimension to this practice. Exodus requires that anything growing naturally on the unworked fields be available to the poor, while Leviticus gives it to slaves and workers. Deuteronomy, however, focuses not only on the land but especially on those who worked the land: the peasant farmers. It requires that their outstanding debts be forgiven during the year of release. Deuteronomy does not treat loans as business transactions but as a form of help to those in need.[8] An alternative view holds that Deuteronomy does not require the cancellation of the debt but merely allows deferment of repayment until after the year of release. What is forbidden is the confiscation of collateral ("the pledge" of 15:2) if the farmer is unable to pay because of the economic strictures of the fallow year.[9] A third possibility is that the kinds of loans that this Deuteronomic law had in mind are the ones that involved the pledge of personal services as security against nonpayment. Apparently creditors were within their rights to compel delinquent debtors to become bond servants in case of default. Deuteronomy not only requires that the debt be cancelled but, in effect, it also frees those who had become bond servants in order to work off their debts.

Of course, an obvious problem with a law that cancelled outstanding debts during "the year of release" is that needed loans would not be given as that year approached. Deuteronomy foresaw this and enjoined people of means to lend to the poor even as the year of release was near (15:9). The book characterizes the failure to be generous with those in need as sinful (15:9*b*), using the same language to condemn those who withhold the wages of their workers (24:15*b*). The theological support for such a characterization is that God expects the wealthy to help the poor. Any failure to do so brings divine judgment on the Israelite community because God is the defender of the poor. But Deuteronomy uses positive motivation as well. It suggests that the result of releasing the poor from their debts will be nothing less than the elimination of poverty in the land that is God's gift to Israel (15:4). Further, Israel's prosperity will be such that it can offer loans to other nations (15:6). Israel, however, is never to seek financial assistance from other nations since such a course of action would be a breach of faith. God will not only provide for Israel's material needs but will eliminate poverty completely if Israel were just obedient. This approach is typical of Deuteronomy, which does not simply codify ancient Israel's legal traditions, but also seeks to motivate its readers to obey.

Another of Deuteronomy's fundamental assumptions about the relations between the wealthy and the poor is that all Israelites—rich and poor—belong to one family. The law of release refers to debtors as "brothers" of their creditors no less than six times in its eleven verses (15:2, 3, 7[2x], 9, 11). That some members of the one Israelite family were without the material blessings promised to all was simply not right in Deuteronomy's view, so the book calls for generosity toward the poor (15:11).[10] Deuteronomy sees no positive value in poverty. It never characterizes the poor as those who have a closer relationship with God because they are poor. The book sees the deprivation of the blessings that God has given to all Israel as an evil that must be eliminated by the generosity of the wealthy. Clearly Deuteronomy reflects a socioeconomic situation that needed a more equitable distribution of resources, a goal that the book sees as attainable.

The law concerning the year of release shows that Deuteronomy defined the poor person as one without the kind of material prosperity that made for economic security. The poor are those who need economic support from others. Occasionally the needs of the poor become so acute that they could be forced into bond slavery by their creditors. The permanent division of the Israelite community into a debtor and a creditor class must not be allowed to occur. Such an economic rift is incompatible with the community's character as a family. If all Israelites could think of themselves as members of a single family and act accordingly, the effects of poverty could be minimized if not eliminated from Israel.

By naming the unwillingness to aid the poor a sin (15:9), Deuteronomy asserts that Israel's relationship with God was reflected in the kind of relationship that existed among the Israelites themselves. The Chronicler, by way of contrast, assumes that Israel's relationship with God was determined by how it worshiped (cf. 2 Chr 13:8-12). While Deuteronomy does not ignore the importance of worship, it chooses to emphasize the moral dimension of a life with God. Perhaps Deuteronomy here reflects a belief that the fall of the Judahite national state and dynasty, the destruction of Jerusalem and its temple, the scattering of the priesthood, and the exile were consequences of the conflict between rich and poor in Israelite society. In other words, the Deuteronomist believes that the existence of poverty in Israel is more than a socioeconomic issue.

Though Deuteronomy devotes more attention to the year of release, Exodus and Leviticus also describe this institution in humanitarian terms. It provided an opportunity for Israelites to care for the most economically vulnerable in their society: the poor. The theological support for this practice was the belief that God retained the ownership of the land (Lev 25:23), though Israel did possess it in fulfillment of the promises that God made to its ancestors. Deuteronomy makes explicit the connection between the year of release and God's sovereignty by requiring that the Torah be read publicly during the pilgrimage made to the central sanctuary for the Feast of Booths during the year of release (31:9-13).

The Year of Jubilee

Leviticus 25 describes another Israelite practice that was designed to eliminate social and economic stratification: the Year of Jubilee, which was the seventh in a series of sabbatical years. The Year of Jubilee would be marked not only by the release of Israelites in bond slavery but also by the restoration of land to families forced to sell their ancestral holdings during the previous forty-nine years. The Year of Jubilee was a social and economic institution with a strong theological foundation. Its purpose was to bolster the economic viability of the family by ensuring that land that had been sold would revert to the family whose economic circumstances necessitated its sale. This practice was grounded in the belief that the land actually belonged to God, who was free to redistribute it without concern for prior human dispositions. The Year of Jubilee sought to preserve two central Israelite values. First, the land was to be distributed among the Israelites equitably, as exemplified in the story of the division of the land among the tribes (Josh 13–24). Second, to preserve this equity the land must be inalienable, as exemplified in the story of Naboth's vineyard (1 Kgs 21). Indeed, Lev 25:23 expressly prohibits any permanent sale of the land. While the land was Israel's inheritance from God (Deut 1:8 + 18x throughout the book), it remained God's. For the people of ancient Israel, the land from which they derived what was necessary to live in freedom and prosperity was the sacrament of their encounter with God. The land made God tangible for ancient Israel; consequently, nothing that affected the land could remain free of theological and ethical import.

Leviticus 25 uses two images in speaking about Israelites. First, they are aliens and tenants (v. 23). The aliens and tenants who lived in Israel but were not native Israelites were completely dependent upon the Israelites for their economic well-being since they could not own land. They survived as farm laborers, artisans, and servants. Just so, the Israelites were to think of themselves as completely dependent upon God for their survival. Second, the same chapter speaks of the Israelites as slaves who have been set free by God (vv. 38, 42, 55). These descriptions imply that Israelites should never exploit or enslave each other. All are God's tenants—all are former slaves set free by the mercy of God.

The purpose of the Jubilee Year was to restore the economic equilibrium of Israelite society, ensuring a right relationship to God. But was this legislation simply a utopian formulation that was never implemented? Roland de Vaux, O.P., maintained that the Jubilee Year was a late and ultimately unsuccessful attempt to radicalize the Sabbath Year by extending it to cover property.[11] There is no biblical text that tells of its implementation, though Isa 37:30 is sometimes suggested as implying the observance of the Jubilee. Still, the very existence of Lev 25 shows how central a just and equitable economy was in ancient Israel's legal traditions. It is likely, however, that the establishment of the Israelite national states made this law meaningless. The economic system that supported an ancient Near Eastern monarchy could hardly envision a person burdened by great debt still holding title to his family's land, making it possible for it to be restored to him. One result of the economic system of Israel's monarchy was the royal confiscation of land through taxation, which reduced many Israelite families to poverty. Still, the legislation regarding the Jubilee Year demonstrates that one purpose of the Torah was to instruct the people of Israel regarding their obligations to each other, especially their obligations to the needy and economically vulnerable among them.

The Wages of the Poor

One cause of the type of economic distress that required the poor to take out loans, to place themselves at the mercy of their creditors, and to sell themselves into debt-slavery was the oppression and injustice perpetrated by people of means. A particularly egregious example of such behavior is the withholding of a laborer's wages. Persons who no longer owned land were forced to support themselves and their families as hired workers. Some employers were aware of their workers' absolute dependence and some did not hesitate to exploit this situation to their advantage. One tactic was to withhold their workers' wages. A laborer whose wages were withheld could not purchase food for his family for the evening meal and for the next day. Both Lev 19:13 and Deut 24:14-15 explicitly forbid this practice. Leviticus calls such a practice oppression and robbery. Deuteronomy characterizes the laborers in question as "poor and needy" (Deut 24:14). Clearly such persons found it difficult to forego their wages until their employers deemed it convenient to make payment. In effect, the wealthy employers were extracting an unauthorized loan from their needy employees. Deuteronomy also extends its protection in this instance to foreign workers, perhaps specifying the prohibition of oppressing aliens found in Exod 22:21.

Deuteronomy warns those who exploit workers that the cries of the poor will be heard by God, who will regard the oppression of the poor as a sin (24:15). While Exod 22:23-24 describes the consequences of this sin, Deuteronomy allows its readers to draw their own conclusions about the effects of withholding the wages of the poor. Deuteronomy does contend that some sins are so serious as to be punishable by death (e.g., 21:22; 24:16), but in this instance the reader is left to speculate about the punishment that will come upon those who commit this sin. But here Deuteronomy is less concerned with the fate of the employer than with justice for the employee. The book wishes to break the cycle of poverty. Withholding the wages of the poor makes their poverty all the more burdensome, and unnecessarily so. It may lead the poor to go into debt in order to survive when justice demands that they enjoy the fruits of their labor. Withholding wages keeps the poor in the cycle of poverty and deepens the economic divisions of Israelite society.

The Judicial System

When the poor are subject to unjust practices such as the withholding of wages, they ought to be able to seek redress in the judicial system. Unfortunately, people of means were often able to use their influence and power to subvert the legal process to their benefit. The Torah is explicit in condemning such corruption of the judicial system: Exod 23:1-9; Lev 19:15; Deut 16:18-20. Exodus explicitly forbids the use of the courts to present justice to the poor: "You shall not pervert the justice due to your poor in their lawsuits" (Exod 23:6).

In fact, the entire series of laws in Exod 23:1-9 probably originated to counter the influence of the wealthy and the powerful over ancient Israel's judicial system. Exodus 23:3 ("nor shall you be partial to the poor in a lawsuit") seems out of place in the context of 23:1-9, which seeks to protect the powerless from the powerful. Martin Noth suggested emending *dl*, the Hebrew word for "poor" in verse 3, to *gdl*, a word meaning powerful, influential.[12] Leviticus 19:15 reads: "You shall not render an unjust judgment; you shall not be partial to the poor or defer to the great: with justice you shall judge your neighbor." Here there is no attempt to protect the rich from the poor, only an assertion that justice should be blind, a fundamental requirement of a judicial system's impartiality. The reason for the legislation on the judicial system is that Israel's was corrupted by the powerful, not that decisions favoring the poor were subverting the system.

The book of Deuteronomy devotes significant attention to the judicial system because it recognizes that the courts can prevent conditions from developing that could make poverty and oppression permanent components of the Israelite social, political, and economic system. Three passages are especially significant: 1:9-18, which describes Moses' appointment of judges; 16:18-20, the law for the judiciary; and 17:14-20, the law for the king. While none of these laws explicitly mentions the poor, ancient Israel's experience testifies that nothing facilitates the destruction of the social order more than a corrupt judicial and political system. Ancient Israel's monarchy and judiciary helped create and maintain poverty, as the prophetic judgment on these institutions makes clear. Deuteronomy's hope for Israel's future gives rise to specific legislation on what needs to be done to keep these two institutions free from the type of corruption that affects the poor most of all.

The narrative describing Moses' appointment of judges sets out some of the characteristics of a good judicial system (Deut 1:9-18). First, it is representative (v. 13). Moses does not choose the judges; they are nominated by the people themselves. The judges appointed by the king (see 2 Chr 19:5) were especially vulnerable to finding in favor of the powerful and wealthy. Second, the judiciary is to be composed of people who are wise, prudent, and experienced (v. 13). Third, the judicial system is to be characterized by fairness and impartiality for both Israelite and alien (vv. 16-17). Finally, there must be a provision for appeal in matters of particular complexity (v. 17). Verse 16 refers to the Israelites as "brothers." This is Deuteronomy's characteristic manner of referring to the members of the Israelite community.[13] Such usage ignores the kind of social stratification that reflects differences in the level of people's economic prosperity. An equitable administration of the judicial office, then, is crucial to Deuteronomy's conception of what Israel is to be.

Deuteronomy's law on the appointment of judges (16:18-20) reflects ideals similar to Exod 23:6-8, which is concerned with problems in the administration of justice. The scope of the law in Exodus is broader since it is not directed at judges alone but forbids anyone from tampering with justice. Deuteronomy 16:19b is almost a verbatim citation of Exod 23:8. Both texts outlaw bribery since impartiality is an essential characteristic of any judge (Deut 16:19*a*). Deuteronomy follows the prohibition of bribery with a positive command to do justice because a just society is one that will endure (v. 20).

Ancient Israel's first judges were the elders who sat at the town gate. They not only settled disputes but facilitated the restoration of harmony between the litigants. With the establishment of the monarchy, a new type of judicial authority made its appearance. There were judges, appointed by the king, to ensure that the king's law was enforced. But the king was to serve as the model of judicial authority. His conduct set the tone for the entire monarchic judicial system. Deuteronomy describes how an Israelite monarchy is to function. According to the law of the king in Deut 17:14-20, God allows Israel to establish a monarchy under certain conditions. Verses 16-17 describe what the king must not do. He is not to amass a great chariot army, nor is he to amass great wealth. He is even to avoid gathering a large harem. The one positive responsibility of an Israelite king, according to Deuteronomy, is to study and observe the Torah. The purpose of these conditions, both negative and positive, is to prevent the monarchy in Israel from becoming an institution that models and facilitates economic and social stratification. The king is never to think of himself as superior to his "brothers," in other words, other Israelites (v. 20). Of course, no ancient Near Eastern monarch would ever consent to rule under the conditions that Deuteronomy suggests. The "law of the king" is less a practical piece of legislation and more of an assertion of Deuteronomy's social idealism. More than any other institution in ancient Israel's life, the monarchy brought within its wake social stratification and economic pressures that made poverty almost inevitable. That a society made up of subsistence farmers support a full-blown monarchy is simply unrealistic. Samuel's description of the "ways of the king" (1 Sam 8:10-18) warns the Israelites that the monarchy will result in their enslavement. Deuteronomy describes a monarchy based on an equitable social and economic system. If only the king would study and observe the Torah, poverty would not exist since the observance of the Torah is a guarantee against poverty (15:4).

Feeding the Poor

In a less idealistic vein, Deuteronomy deals with the symptoms rather than the causes of poverty as it attempts to move people of means to aid the poor, whose numbers never seem to diminish: "Since there will never cease to be some in need on the earth, I therefore command you, 'Open your hand to the poor and needy neighbor in your land'" (Deut 15:11). The most pressing need for the poor was simply survival. Usually that meant having enough food to eat. One way to make food available for the poor without any great expense to the people of means is to allow the poor to glean from fields that have been harvested. Both Leviticus (19:9-10; 23:22) and Deuteronomy (24:19-22) require harvesters to refrain from being overly efficient in their work. A generous farmer may even leave more than the law required, as Boaz did for Ruth (see Ruth 2:15-16). Apparently this studied inefficiency was an ancient custom that the Bible's legal traditions invest with new meaning. Gerhard von Rad suggests that not harvesting a field completely at first was intended to placate the spirit of the field in order to ensure continued good harvests.[14] The Torah demythologizes this custom by having the unharvested crops benefit the poor.

The laws permitting gleaning benefit the poor not only by offering them a supply of food without charge but also by permitting them to maintain some degree of dignity at the same time. The poor were not simply receiving a handout but were working to support themselves. Still, the greater benefit came to the people of means who kept the commandment regarding gleaning. This law reminded successful farmers that the land and its bounty were theirs in trust from God. They should never think that their harvests of grain, grapes, and olives belonged to them by right, for they belong to the poor as well. This commandment was meant to develop a generous attitude on the part of the wealthy and successful. What better way to express one's generosity than to give without knowing to whom one is giving and without the recipients knowing from whom their good fortune comes? The theological assumption supporting this law is the denial of absolute proprietorship over the land by human beings. The land and its bounty belong to God, who commands that the people of means share their harvest with the poor. The early rabbinic tradition attempted to quantify the observance of this command by asserting that it was to be fulfilled by leaving at least a sixtieth part of the harvest for the poor (*m. Pe'ah* 1.1-2).

In addition to enjoining farmers to permit the gleaning of their fields, Deuteronomy suggests two other ways to ensure that the poor have enough food: the triennial tithe (Deut 14:28-29) and festal meals associated with pilgrimage feasts (Deut 16:11, 14). The triennial tithe is Deuteronomy's attempt at providing relief for the poor on a regular basis. The Deuteronomic law is similar to one in Exodus that allows the poor to take the crops that grow without cultivation during the Sabbath Year, when Israelite farmers were forbidden to work their fields (Exod 23:10-11). The law in Exodus, which requires forgoing an entire year's harvest, may have become impractical once the Israelite economy became more complex. Deuteronomy's requirement that the triennial tithe be given to the poor is certainly more realistic in its expectations regarding how successful farmers may contribute to people without land of their own.

There is a marked difference between Deuteronomy's regulations about tithes and those found in Lev 27:30-33 and Num 18:20-32. The latter texts regard the tithe as belonging to God. The Israelite farmer gives the tenth part of his crops and animals to the Levites, who use it for their support. The Levites give a tenth of the tithes that they receive to the priests. Deuteronomy's extensive treatment of tithes (Deut 12:6, 11, 17-19; 14:22-29; 26:1-13) does not describe the tithe as dedicated to the support of the temple's personnel. The tithe is to provide a sacrificial meal that is to be eaten by the Israelite farmer and his family at the central sanctuary, where the tithe is to be presented in acknowledgment that the land and its abundance are gifts from God. The Israelite farmer is to invite a Levite from his town to share in this meal since the Levites have no land from which to make their own tithes (Deut 14:27). The Israelite farmers are to enjoy this meal at the central sanctuary for two consecutive years out of every three. During the third year the tithe is to be kept within the town and given to the Levites, aliens, orphans, and widows because they do not own land (Deut 14:28-29; 26:12). Deuteronomy was able to transform the practice of tithing because its law centralizing all sacrificial worship at a single sanctuary (Deut 12:2-12), eliminating the need to support a large number of places of sacrificial worship. In Deuteronomy, then, tithing became a way to support the poor rather than to support sanctuaries.[15]

Besides the triennial tithe Deuteronomy mandates two other occasions for the successful Israelite farmer to share the land's bounty with the poor. Of the three pilgrimage festivals, Passover, Weeks, and Booths, the latter two maintained a close connection with the celebration of a bountiful harvest. The Passover festival, no matter what its origins, became focused on the celebration of the Exodus. The Feast of Weeks, at the end of the wheat harvest, and the Feast of Booths, at the end of the fall harvest, were occasions to celebrate God's gift of fertility and bounty as evidenced by the harvest of food that ensured the people's well-being. Deuteronomy "commands" the Israelite farmer to rejoice at these feasts along with his family. But the poor are also to be included in these celebrations. Deuteronomy explicitly commands that the Israelite farmers include their servants, plus widows, orphans, aliens, and Levites in their celebration (Deut 16:11, 14). These people had no land from which to provide the food to celebrate God's goodness to Israel. This is another example of a Deuteronomic transformation of religious practices into opportunities to make the people of means aware of what it means to be poor—in other words, to be without the resources that are necessary for survival. Surely the Deuteronomic legislator did not intend a minimalist fulfillment of this law. Once made aware of the needs of the poor, people of means should be willing to share the blessings with those without resources of their own.

The Tenth Commandment

"Neither shall you covet your neighbor's wife. Neither shall you desire your neighbor's house, or field, or male or female slave, or ox, or donkey, or anything that belongs to your neighbor" (Deut 5:21).

It is important to see this commandment against the background of ancient Israel's agrarian economy. The challenges that the Israelite farmer faced were many. A year without sufficient rain meant a poor harvest; two years of drought usually was disastrous. The quality of the soil was not the best. It was quite rocky and the hills of the central highlands required a very labor-intensive form of agriculture. The Canaanites and the Philistines controlled the fertile valleys and the coastal plain. There was the danger of raids and invasions. After months of hard work, a harvest could be lost because of the fortunes of war. In the low-yield agriculture of Israel, one way to make the odds of survival better was to increase one's holdings. The more land one possessed, the greater likelihood of holding up under the vagaries of the agricultural enterprise. But increasing one's holdings always came at the expense of another. The tenth commandment prohibits the kind of covetousness that ensures one's security while diminishing that of one's fellow Israelite. The intended effect of the tenth commandment is to reverse the tendency to make self-interest the guiding principle of one's actions. What the Torah expects of the wealthy is the willingness to give up what is rightfully theirs in order to help the poor. Clearly the desire to take what rightfully belongs to another impedes the type of selfless act that the Torah believes can overcome the economic divisions in the Israelite community.

Conclusion

Focusing on the number of times that the several Hebrew words that are translated as "the poor" occur in the Torah might lead one to think that the poor are only a subsidiary concern in the Torah. Actually, it is clear that concern for the poor, for a just economic system, and for the elimination of the exploitation of the vulnerable members of society is at the heart of the Torah. But it is important to note that the Torah does not idealize poverty as a state that brings a person closer to God. Poverty is a curse (Lev 26:14-26). It should not exist in Israelite society. It is an anomaly that in the bountiful land that God has given Israel as its inheritance there should be people who are hungry and homeless.

The Torah offers three solutions to the problem of poverty. First, the Torah makes it clear that the people of means have certain obligations toward the poor and the economically vulnerable in Israelite society. Priests are not to expect the poor to make the same type of offerings that the wealthy bring to the temple (Lev 5:7-13; 14:21-32). During the harvest, farmers are to be careful to leave something in the fields for the poor to glean. Every third year, farmers are not to take their tithe to the central sanctuary but are to leave it in their town, making it available to the poor. In addition, the more successful farmers are to include the poor in their festal meals during the Feasts of Weeks and Booths. The most immediate needs of the poor relate to the question of their survival. The wealthy are obliged to ensure that survival.

Other legislation goes beyond simply alleviating the immediate needs of the poor. It forbids the exploitation of the economically vulnerable. In the Bible as a whole, the poor are not simply those with little or no economic resources but also those who are powerless to control their own destiny. They are poor precisely because the people of means can take advantage of them. Employers, then, are directed by the Torah to pay their workers each day so that their workers will be able to provide for their family. Creditors are not to embarrass or inconvenience their debtors in the manner they choose to secure the repayment of loans. Judges are obligated to avoid favoring the people of means in matters of legal dispute.

Finally, the most significant of the Torah's legislation regarding the poor seeks to prevent the emergence of a permanent debtor class in Israel. The Torah does not wish to have the people of Israel divided between the landowning wealthy and poor laborers who must beg from the people of means. While creditors do have legitimate claims on their debtors, they must remember that the purpose of a loan is not to make a profit for the creditor but to aid those who have experienced some economic setback. Loans to fellow Israelites, then, are to be interest-free. If debtors do default and are forced to work off their debts, they are to be treated as hired workers, not as slaves. Their service is not to exceed six years. When they are set free, they are to receive economic help in making a new start. Land that is sold in payment of loans is to return to the original owners during the Jubilee Year.

The Torah's approach to the poor is both comprehensive and enlightened. It recognizes that poverty is the result of economic exploitation, a corrupt legal system, and lack of resources. The Torah's views are based on two fundamental assumptions. First, God remains the owner of the land. Israel receives that land as an "inheritance" but not as a permanent possession. The land, then, can be held only in accordance with the prescriptions of the Torah, in which God's will is manifest. Second, the Israelite community is a family. All the members of that family are to have access to the land and its bounty. It is wrong for some members of the Israelite family to enjoy the bounty of the land while others live in poverty. Alleviating the suffering of the poor, then, is not a matter of charity but of justice.

Questions for Reflection

1. What are some of the basic theological assumptions that undergird the Torah's treatment of the poor? Are these helpful as people today respond to the poor?

2. What is the fundamental goal of the Torah's legislation about the poor? How does it differ from contemporary attitudes toward poverty?

3. Contrast the Torah's understanding of the origins of poverty with contemporary attitudes toward the poor.

4. What is the difference between the purpose of loans in the ancient Israelite economic system and the capitalist economies of today?

5. Why were Hagar and Ishmael vulnerable to abuse and exploitation by Abraham and Sarah? How did they survive?

6. Why does Deuteronomy describe the Hebrew slaves' situation as one of "poverty"?

7. How does the Torah's legislation seek to prevent the development of a permanent underclass in Israel?

THE FORMER PROPHETS

The books that the rabbis called the "Former Prophets" (Joshua, Judges, Samuel, and Kings) tell a tragic story. They describe the odyssey of the people of Israel in the land that was promised to their ancestors. The story begins by telling how Israel came to possess that land and goes on to relate how Israel came to lose it. The story ends with the fall of Jerusalem, the collapse of the Judahite national state, and the exile of many people. What began with so much hope and promise ends in despair. To explain this tragedy to his readers the author uses the theological perspectives that undergird the book of Deuteronomy; hence, the Former Prophets have also come to be known as the Deuteronomistic History.[1]

The most fundamental of these principles is that Israel's future depends on its absolute fidelity to God expressed through obedience to the written, authoritative Torah—in other words, the book of Deuteronomy. The Deuteronomistic History explains that what befell the people of Israel was a consequence of their infidelity and disobedience. The purpose of relating the stories that make up the Deuteronomistic History is to provide the people with example stories from their past about the vital importance of shaping their lives in accordance with the Torah. The Deuteronomist sought to turn Israel's past into a sermon. Calling the Former Prophets a *historical* work is unfortunate because it is not a history—at least not in the modern sense. The Former Prophets appear to have a homiletic purpose: to turn the past into a sermon on fidelity and obedience.

If one focuses on the number of times words for "the poor" appear in the Deuteronomistic History, one could conclude that the oppression of the poor and the need for a just society were not part of the Deuteronomist's agenda.[2] But that would be to misjudge the writer who wished to tell the story of how Israel acquired and then lost the land. What happened to the poor and the oppressed is at the heart of that story.

Joshua

The story of Israel in the land begins with Joshua assuming the leadership of the Israelites, who were on the verge of entering Canaan (Josh 1). After a series of swift military campaigns in the center, in the south, and finally in the north, Joshua and the Israelite armies succeed in taking control of the land promised to their ancestors (Josh 2–11). A good portion of the book then is devoted to the distribution of the land (Josh 13–21). Toward the end of the book of Joshua, the Deuteronomistic Historian expresses his evaluation of Israel's first years in the land under Joshua's leadership: "Israel served the LORD all the days of Joshua, and all the days of the elders who outlived Joshua and had known all the work that the LORD did for Israel" (Josh 24:31).

Joshua and Israel were victorious despite long odds precisely because "Israel served the LORD." How much of the book of Joshua can be used to reconstruct the early history of Israel is still a matter of debate. But there is a growing consensus that ancient Israelite society emerged in the central highlands of Canaan, in part, as a reaction against the economic and political oppression that characterized the rule of the Canaanite city-states during the transition from the Late Bronze Age to the Early Iron Age in Palestine.[3] The Deuteronomist's narratives, however, attribute Israel's acquisition of the land that was to be the scene of its subsequent history as the result of a series of miracles by which God gave Israel military victories over the indigenous population of Canaan. The conclusion that the Israelite tribes emerged in the midst of social and economic conflict is based less on the book of Joshua and more on the results of archaeological excavation and study of ancient Near Eastern texts as interpreted through the lens of the social sciences.

Rahab and the Spies

The book of Joshua provides some interesting indications of social conflict that was endemic during the Late Bronze Age as well as in the period of the Israelite national states. For example, the story of the Israelite spies in Josh 2 introduces a Canaanite prostitute named Rahab into the narrative about Israel's taking of Jericho. Two spies, sent by Joshua, spent the night in her house. She hid them from the king of Jericho and so saved their lives. The story gives no specific motive for her action, though her comments—set in typical Deuteronomistic phraseology—about the power of the God of Israel in Josh 2:9-11 are meant to provide a reason. But the careful reader recognizes that Rahab represents the urban lower classes, who had no reason to support the royal establishment. As a prostitute, she was among the debased and expendable elements of the city. When the immediate threat from the king of Jericho passed, the spies left Rahab's house and "went into the hill country" (Josh 2:22). The hill country provided a safe haven for the Israelite revolutionaries. The story of Rahab and the spies reflects the alliance between the urban lower classes and the rural peasants in opposition to the royal establishment. The urban poor want to ensure that the revolution will succeed (Josh 2:9a, 14b, 24a) and that they will survive the conflict (Josh 2:12-14, 18-19). The rural peasants, on the other hand, want to avoid being betrayed by those urban dwellers who are loyal to the king (Josh 2:14, 20-21). Both Rahab and the spies were in conflict with the king and his servants and this story celebrates the small victory of these representatives of the lower social classes as they made the king of Jericho look foolish.

The literary connection between Rahab's story and that of the taking of Jericho is artificial. Joshua 6 describes the fall of the city as the result of a miracle. If the town was to be taken by miraculous means, why send out spies? Since no military maneuvers were involved in the city's conquest, what was the purpose of the reconnaissance? The description of Jericho's fall in Josh 6 is a thinly disguised account of the liturgical celebration of an Israelite victory over a powerful Canaanite city-state. One can certainly visualize the peasant farmers and the urban poor of Canaan celebrating their victory by marching around the ruins of Jericho, which had become a symbol of the demise of the ruling elite. The Deuteronomist transformed the description of a popular liturgical celebration into an account of the miraculous defeat of Jericho to show what God will do for an obedient people. Still, the subtext is clear enough. The lower urban classes and the rural peasants unite in their opposition to the ruling elite, whose wealth and power undergird their social, economic, and political dominance.

The Covenants with Gibeon and Shechem

Not all the stories in Joshua ascribe the taking of the land of Canaan to military victories by the Israelite armies. Joshua 9–10 tells the story of a covenant between the Israelites and the Gibeonites and Josh 24 that of a covenant with the Shechemites. In the century before the emergence of the Israelite tribes in the central hill country of Canaan where Gibeon and Shechem were located, that region was marked by revolutionary activity against the Canaanite political system. There was a growing rift between the Canaanite cities and the surrounding villages in the countryside. Because of Egypt's internal problems, the hegemony it exercised over Canaan was diminishing in the Late Bronze Age. The population of the rural areas virtually ignored Egyptian authority and they began to withhold their allegiance from the aristocrats in the cities because their rule was supported by the Egyptians. These ruling elites in the cities were concerned about the collection of taxes and the enforcement of the corvée.[4] Of course, both oppressive measures were directed at the rural population. The covenants with the Gibeonites and Shechemites helped the Israelites overcome the greatest danger to their continued existence in the central highlands: coalitions among the Canaanite city-states. The story of the covenants with Gibeon and Shechem illustrate how the oppressed can unite to defeat their oppressors.[5]

The Bible includes the people of both Gibeon and Shechem among the Amorites (western Semites) who have a Hivite identity (see Gen 34:2; 48:22; Josh 9:1-2; 2 Sam 21:2). Both were listed among the Levitical cities (Josh 17:2, 7; 21:17) and both are associated with failed attempts at establishing a hereditary monarchy in Israel (Judg 9; 1 Sam 13:13, 16, where Geba may be an alternate designation for Gibeon). These associations suggest a concern for those whose social position placed them in economic peril and fit the antiestablishment undercurrent of the story of ancient Israel's origins in Canaan. As non-Israelites, the people of Gibeon and Shechem fall under the protection that Deuteronomy affords to aliens. Similarly, that both become Levitical cities connects with the special consideration Deuteronomy gives to the Levites. Finally, Shechem witnessed Abimelech's failure to establish a monarchy while Gibeon was probably the location of Saul's ill-fated court.

The Victories of the Peasants

The Deuteronomist ends the story of Joshua's victories with a summary found in chapter 12. Thirty-three kings are named: two from east of the Jordan River and thirty-one from west of the river. The historical value of this list is not as important as the ideological statement it makes. It shows that the first Israelites under the leadership of Joshua opposed the political, economic, and social system of Canaan as represented by the defeated kings. The book of Joshua, then, presents Israel beginning its life in the land without the burdens that come with a monarchic system. There were no taxes to pay, no forced labor to endure. The labor of the peasants did not have to support the king and his entourage. They did not have to serve in his armies but were free to work the land that God gave to Israel, ensuring their survival.

Chapters 13 to 21 describe the distribution of the land among the Israelite tribes. To the modern reader the text goes into numbing detail, listing some place-names whose precise location is no longer known. But this list is theologically significant in the Deuteronomic scheme, for it shows the basis for the assertion in Deut 15:4: "There will, however, be no one in need among you, because the LORD is sure to bless you in the land that the LORD your God is giving you as a possession to occupy." The equitable distribution of the land meant that all Israelites had access to the means of production. There were to be no poor in Israel because of the gift of the land, which made it possible for every Israelite family to produce what was necessary to sustain life. The implication that the Deuteronomist wishes readers to draw is that poverty is a human creation. The choices that human beings make lead to a redistribution of resources that enrich some people and impoverish many.

The book of Joshua sets the scene for the rest of the story about Israel's life in its land:

> Thus the LORD gave to Israel all the land that he swore to their ancestors that he would give them; and having taken possession of it, they settled there. And the LORD gave them rest on every side just as he had sworn to their ancestors; not one of all their enemies had withstood them, for the LORD had given all their enemies into their hands. Not one of all the good promises that the LORD had made to the house of Israel had failed; all came to pass. (Josh 21:43-45)

The story begins with great promise. The people have their land. They can live in that land without external threats. Peace and prosperity are within their grasp. Unfortunately, the rest of the Deuteronomistic History tells the sad tale of how Israel let these slip away. The Deuteronomist lays the blame for this tragedy at Israel's feet. Its choice to serve other gods sealed its fate, for these gods were not responsible for giving Israel its land and obviously could not maintain Israel there. At the end of the story, Israel finds itself in exile from the land that God had given it. While it is true that the Deuteronomist does not focus on the social conflict that was tearing Israel apart, as did the classical prophets, still that conflict is not very far from the surface of the Deuteronomist's story.

Deuteronomy asserts that there are to be no poor within Israel (15:4). The book of Joshua shows that this assertion was not some idealistic dream but a genuine possibility, because in giving the land to Israel, God made it possible for Israelite society to be free of the social cleavages and economic inequities that marked Canaanite society. The stories of military conflict in Joshua show how absolute was the rejection of the Canaanite social, political, and economic system by the first Israelites. Historians continue to study to what extent the narratives in Joshua can be used to reconstruct the history of early Israel, but the ideological intent of these stories is clear. One conclusion that clearly flows from the book is that all Israelites were to share equally in the gift of the land that God had given them in fulfillment of the promises made to Israel's ancestors. Poverty, want, and deprivation were not to be part of Israel's experience.

Judges

The Deuteronomist has collected several stories about local tribal heroes, arranged them in a chronological framework, and used them to bridge the gap between Israel's entrance into the land and the rise of the Israelite national states. The transition from the book of Joshua to the book of Judges is abrupt. Toward the end of Joshua the Deuteronomist asserts that God had given Israel "rest on every side" (Josh 21:44), but toward the beginning of Judges the Deuteronomist has a messenger from God warn the Israelites that the nations will oppress them (Judg 2:3). The Deuteronomist blames this ominous turn of events on the infidelity of the Israelites: "Then the Israelites did what was evil in the sight of the LORD and worshiped the Baals; and they abandoned the LORD, the God of their ancestors, who had brought them out of the land of Egypt; they followed other gods . . . " (Judg 2:11-12). The oppression that comes as a consequence of this infidelity usually expresses itself in socioeconomic terms. While the oppressors are Canaanite kings, certainly the oppression of the Israelite peasants under their own political and social system was not much different. Several of the stories in Judges describe successful acts of resistance. The resistance is successful not because of force of arms but because it is offered by people who repent of their infidelity. The stories in Judges subvert any system of political and social oppression and offer support to those who protest the status quo. The political systems of both Israelite national states were quite unstable[6] and it is likely that one reason was their unjust social and economic systems, which were decried by the prophets. The stories in the book of Judges are thinly veiled critiques of the type of injustice that was endemic to the two Israelite kingdoms.

Ehud

The first detailed narrative of a "judge" who led the Israelite peasants against their oppressors appears in Judg 3:12-30. This is the type of traditional story that is told and retold, as it relates the tale of one of their own who was able to outwit a king and his courtiers and then defeat a demoralized army. It is a story in which irony and wordplay abound.[7] It is a story about economic oppression. Eglon, the king of Moab, crossed the Jordan River and took up temporary residence at Jericho. He came there to receive taxes from the tribe of Benjamin, whose territory he controlled. Ehud, who brought Benjamin's tribute, also brought a dagger and assassinated Eglon. Ehud followed up his act of assassination by leading the Israelites against the Moabite army, which he virtually destroyed. Of course, the Deuteronomist notes that Ehud's victories followed the repentance of the Israelites (Judg 13:12, 15). Still, the subtext of this story justifies resistance to economic oppression. While the Deuteronomist is clear that the oppression was a consequence of Israel's infidelity, it is also clear that Israel experienced that oppression in the economic and political spheres. A renewed commitment to fidelity meant the end of economic deprivation and political subjugation.

Deborah

The story of Deborah, told in both prose and poetry (Judg 4–5), is another tale of a peasants' uprising against a coalition of Canaanite kings. Their combined armies were led by Sisera, who served Jabin of Hazor.[8] The Israelites probably wanted to gain a foothold in the fertile and strategic Jezreel Valley. The Canaanites were determined to keep them out. Of course, the Deuteronomist identifies the cause of the peasants' economic problems as their infidelity to their ancestral religious traditions (Judg 4:1-3). Under the leadership of Jabin, the Canaanites were able to keep the Israelites hemmed in the highlands. But urged on by Deborah, the Israelites decided to take their fate in their hands and move against the Canaanites. The Israelite peasants, with only hand weapons, had to face a professional army spearheaded by a formidable chariot force. Some Israelites thought the odds were too long and stayed away (Judg 5:15b-17). But then the rains came (Judg 5:20-21), making it impossible for the chariots to maneuver. The Canaanites lost their edge and the Israelite peasants were victorious. This story shows that peasants under the unlikely leadership of a woman can overcome even a coalition of kings. In addition, the victory of the Israelites was sealed by the action of Jael, a Kenite woman who assassinated Sisera, the Canaanite general, as he sought her help in evading capture by the victorious Israelites (Judg 4:17-22; 5:24-27). The Kenites were metal workers. This may reflect that artisans found themselves as hard pressed by the economy of monarchy as did the peasant farmers.

While the Canaanites had their coalition, so did the Israelite peasants. The prose account mentions only two tribes, Naphtali and Zebulon (Judg 4:6), while the poem describes a broader coalition (Judg 5:13-18). Even a non-Israelite joined in the struggle against oppression. While the Deuteronomist uses this story to support his notion that fidelity to Israel's God brings the blessings of victory, the story itself is another protest against the economic system characteristic of the stratified social and political system represented by the Canaanites. As such, it subverts the Israelite versions of that system by showing that with God's help, the peasants will overcome those who oppress the poor.

Gideon

In the story of Gideon (Judg 6–8), the Deuteronomist asserts that the pressure brought to bear on Israel by Midian reduced Israel to poverty (Judg 6:6).[9] The home of the Midianites in the southern Transjordan probably did not produce enough food for their growing population, so they used their military might to tax the Israelite farmers in the central highlands west of the Jordan. To feed their people the Midianites simply confiscated the Israelite harvest on a regular basis. It is likely that the Midianites dominated much of the central highlands on both sides of the Jordan in the early years of Israel's existence. The effects of Midianite hegemony were devastating on the Israelite economy (Judg 6:4-5). But the Israelites resisted their oppressors under the leadership of Gideon, who maintained that he belonged to the *poorest* clan in the tribe of Manasseh (Judg 6:15).[10] Gideon was successful in ending Midianite domination of the Israelite central highlands. Of course, the Deuteronomist's telling of Gideon's story emphasizes God's role in responding to Israel's repentance and in defeating the Midianites and their allies. Still, this story, like the others in Judges, implies that the oppression of the Israelite peasants was going to end by the neutralization of those responsible for it. The Deuteronomist does not commend the beleaguered tribe of Manasseh to the charity of their fellow Israelites. The Midianite raids end because the peasant farmers defend themselves by force of arms. Certainly this story subverts any oppressive regime, including that of the two Israelite kingdoms, by encouraging the oppressed to stand up to their oppressors with the assurance that God will defeat their enemies. And the story of Gideon was well-known; Isaiah alludes to it as he encourages the people of Zebulon and Naphtali to expect a similar act of deliverance (Isa 8:23*b*; ET 9:1).

The Deuteronomist notes that Gideon's success led the Israelites to ask Gideon to rule over them as king and to set up a royal dynasty (Judg 8:22). While Gideon declined the offer, his son Abimelech attempted to establish an Israelite monarchy at Shechem (Judg 9:1-6) after murdering his seventy brothers, whom he considered potential rivals. One survivor of the massacre of Gideon's children was his youngest son, Jotham. Using a fable, he tells all who would hear what he thought of kingship: only the unqualified seek it and it will destroy all who rely on it (Judg 9:7-15). Of course, the Deuteronomist voices his concerns through the character of Jotham. What the fable reflects is Israel's experience of the monarchy. It not only failed to deal with Israel's problems, it was responsible for most of them. What the Deuteronomist objects to is not simply a form of government but the social stratification and economic exploitation that the Israelite monarchy brought with it. The memory of Abimelech's short-lived rule in Shechem gave the Deuteronomist the opportunity to protest Israel's monarchy as it was experienced, especially by the poor. Instead of maintaining Israel as a community of brothers (see Deut 17:20), the monarchy turned brothers into fratricides.

Jephthah

Another way that the Deuteronomist chooses to comment on ancient Israel's social structure occurs in the story of Jephthah (Judg 11:1–12:7). The hero of the story belongs to a class of social outcasts since he was the son of a prostitute. Though his father, Gilead, apparently acknowledged paternity, Jephthah's brothers were not so generous. They did not want to share their inheritance with a brother born on the wrong side of the bed (Judg 11:1-2). Because Jephthah's mother was a prostitute, his parentage on his father's side was open to dispute. Prevented by his brothers from acquiring any part of the family's land, Jephthah was forced to support himself from banditry (Judg 11:3). But when the Ammonites were harassing the people of Gilead, their elders turned to Jephthah, who reminded them of their complicity in his degradation. The Deuteronomist suggests that when the social and economic system makes it impossible for a person to have access to the means of production for self-support, those who are deprived will support themselves in other ways. Jephthah was not content to become an object of charity but resorted to raiding along with others like himself. The experience that Jephthah gained as a raider prepared him to lead the people of Gilead against the Ammonites who were threatening them. His military success led to a dramatic change in his social status (see Judg 12:7).

The Levite's Concubine

Another person who was "outside" the system was the unnamed secondary wife (concubine) of a Levite from Ephraim. Judges 19 tells her horrific story.

Often concubines were purchased slaves. The Bible usually portrays the presence of a concubine as a source of problems in a household. For example, there is the tension between Sarah and Hagar (Gen 16), and the murder of Gideon's seventy sons by Abimelech, a son Gideon had with a concubine (Judg 8:31; 9:5). There was an unspecified problem between the Levite and his concubine that led her to return to her father in Bethlehem. After reconciling, the two were returning to Ephraim when they were forced to spend the night in Gibeah as the guest of an old man. While the Levite was given the protection due to a traveler, the concubine was not. To assuage a gang that was roving about terrorizing the populace, the old man was ready to give them his daughter, but the gang refused, so the Levite gave them his concubine. She died after a night of sexual abuse at the hands of the gang (Judg 19:25). While the story explicitly states that the Levite and his concubine lacked nothing (Judg 19:19), the Levite's wealth did not protect his concubine from being raped and murdered. What is even more horrible is that the Levite was an accomplice to his concubine's suffering. She was particularly vulnerable, not even enjoying the status of a wife. She was expendable. The Deuteronomist does not have to comment on the Levite's crime. The story speaks for itself. Here is a woman—a concubine and probably a slave—who had no social standing. Society did not offer her any protection. This is the kind of society that was under divine judgment. While the concubine did not suffer any privations because she belonged to the household of a wealthy man, she was poor because she did not control her own person and her own destiny. This is not the kind of society that the Deuteronomist envisioned for Israel.

In telling the stories of early Israel's heroes, the Deuteronomist repeatedly notes that the problems faced by the Israelite tribes stemmed from their lack of fidelity and commitment. Still, in the course of telling these old stories, the Deuteronomist describes the oppression of the weak and powerless. The stories of Ehud, Deborah, and Gideon show that ending oppression may require armed rebellion against a political system that is responsible for that oppression. With the story of Abimelech, the Deuteronomist's narrative takes an ominous turn because the oppression comes not from the outside but from within. Abimelech's attempt to establish a monarchy reveals how destructive such a political system can be. Finally, the Deuteronomist focuses on two people who were on the margins of ancient Israel's social system: Jephthah and the Levite's concubine. The Deuteronomist implies that a social system that relegates some people to the margins of society can lead to the destruction of that society. The book of Judges ends with the Israelite tribes on the brink of self-destruction. Certainly the Deuteronomist's audience recognized that the unjust social and economic system of the Israelite kingdoms made the fall of those kingdoms predictable.

Samuel

Hannah

The books of Samuel and Kings tell the story of the rise and fall of the two Israelite kingdoms. The story revolves around the failed monarchies of these states. But the story begins with someone on the margins of Israelite society: an infertile woman. In the agrarian economy of ancient Israel, every person available for work was an asset, while every unproductive mouth to feed was a liability. For the peasant farmer, children were a guarantee of survival. First Samuel begins with the story of Samuel's birth. To underscore Samuel's significance the Deuteronomist describes his birth as little short of miraculous (1 Sam 1:1-20). Though Hannah and her husband, Elkanah, had no children, he was devoted to her (1 Sam 1:8). The Deuteronomist notes that Elkanah had a second wife: Peninnah. His first readers would have concluded that Elkanah took this second wife so that he might have children. In addition to the help older children provided the peasant farmer, having children ensured that, upon his death, his land would remain in the family and be transferred in an orderly fashion.

Of course, the Deuteronomist presents Hannah as upset at her infertility. That Peninnah had children only added to her misery. In lamenting her situation in prayer, Hannah uses the language of the poor. She begs God to consider her "poverty" (*'ŏnî;* 1 Sam 1:11). Here, of course, Hannah does not refer to the debilitating effects of material poverty but to the abasement and humiliation she experienced because of her infertility, which led to Peninnah's taunts. God heard Hannah's prayer. She conceived and bore a son whom she named Samuel. Because the Deuteronomist used the vocabulary of the poor in composing Hannah's prayer for a child, he chose a prayer of thanksgiving for Hannah that used the vocabulary of the poor as well (1 Sam 2:1-10). This prayer has come to be known as "Hannah's Song."

Even a cursory reading of Hannah's Song reveals that the Deuteronomist chose a prayer that had a different setting and function than those it came to have in 1 Samuel. The prayer originally celebrated a military victory by Israel's king and army. Verses 4 and 10 are certainly martial in tone and imagery, which, of course, is not appropriate to Hannah's situation. The song concludes with a prayer for the king (v. 10*b*), which is an anachronism in Hannah's time since the Israelite monarchy had not been established as yet. Also, 1 Sam 2:11 can follow 1 Sam 1:28 without any difficulty—another indication that the song was introduced into this story of Hannah by the Deuteronomist. Still, it is not very hard to appreciate the reason for the insertion of this hymn of thanksgiving. The song speaks about a barren woman who has seven children while "she who has many children is forlorn" (1 Sam 2:5),[11] and the antagonisms described in verses 1 and 3 could easily be taken as allusions to Peninnah's cruelty toward Hannah.

Surely, Hannah's prayer that God consider her "poverty" ('ŏnî; 1 Sam 1:11) made 1 Sam 2:6-8 particularly appropriate:

> The LORD kills and brings to life;
> > he brings down to Sheol and raises up.
> The LORD makes poor and makes rich;
> > he brings low, he also exalts.
> He raises up the poor from the dust;
> > he lifts the needy from the ash heap,
> to make them sit with princes and inherit a seat of honor.
> For the pillars of the earth are the LORD's,
> > and on them he has set the world.

Verses 6 and 7 are made up of a series of four lines in which a negative action by God is followed by a positive one. Verse 8a is an extended description of God's positive action on behalf of the poor. This departure from the pattern of verses 6-7 serves to set off God's goodness toward the poor in verse 8a. Also, verses 6-7 and 8b frame this assertion of God's special care for the poor by stressing the comprehensiveness of God's rule. These verses also reflect the reversal of fortunes motif, which fits Hannah's situation and expresses the hopes of the poor. The imagery of verse 8 underscores this dramatically. The town dumps (the "ash heaps" of v. 8) provided a place for the poor to spend the night (see Lam 4:5; Job 2:8; 30:19). God so reverses the status of the poor that they will no longer sit in town dumps but among royalty on thrones.[12]

Verse 8b establishes God's care for the poor in the context of God's role as the Creator of the world. Because God made this world and is the ultimate source of its bounty, God has the right to ensure that the poor have a share in that bounty. If necessary, God will take specific action to do just that. The Song of Hannah, then, reflects an understanding of deity that is fundamental to the biblical tradition. The God that Israel is to serve is a God who takes the side of the poor so that they too can enjoy the benefits of God's creative work. The text does not call for understanding of and charity toward the poor. It does not idealize poverty as a state that places the poor in a closer relationship with God. Hannah's Song acclaims a God who reverses the fortunes of the poor so that they can enjoy the good things of this world.

The Establishment of the Monarchy

While it is true that the Deuteronomistic Historian blames Israel's kings for the fall of the two Israelite national states, one of the principal specifications of the Deuteronomistic indictment of the Israelite monarchy was its failure to maintain a just society based on an equitable distribution of the nation's resources. The monarchy abetted the concentration of wealth in the hands of a privileged elite and the reduction of many—especially subsistence farmers—to poverty. This is clear enough from 1 Sam 8, which describes the request of Israel's elders for a king, Samuel's reaction to that request, and God's instructions to Samuel on responding to the elders. The immediate circumstances that led the elders to ask for a king were the corruption of Samuel's sons. The prophet had appointed them as judges and they showed themselves to be only concerned with using their office to enrich themselves (1 Sam 8:1-3).

From a theological perspective, the elders' request was tantamount to a rejection of God as king over Israel (1 Sam 8:7-8) but from a political standpoint, it was an act of counterrevolution. When the Israelite tribes began taking control of the central highlands, they did so as an act of rejecting the political and economic hegemony of the Canaanite city-states, which the peasant farmers of Canaan experienced as oppressive. The Israelites denied royal prerogatives to any human lord and ascribed them to their patron deity alone. Yahweh was king of the Israelites and Yahweh ruled Israel without any human intermediary. Thus, the Israelites were freed from having to support the people at the top of a hierarchical social and political system. Such a course of action was possible because of the collapse of Egyptian imperial power in Canaan and the subsequent internecine warfare among the Canaanite city-states toward the end of the Late Bronze Age (ca. fourteenth to twelfth centuries BCE). The elders' request for a king meant a return to a social, political, and economic order that the early Israelites had rejected precisely because they experienced its oppression. The elders, however, justified their request by asserting that a *human* king would maintain justice in society—something that Samuel's corrupt sons were undermining.

While God instructed Samuel to accede to the elders' request, God also told him to advise the people about the consequences of their choice (1 Sam 8:7-9). Samuel's warning focuses on the claims that the king will make upon the people (1 Sam 8:10-18). Unfortunately, English translations do not render the play on words that is critical to appreciating the Deuteronomist's message. Verses 9 and 11 both speak about "the ways of the king." The Hebrew word that the RSV renders as "the ways" is *mišpāt* and is derived from the Hebrew root *špt*, whose semantic field includes justice, right, judgment. Words from this root are found in 7:17 and 8:2, 3, 5, 6, and 20. The wordplay involves a rather bitter irony. Certainly, the elders had legitimate grievances against Samuel's sons, who as judges (*šōfᵉtîm*, vv. 1-2) allowed their greed to pervert the justice (*mišpāt*, v. 3) that they were to administer. But the "ways" (*mišpāt*) of the king (vv. 9, 11) will mean an even greater perversion of justice. The king will appropriate people and property through forced labor and heavy taxation, all to support his lavish lifestyle. Everyone living under the king's brand of justice (*mišpāt*) will be little more than royal slaves (1 Sam 8:16).[13] Instead of being content to be God's servants, the Israelites were choosing to become servants to a human lord.

The irony of the story in 1 Sam 8 is that the Israelites were intent on choosing the kind of life that they found oppressive in Egypt and in Canaan. Giving absolute authority to a human king turns that king's subjects into slaves and creates both poverty and oppression. The Israelites lost confidence in God despite their experience of God's power to save them from their enemies (see 1 Sam 12:8-11). This loss of confidence led the elders to ask Samuel for a king. The Deuteronomist suggests that there is no other way to view this request than as a rejection of God's kingship. The implications of this rejection for Israel's social and economic order were serious because Israel's monarchy brought with it old forms of oppression. The Deuteronomist portrays the rise of the Israelite monarchy as a genuine counterrevolution, for the monarchic system effectively negated most of what the early Israelites achieved when they withdrew their support from the kings of Canaan.

The story of the elders' request for a king in 1 Sam 8 portrays the monarchy as a prime cause for poverty in Israel. This text likely reflects the experience of monarchy and the economic system that it spawned. Instead of preserving justice, the monarchy creates injustice. The forced labor, burdensome taxes, and confiscation of property made life very difficult for the Israelite peasant farmer. The forced labor took him away from his land when it needed to be worked. Taxes amounted to a royal confiscation of what subsistence farmers needed for survival. The confiscation of land turned these farmers into hired workers at best and beggars at worst. The monarchy, in the view of the Deuteronomist, created poverty in Israel.

David

First Samuel includes an interesting use of the vocabulary of the poor. In 1 Sam 18:23, David refers to himself as "poor man." The Deuteronomist does not paint an entirely flattering portrait of David. For example, in 1 Sam 18:17-27, the storyteller has David jumping at the chance to marry into Saul's family—though Saul's offer of his daughter Michal to David does not appear to make sense, since it did not seem to serve Saul's purpose in his struggle with David for popular support. But David's describing himself as poor may not be simply metaphorical. He may have been unable to pay the bride-price that was appropriate for someone who was to marry the daughter of a king.[14] The Deuteronomist implies that Saul was aware of David's economic position and his ambition and attempted to use these to his advantage by suggesting that he would waive the conventional bride-price if David were to kill one hundred Philistine men.[15] The clear implication is that Saul expected David to be killed in the attempt. This shows how people of means could exploit the economically poor. Instead of serving as the protector of the poor, Saul abused his power to manipulate David. Saul's plan, however, worked to his disadvantage since David was successful and brought Saul the proof demanded by the king. Saul had no other choice but to give his daughter to David in marriage. In this case, the poor person was able to triumph over his circumstances, but most often such abuses of power do not turn out this way.

While this story may add to David's reputation as a highly resourceful and successful fighter, it is the first of at least three attempts made by David to increase his social standing and popular approval through marriage into influential families. The marriage to Saul's daughter finds parallels in David's marriages to Abigail (1 Sam 25) and Bathsheba (2 Sam 11).[16] It is likely that the Deuteronomist meant the word "poor" in 1 Sam 18:23 to be taken literally.[17] There is no idealization of poverty here. The social stratification that came with the monarchy turned people into schemers in order to improve their social position. David was the most successful social climber of all. He was the youngest son of a man from an obscure village who eventually came to rule over all Israel.

The stories of Hannah in 1 Sam 1 and of David in 1 Sam 18 offer some important contrasts. Both characters identify themselves as poor and in neither case is their poverty idealized. Hannah laments the infertility that has brought her such grief. Not having given her husband any children was a difficult enough burden for her to bear, but Peninnah's taunts made Hannah's situation unbearable. Her laments were heard. She had a child who was destined to play a central role in the rise of the Israelite monarchy. This prompts her to praise God, who always takes the side of the poor. David, however, takes control over his own destiny. He takes advantage of the opportunity given him by Saul to improve his social and economic position. David learns that marriage to the right women can help one's climb to the top. While the Deuteronomist clearly approves of Hannah's behavior, he lets David's speak for itself. David overcame poverty and low social standing by marrying into the royal family. Poverty led one person to prayer and another to scheming.

The darkest colors in the Deuteronomist's unflattering portrait of David are painted in the story of his affair with Bathsheba (2 Sam 11–12). David's own manipulation by Saul, who offered him the hand of Michal if he were to survive what was apparently a suicidal mission, should have made David sensitive to those who were in no position to resist the power of the wealthy. Unfortunately, this experience did not prevent David from abusing his power when he succeeded Saul as king. David's crime surfaced at a critical moment and brought his guilt under public scrutiny. Whether David's affair with Bathsheba was an abuse of power or a conspiracy between the two lovers is a matter of some discussion.[18] But the elimination of Bathsheba's husband, Uriah, certainly was an act of arrogant royal power. It is ironic that, like Saul, David tried to resolve his problem by sending his rival on a suicidal mission. But unlike Saul's plan, David's was successful and Uriah died in battle (2 Sam 11:14-25). After the usual mourning period was over, David and Bathsheba married. But David's troubles over the whole affair were far from over.

The prophet Nathan, whom the Deuteronomist presents as a vocal supporter of the Davidic monarchy (see 2 Sam 7), frustrated David's attempt at covering up the conspiracy to have Uriah murdered. Nathan approached the king with a case of a poor man from whom a rich man stole a pet lamb (2 Sam 12:1-4). It is ironic that Nathan used the same word ($rā\ʾš$) to describe the abused individual as David used to describe himself when he said that he was too poor to marry into Saul's family. But the prophet's case was fictional—to a point. The case that Nathan presented was a parable that underscored the outrageous character of David's crimes of adultery and murder.[19] This parable is certainly a composition of the Deuteronomist, since a case for judgment would not have been presented without actually naming the accused and the injured party. "Rich man" and "poor man" are simply too vague. Also, as callous as the rich man's crime was, stealing a lamb was not a capital offense. There is no clearer protest against royal absolutism and the oppression of the poor under the monarchy than in this parable. It leads the reader to feelings of disgust at the behavior of the king as it contrasts the rich man, who had flocks and herds, with the poor man, who had just a single pet lamb. The rich man took what little the poor man had. What makes this crime even worse is that those who benefited from the rich man's hospitality would speak well of his generosity, not knowing how he acquired the lamb that he served them. If this despicable person is worthy of death, how much more should David pay for his crimes?

For the Deuteronomist, David's adultery and murder were not simply irrational acts of a man trapped by his own passions. They were the actions of a king who was ready to use all his power to achieve his ends, despite the cost to anyone else. The warnings about the abuse of royal power that the Deuteronomist put on Samuel's lips (1 Sam 8:10-18) were well founded. The first two occupants of Israel's throne were guilty of precisely the kind of abuses that the prophet foresaw. David, however, was simply better at the game than was Saul. The king's subjects became little more than pawns in his service who could be manipulated and even murdered to suit the king's convenience. Of course, no other group suffered more from the effects of royal absolutism than the poor. Uriah was not poor by any means, but if he could be eliminated by a king intent on making life easier for himself, what could those who did not enjoy the immunity that wealth and power conferred do? Nathan's parable, then, makes it clear that the Deuteronomist had serious problems with a political system that could abuse people in the manner described in 2 Sam 11–12. Before the Deuteronomist tells the story of David's adultery with Bathsheba and his murder of her husband, Uriah, he remarks that "David administered justice and equity to all his people" (2 Sam 8:15a). The Deuteronomist clearly wanted his readers to consider the Bathsheba incident a turning point in David's reign. The statement made in 2 Sam 8:15a could not be made after the events narrated in 2 Sam 11–12.

David used his absolute royal power to secure his own position at the cost of another man's marriage and life. Such abuse of power often leads to popular discontent, so the Deuteronomist tells the story of two revolutions that David had to put down in order to remain on the throne of Israel. While later generations may have idealized David, the Deuteronomist reminds his readers of the high level of dissatisfaction with David. One of the revolts was led by Absalom, one of David's own sons (2 Sam 15:1–18:18). The other was led by Sheba, a member of the tribe of Benjamin, to which Saul belonged (2 Sam 20:1-22). To quell these revolts David had to rely on non-Israelite mercenaries whose loyalty was purchased (2 Sam 20:6-7). Apparently David could not trust the tribal militia, whose sympathies would have been with the revolutionaries.

Second Samuel describes the cost that Israelites had to pay in order to have a king to rule over them. A social and political system of hierarchy will defend itself against the grievances of the poor and powerless. The Deuteronomist asserts that David had to deal with at least two revolutions that arose because of his centralizing and absolutist rule. The clear implication is that the Israelite experiment with monarchy brought injustice and oppression in its wake. While the Deuteronomist here does not deal with specific acts of oppression against the poor, it is obvious that he wants to deal with a systemic issue. He portrays the monarchy—even under David—as a political system that invariably leads to social stratification, which in turn brings oppression and poverty. The two popular revolutions against Davidic rule imply that the Israelite peasants were desperate enough to attempt to overthrow David. The king in turn recognized that he had lost all popular support and turned to mercenary forces to maintain his power.

Kings

Solomon

Revolutions against the monarchy's political and economic system continued after David. The Deuteronomist suggests that the glory of Solomon's reign was, in large measure, based on taxing the peasants in order to provide for the king and his court. The list of the twelve "officials" who were responsible for collecting the produce from the peasants to support the royal establishment implies that there was a definite organization and procedure for the collecting of taxes (1 Kgs 4:7-19).[20] While the biblical text does not go into detail about these taxes, they must have posed a hardship on subsistence farmers, especially in years when the rainfall was below normal. Of course, the lifestyle of the court had to be maintained in both good and bad years.

Two other features of Solomon's administration also fostered resentment that fed the revolutionary fever. First, Judah, Solomon's tribe, appears to have been exempted from this form of taxation since there was no official named to collect provisions from that region. Second, two of the officials were Solomon's sons-in-law (1 Kgs 4:11, 15). While such favoritism was not unusual, it did run contrary to the supposed equality of all Israelites.

As burdensome as the requirement to provision the royal court was, a still more onerous form of taxation was the system of forced labor. Usually prisoners of war and aliens were required to work on government projects (e.g., Josh 16:10; 1 Kgs 20–21), but Solomon also required that Israelites submit to forced labor (see 1 Kgs 5:27 [ET 5:13]). Among the projects completed by conscripted labor were the temple, the royal palace, and fortifications in Jerusalem, Hazor, Megiddo, and Gezer (1 Kgs 9:15). Jeroboam, who administered a portion of Solomon's forced labor (1 Kgs 11:28), was in a position to recognize the rising level of discontent that this system of taxing human labor was causing among the people. Eventually he broke with Solomon. Jeroboam's revolt was unsuccessful and he sought asylum in Egypt, where he remained until Solomon's death (1 Kgs 11:40).

Rehoboam

The most successful revolution against the house of David occurred shortly after Solomon's death and was occasioned by the refusal of Solomon's son and successor, Rehoboam, to lighten the burden of taxation. Jeroboam returned from exile in Egypt to lead the revolt, which brought an end to the rule of the Davidic dynasty over Israel except for the territory of Judah. Among the first actions taken by the revolutionaries was the assassination of Adoram, who was the royal official in charge of forced labor (1 Kgs 12:18)—so great was popular resentment against the requirement of forced labor. According to Kings, the result of Jeroboam's revolution against Rehoboam was the creation of two Israelite national states: Judah, which was ruled by Davidic dynasty, and Israel, which was ruled by a succession of dynasties.

It is unclear to what extent the kings of the two Israelite national states made use of forced labor. The only explicit allusion occurs with reference to building projects undertaken by Asa of Judah (908–867 BCE; see 1 Kgs 15:22). That the people of Israel and Judah were dissatisfied with the economic policies of their kings was clear enough. Political instability leading at times to violent revolution continued. Revolutions occurred, in part, because of the economic abuse described in 1 Sam 8:10-18. Though ancient Israel emerged in Canaan because of popular rejection of the oppressive economic and social system that was characteristic of the Canaanite city-states, the establishment of the Israelite monarchy was, in effect, a counterrevolution. Still, the people of Israel never fully accommodated themselves to the monarchy, so revolutions continued. Of the first five men to rule over the northern kingdom, two were assassinated (1 Kgs 15:25-27; 1 Kgs 16:8-10) and one committed suicide during a revolution after just one week on the throne (1 Kgs 16:15-20). This revolution was led by Omri (879–869 BCE). Though 1 Kings dismisses him in a few verses (16:21-28), Omri founded a dynasty that produced four kings over three generations. Almost two hundred years later, the Assyrians would call the northern kingdom "the land of Omri" (*ANET*, 280-81, 284-85).

The Dynasty of Omri

The Omride period in Israel (876–842 BCE) was a prosperous time, if one is to judge by the building activity in places like Samaria, Megiddo, and Hazor. But the achievements of the Omrides were paid for by the poor. Both textual and archaeological evidence suggests that the gap between rich and poor was growing ever wider at that time. To survive the poor had to borrow at a very high interest rate. To repay their debts they sometimes had to mortgage their land or sell themselves and their children into slavery (see 2 Kgs 4:1). It is very likely that the great drought during Ahab's reign (1 Kgs 17–18) drove many poor peasants into bankruptcy.[21] They forfeited their land to their wealthy creditors, who began amassing large estates. Crops such as olives and grapes replaced the grain that the peasants grew. The olives were grown for their oil and the grapes for the wine that was produced from their juice. Both were important export crops. But with less land devoted to staples like wheat and barley, the price of grain sky-rocketed. The poor were driven even more deeply into debt. One hundred years later, Amos would criticize the activities of the wealthy that produced a cycle of poverty from which the peasants could not escape (Amos 8:4-6).

The story of Naboth's vineyard (1 Kgs 21) illustrates the relationship between rich and poor during the Omride period. The principal characters in the story are Naboth, an Israelite peasant, Ahab, the king of Israel, and his wife Jezebel. It is likely that the marriage between Ahab and Jezebel was designed to ensure good economic and commercial relations between Israel and Sidon. Jezebel was the daughter of Sidon's king (1 Kgs 16:31). Jezebel probably knew very little of Israelite tradition and cared for it even less, especially when it limited what she believed were the prerogatives that she and Ahab should enjoy as sovereigns. This is especially clear from her behavior in the incident with Naboth.

Ahab wished to enlarge the vegetable garden near his palace. To do this he sought to buy Naboth's vineyard, which abutted the royal holdings. Naboth refused to sell, citing the legal and religious obligations that required him to keep ancestral property within his family (1 Kgs 21:3; see Lev 25:10, 13-17, 23-24, 34). While Ahab was bitterly disappointed at Naboth's refusal, he understood the reasons that prompted it. Jezebel was not so understanding. She mockingly asked her husband: "Do you now govern Israel?" (1 Kgs 21:7). Jezebel was asking her husband to act like the king he was. Unfettered by the limitations that Israelite tradition placed on a sovereign's power, Jezebel gave Ahab an object lesson on asserting the prerogatives of royalty. She coopted the elders of Naboth's town into convicting him on trumped-up charges of treason. After Naboth's execution, his property was forfeit to the crown. Ahab was able to plant his vegetables (1 Kgs 21:8-16). The ease with which Jezebel brought the elders into her plan shows the ability of wealth and power to corrupt. Perhaps the elders believed that their cooperation would preserve or even enhance their social and economic position. Elijah, the great defender of traditional Yahwism, entered the story after Naboth's execution. The prophet could not allow this exercise of raw power to go unchallenged. He accused Ahab of the judicial murder of Naboth (1 Kgs 21:17-19).

What happened to Naboth happened too often, especially in times of economic difficulty when peasants were forced to go into debt simply to survive. Land was their only truly valuable possession, but selling it meant that their descendants faced the prospect of a life of poverty in an economy based on agriculture. The custom requiring that ancestral holdings remain in the family's possession was designed to prevent the creation of a permanent class of poor people in Israel. Land, which was the basis of prosperity, was to remain the inheritance of *all* Israel. Elijah represented the Israelite tradition that viewed actions like those of Ahab and Jezebel as rejecting the divinely established social and economic order. It was the Lord who owned the land and it was the Lord who gave it as an inheritance to all Israel. Crimes such as those committed against Naboth not only condemned entire families to poverty but also were a rejection of Yahweh's rights as well. The only true sovereign in Israel was Yahweh—not Ahab or any other monarch.

Jehu

Given the despotism exemplified by Ahab and Jezebel, it is little wonder, then, that the prophet Elisha considered it the divine will that the Omride dynasty should come to an end. He fomented the revolution led by Jehu, who saw himself as dealing with the kind of injustice that consumed Naboth (2 Kgs 9:21-26). Jehu led a military *coup* against Jehoram king of Israel (851–843 BCE), the last king of the Omride dynasty. Jehu replaced Jehoram as king. But the level of violence (see 2 Kgs 9–10) indicates that this was no ordinary military *coup*. No doubt the revolution released years of pent-up anger and frustration. Not only were the kings of both Israel and Judah assassinated, the entire Israelite royal family and court were exterminated. Jezebel's supporters were lured into the temple of Baal, which Ahab built for her, and killed. The temple itself was razed. Everyone remotely connected with the house of Omri was eliminated. While such a bloodbath cannot be justified on moral grounds, it does show the depth of alienation the people felt. The revolution was a bloody affair whose ferocity was still remembered and condemned by the prophet Hosea one hundred years later: "I will punish the house of Jehu for the blood of Jezreel, and I will put an end to the kingdom of the house of Israel" (Hos 1:4).

Such ferocity can be explained only by popular anger caused by injustice over a long time. Ancient Israel arose as a protest against an unjust economic and social system. It was folly for Israel's kings to expect that the people would endure injustice.

Jehu (839–822 BCE) did not take any effective action to end the oppression of the poor. He was distracted by war with the Arameans, who took advantage of the disruptions caused by the revolution to strip Israel of a significant amount of territory. Eventually, however, the Aramean advance was checked by the Assyrians. When the Assyrians had to withdraw from the region because of internal problems, Israel under Jeroboam II (788–748 BCE) was able to reclaim lost territory (2 Kgs 14:25). But the king gave these lands to his retainers, who became owners of large estates. The small subsistence farmers who made up the bulk of Israel's population could not compete with the great landowners, so the "prosperity" that Israel's resurgence brought created a class of servants and slaves.

Jeroboam II

Excavations at Samaria reveal the wealth of Jeroboam's Israel, a wealth not shared by all.[22] The prophet Amos, whose ministry took place during Jeroboam's reign, makes it clear that beneath the veneer of prosperity, the poor suffered. The ordinary folk provided the wealthy with their high standard of living. For example, the prophet describes the plight of the peasant farmer whose survival depended on the vagaries of nature and the forbearance of moneylenders. Whenever there was a drought or other natural calamity, the farmers were certain to be visited by their creditors, who were unmerciful in their dealings with the poor. But the people of means were not satisfied with simply benefiting from the ill fortune of the peasants; they also resorted to all sorts of schemes to wrest land from the poor in order to increase their own holdings. They used the judicial system to strip the poor of their land, homes, and sometimes even their very persons (Amos 5:10-12).

The portrait of Israel's social and economic system under Jeroboam II shows how completely ancient Israelite society was transformed by the monarchy. Israel began as a society without class distinctions. All Israelites had access to the means of production, the land. This is not to suggest that this system was without problems, but all controversies were dealt with by the elders of the village, who ensured that equity prevailed. The monarchy brought with it a privileged class made up of royal retainers, whose lifestyles were supported by the labor of the peasants. This served to rend the fabric of ancient Israelite society. In spite of violent revolution and prophetic protest, the people of means insisted on their privileges and used their economic and political power to preserve them. Eventually Israelite society was so divided that the kingdom of Israel was easy prey for the Assyrians.

The Fall of the Kingdom of Israel

After the death of Jeroboam II, chaos came to reign in Israel (2 Kgs 15:8-28). Within ten years Israel had five kings, three of whom seized the throne by violence. There was a complete collapse of law and order (see Hos 4:1-3), with the poor suffering the most because of the state's disintegration. The prophets also describe the breakdown of Israel's religious values, which should have served to unite the people and forestall the deterioration of the

Israelite state. The final step in the northern kingdom's march toward self-destruction was a fatal miscalculation by Pekah (737–732 BCE). He led Israel into a coalition of petty states from the Levant against the mighty Assyrian Empire. The Assyrians did not hesitate in reducing the kingdom of Israel to a tiny vassal state that was allowed to survive as long as it did nothing to irritate Israel's Assyrian masters. Israel's last king, Hoshea (732–724 BCE), signed the nation's death warrant when he attempted an ill-advised revolution (2 Kgs 17:1-6). The Assyrians absorbed what remained of the northern kingdom into their provincial system in 721 BCE. They deported Israel's upper class to forestall any more revolutionary activity. The devastated land was repopulated with people from Mesopotamia (2 Kgs 17:24).

Perhaps the kingdom of Israel would have fallen to the expansionist and militarist Assyrian Empire under the best of conditions. What made this fall even more tragic was that it was preceded by the complete rupture of the kingdom's unity. The nation divided itself into two groups. The first was made up of the king and his supporters. The latter believed that their prosperity was a direct result of royal policies. The king, eager for the support of the powerful and wealthy, allowed them to get away with the grossest of injustices against the lower class. In fact, as the Naboth incident shows, even kings were not above judicial murder as they sought to better their economic status. The peasant farmers made up the bulk of the northern kingdom's populace. Their existence was always precarious since they were defenseless against the avarice of the people of means, who used every mishap suffered by the peasants along with every legal and illegal means to turn the disadvantages of the poor into advantages for themselves. As long as Israel was divided into these two classes, it could not long survive.

The Fall of the Kingdom of Judah

The kingdom of Judah survived 134 years longer than the northern kingdom. This was not because the social and economic situation in the south was any better than it was in the north. Because the Davidic dynasty managed to maintain its control in the south, Judah did not suffer the consequences of the often violent dynastic changes that plagued Israel. Further, Judah's kings took a less aggressive stance in international politics than did their counterparts in Israel. Josiah, the one Judahite king who attempted to become a player on the international scene, died in the attempt (2 Kgs 23:29-30). The southern kingdom also made some attempts at reform. While the Deuteronomist focuses on the cultic aspects of the several reform movements (e.g., the reforms under Hezekiah, 2 Kgs 18:3-6), these must have had some repercussion on the socioeconomic level as well. A return to strict Yahwism likely limited some of the grosser forms of social injustice. Perhaps that is the reason for Isaiah's support of Hezekiah (2 Kgs 19:1–20:11). Such prophetic support would be unthinkable were the king guilty of practicing or condoning the oppression of the poor.

Unfortunately, Hezekiah's reforms did not survive him. Hezekiah made some unwise political and military decisions when confronted by the threat from Assyria. He joined a coalition of petty states in the Levant in resisting Assyrian hegemony in the region. Sennacherib moved quickly against the rebels. He first subdued the Phoenician and Philistine cities and then turned his attention to Judah. He focused on its principal towns and, after overcoming all resistance, moved on Jerusalem. Hezekiah surrendered and had to pay a heavy indemnity (2 Kgs 18:13-16). The Assyrians stripped Judah of much of its territory, leaving Hezekiah to rule over Jerusalem and its environs (*ANET*, 287-88). Hezekiah and Judah survived the Assyrian onslaught—but barely. Of course, the peasants suffered most from the disruptions caused by the Assyrian invasion and Sennacherib's demands for tribute. Judah's farmers not only had to support the Judahite monarchy but also had to pay additional taxes as tribute to Assyria.

Judah's economic situation deteriorated even more during the reign of Hezekiah's two successors: Manasseh (698–644 BCE) and Amon (643–642 BCE). Again, the Deuteronomistic account of the reigns of these two kings focuses on cultic matters, though the account of Manasseh's reign contains the cryptic note that "Manasseh shed very much innocent blood" (2 Kgs 21:1-26, see especially v. 16). Manasseh decided not to repeat his father's anti-Assyrian policies and chose to be Assyria's most loyal vassal. Besides paying regular tribute, Manasseh also sent laborers from Judah to help build the royal palace in Nineveh and soldiers to fight alongside the Assyrians in Egypt. While all sectors of the Judahite economy were likely affected by Manasseh's policies, the people with the fewest economic resources had to bear the heaviest burden. The peasants had to provide the material for the tribute as well as providing the laborers and soldiers that Manasseh sent to the Assyrians. There was resistance to Manasseh's policies, but he put down all opposition ruthlessly and quickly (2 Kgs 21:16). Upon succeeding Manasseh, Amon determined to follow his father's policies, but the pressure on Judah became so unbearable that Amon was assassinated by his own courtiers after just two years on the throne (2 Kgs 21:23).

Josiah (641–610 BCE) came to the throne at the age of eight and those who ruled Judah in his name had little choice but to continue Judah's subservience to Assyria. The prophet Zephaniah describes the period before Josiah reached the age of majority as a time of injustice and violence (Zeph 1:9; 3:1-7). Fortunately for Judah, the Assyrian Empire began an irreversible decline.

Josiah took advantage of the situation by initiating a cultural revolution, which had as its central feature the reinstatement of Judah's ancestral religious traditions in national life (2 Kgs 22:3–23:27). Josiah sought to expand the area under his control by retaking what once was Judahite territory in the southwest and by extending his authority into areas that were once part of the former kingdom of Israel (2 Kgs 23:19).

Again, the Deuteronomist concentrates on the cultic aspects of Josiah's cultural revolution, but it is clear that the "reform" was not limited to matters liturgical. The Deuteronomistic account of Josiah's reign asserts that the impetus for Josiah's actions came as a result of finding "the book of the law" during the course of repair work on the temple of Jerusalem (2 Kgs 22:1-20). Although the book is not identified specifically, it is clear that the Deuteronomist intends readers to assume the book was Deuteronomy.[23] Now the book of Deuteronomy is only minimally concerned with matters of ritual and cult. Its basic concern is to motivate its readers to live according to traditional Israelite moral values. Among those emphasized in Deuteronomy is the need for just intersocietal relationships and the obligation to care for the poor.

The restoration of a society based on justice was probably not the principal impulse for Josiah's reform. That motivation came from a resurgent nationalism after more than a century of humiliation under Assyrian domination. But once reform was sweeping through Judah, its contours could not be limited by such a narrow purpose. The atmosphere created by Josiah's reform provided an opportunity for prophets such as Zephaniah and Jeremiah to speak out about the abuse of the poor. Jeremiah called for something more than simple reform of Judahite patterns of worship. He urged a return to the ancient values of Yahwism (Jer 6:16-21). Unfortunately, the zeal for reform ended with Josiah's tragic death at Megiddo (2 Kgs 23:29). Judah's short-lived independence ended and its fate was sealed. Within twenty-two years after Josiah's death, the Judahite state fell. Its territory was absorbed into the Babylonian provincial system and its leading citizens were taken into exile (2 Kgs 25:11) to forestall any resistance to Babylonian imperialism.

It is important to note that the Deuteronomist asserts that it was the "poorest people of the land" who remained after the deportation of Jerusalem's elite (2 Kgs 25:12). It is ironic that it took the fall of the Judahite national state to free these people from the rapaciousness of the wealthy and the corruption of the economic system. The people of means schemed and cheated to dispossess the poor but, in the end, the poor were able to repossess what was rightfully theirs. The Former Prophets thus begin and end the same way: those without land receive the land of Canaan as an inheritance from God, the true owner of that land. At the beginning of Israel's story as recounted in the Former Prophets, the gift of the land meant victory and salvation for all Yahweh's people. At the end of the story, it meant exile for the wealthy and the powerful.

Conclusion

The Former Prophets tell a very sad story. What begins with so much promise ends in tragedy. At the beginning and at the end of the story stand the poor and dispossessed. The Former Prophets begin with the book of Joshua, which describes the miracle of divine power that enabled escaped slaves to establish a new social and economic order in the land that God promised to their ancestors—a social order without distinctions based on economic power, for all Israelites were to have their share of the land. The foundation of Israelite society was to be loyalty and commitment to Yahweh. The Former Prophets, however, tell a story that highlights Israel's disloyalty and failure to remain committed to the service of Yahweh alone. The people asked for a king to ensure their security but that institution served only to accelerate the process that led to the fall of the two Israelite national states. These states fell because some Israelites were not content with their share of Israel's inheritance, but sought to accumulate as much as possible for themselves at the expense of the powerless. In the end, however, it was the powerless who were left in the land while the people of means found themselves in exile from the land that was to be Israel's everlasting inheritance.

Questions for Reflection

1. How does the story of Rahab and the spies (Josh 2) reflect the struggle of those who find themselves on the margins of society?

2. How do the stories in the book of Judges reflect the struggles of the poor and oppressed?

3. What argument does 1 Sam 8 use in trying to dissuade Israel from asking for a king?

4. Compare how Hannah and David use the vocabulary of the poor.

5. What caused the revolutions against David's rule?

6. What was the cause of the revolution against the house of David following Solomon's death?

7. What was the fate of the peasants under the kings of the two Israelite national states?

CHAPTER THREE

THE LATTER PROPHETS

While there is some disagreement about the importance of the motifs of "the poor" and "poverty" in the Former Prophets, there can be none regarding the centrality of these themes in the Latter Prophets (Isaiah, Jeremiah, Ezekiel, and the Twelve). Prophecy was not a phenomenon unique to ancient Israel. Other peoples in the ancient Near East had their specialists in the process of divine-human communication. Among the special characteristics of prophecy in ancient Israel is an intense criticism of the monarchy and associated institutions, especially the judicial system (Amos 5:7; Isa 5:23; Mic 3:9-11; Jer 22:13-17). Other objects of prophetic criticism were the wealthy landowners and creditors who foreclosed on peasants who were unable to repay loans. Ancient Israel witnessed the gradual concentration of land in the hands of a few and the creation of a great number of landless farmers who were reduced to hiring themselves out as agricultural workers to survive (Isa 5:8; Mic 2:1-3; Ezek 22:29; Hab 2:5-6). Merchants who defrauded their customers also heard their practices condemned by the prophets (Hos 12:7-8; Amos 8:5; Mic 6:10-11; Isa 3:14; Jer 5:27).

Ancient Israel's prophets were not economic theorists or social critics. What they did was to make Israel appreciate the consequences of the injustice that infested the ancient Israelite social and economic system. The prophets did not regard poverty as the result of chance, destiny, or impersonal forces. Poverty was the creation of the rich who disregarded the norms of traditional Israelite morality because of their greed (Amos 3:9; Hab 2:9; Jer 5:27; Ezek 45:9; Mal 3:5). The wealthy used their economic power and political influence not to build up the community but to advance their goals of becoming wealthier and more powerful. The prophets believed that behavior, which ignored traditional Israelite values, called forth divine judgment. They were certain that God called them to announce the inevitability of that judgment.

Amos

The prophet Amos clearly blamed the royal establishment and the people of means for creating poverty in the kingdom of Israel. On the surface, the extraordinarily long reign of Jeroboam II (788–748 BCE) was a time of great peace and economic prosperity. The nation was poised to exploit its resources for the benefit of its people. Unfortunately, beneath this veneer of prosperity there festered social and class conflict. The upper classes, concentrated in urban areas such as Hazor, Megiddo, Bethel, and Samaria, were manipulating the nation's institutions to amass ever greater wealth at the expense of the peasant farmers. The people of means used their power to control the judicial system, depriving the peasants of their ancestral lands and even their personal liberty. It was one thing to falsify weights and measures in the marketplace and engage in other dishonest commercial practices (Amos 8:5-6). But by corrupting the judicial system, the wealthy were creating poverty and a permanent underclass in Israel (2:7; 5:11). Amos knew of these developments in the kingdom of Israel though he was a native of the kingdom of Judah. He ventured to the royal sanctuary of Bethel (Amos 7:12-13) in order to speak out in the name of God against the injustice that became characteristic of Israel's economic life: "For I [Yahweh] know how many are your transgressions, and how great are your sins—you who afflict the righteous, who take a bribe, and push aside the needy in the gate" (Amos 5:12).

The city gates provided the setting for the settling of disagreements. Before the rise of the monarchy, elders adjudicated cases brought to them, protecting the rights of the poor (e.g., Ps 82; Jer 5:28-29; 22:15; Deut 1:16-17) and serving as arbiters in matters of dispute (e.g., Deut 21:18-21; 22:13-19; Ruth 4:2-12). The elders made their decisions on the basis of traditional values and customs. With the rise of the monarchy, royal appointees sat with the elders to dispense justice. The system depended on the veracity of witnesses and the honesty of the elders who sat in judgment. The clear implication of Amos's words is that the judicial system has broken down. Both witnesses and judges accepted bribes. The result was that the poor had no possibility of receiving equitable treatment. An example of how Israel's judicial system could be corrupted is illustrated by the story of Naboth, which describes Jezebel's success in coopting "the elders and nobles" of Naboth's town into falsely convicting him of treason (1 Kgs 21:8-13).

It is important to note that Amos equated the poor with the righteous in both 2:6 and 5:12. The righteous person is one who fulfills the demands that flow from a particular relationship. Judges and witnesses are righteous when they fulfill their responsibilities with integrity. Above all else, judges are to be righteous. They are to restore the rights of those who have been deprived of them. In doing so, they ensure the restoration of good order to society. Amos believes that judges should declare in favor of the poor because their poverty has been created by the wealthy who have manipulated the system. Because of the judges' failure to declare the needy "righteous," the prophet does so. That judges and witnesses ought to be righteous stems from God's righteousness in taking the side of the Hebrew slaves against their oppressors (Ps 103:6-7). Amos's words imply that what God has done for the people of Israel, God does for the individual members of that community who are poor and oppressed (see Ps 68). God's actions on behalf of the poor declare them to be righteous. For Amos, it was not the judges and elders who were in the right but the poor whose rights they ignored. The poor were entitled to have their rights recognized by the powerful in Israelite society, but that recognition was not forthcoming.[1]

Amos 2:6-7 illustrates the situation that incited the prophet's condemnation of the Israelite economic system:

> Thus says the LORD:
> For three transgressions of Israel,
>   and for four, I will not revoke the punishment;
> because they sell the righteous for silver,
>   and the needy for a pair of sandals—
> they who trample the head of the poor into the dust of the earth,
>   and push the afflicted out of the way. . . .

The prophet's words indict judges for their corruption and the creditors who bring a case against the poor to recover trifles. While Israelite custom permitted bond slavery as a means to pay off debts, Amos castigated lenders who pounced on a poor man's inability to pay off the smallest of debts. The prophet continued his oracle by asserting that the oppression of the poor is a crime that exposes Israel to divine judgment. The basis for the prophet's criticism was his conviction that the protection of the poor and powerless was at the very center of ancient Israel's moral traditions and should have been a priority of the judicial system. Concern for the poor is reflected in ancient law, in the admonitions of the sages, and in the hymns of Israel's worship. Despite the centrality of this tradition, the people of means used their economic power to corrupt judges into pronouncing judgments that deprived the poor of their ancestral land and their freedom simply to settle a minor debt. Of course, the wealthy oppressed the poor in order to support a lifestyle of extravagance (Amos 4:1; 5:11; 8:4). Their pursuit of luxury was made possible by the oppression of the poor.

The prophecy of Amos is an unrelenting attack on the social evils that helped create poverty and a dependent underclass in eighth-century Israel. Amos excoriated the wealthy because they seized the lands of the poor, corrupted the judicial system, and manipulated the economy for their benefit.[2] He painted a picture of the wealthy that made them look heartless and dishonest. Unlike Elisha, who was active a century earlier, Amos did not call for a revolution (see 2 Kgs 9:1-10). Anyone who criticizes the powerful and points out that their wealth and position were stolen from the poor will be accused of fomenting revolution as was Amos, though the prophet vehemently denied that he was a revolutionary (Amos 7:12-15). Amos likely thought that revolution was futile since he seems to have held out no hope for the northern kingdom. At the very least, the prophet believed that Israel would have to experience divine judgment before any restoration might be possible.[3]

Amos did suggest that the kingdom of Israel might again experience God's graciousness if its people "establish justice" in their land (Amos 5:15). On the whole, however, it appears as though the prophet held out little prospect of any change on Israel's part. What the nation had to look forward to was a terrible day of judgment: "Alas for you who desire the day of the LORD! Why do you want the day of the LORD? It is darkness, not light..." (Amos 5:18). The "day of the Lord" was a central theme of prophetic preaching.[4] This expression encapsulated the belief that Yahweh would protect Israel from being destroyed by its enemies. Though these enemies may at times dominate Israel, their power can only be temporary, for on "the day of the Lord" that power will be broken. Amos asserted that Israel was correct to view the day of the Lord as the time for God to move against God's enemies. What Israel failed to understand, however, was that it was numbered among God's enemies because of the oppression of the poor that had become so endemic to its economic system.

Amos did not idealize the poor or poverty. The poor were righteous not because of their poverty but because they had been denied their rights by people of means. The poor were "in the right" while the wealthy were not. The poor were faithful to their covenantal obligations; the rich were not. The purpose of the prophet's oracles is not to set the poor on any pedestal. Amos attempted to make certain that Israel knew the cause of its impending and unavoidable doom. Israel would have to face judgment because of the treatment that the poor were receiving. They were denied their rights as

Israelites for the sake of increasing the wealth and supporting the lifestyle of the ruling class.

It almost appears as though Amos is describing a class conflict in the style of a twentieth-century Marxist. For Amos, however, the poor do not really form a "class" in opposition to the wealthy. The poor are simply those members of Israelite society who are alone and defenseless. They are not in any way organized in opposition to the wealthy in some sort of a class struggle. But the prophet did see the rich not simply as individuals but as a group that marshaled political, judicial, and social forces to undercut the poor and thereby increase their own wealth. Still, the prophet did not see a class struggle or revolution as the outcome of the oppression of the poor by the wealthy. Yahweh and Yahweh alone will bring judgment upon Israel.

Isaiah 1–39

Amos preached in the northern kingdom but he had a "twin" in the south who delivered the kinds of denunciations of social inequities that are remarkably like his own.[5] With an anger that bordered on rage, Isaiah railed against the wealthy landowners and corrupt judges whose scruples did not prevent them from conspiring to rob the poor of their rights, their land, and their freedom:

> Your princes are rebels
> > and companions of thieves.
> Everyone loves a bribe
> > and runs after gifts.
> They do not defend the orphan,
> > and the widow's cause does not come before them. (1:23)

> The LORD enters into judgment
> > with the elders and princes of his people:
> It is you who have devoured the vineyard;
> > the spoil of the poor is in your houses.
> What do you mean by crushing my people,
> > by grinding the face of the poor? says the Lord GOD of hosts.
> > > (3:14-15)

> Ah, you who join house to house,
> > who add field to field,

until there is room for no one but you,
    and you are left to live alone in the midst of the land! (5:8)

Ah, you who are heroes in drinking wine
    and valiant at mixing drink,
who acquit the guilty for a bribe,
    and deprive the innocent of their rights! (5:22-23)

Ah, you who make iniquitous decrees,
    who write oppressive statutes,
to turn aside the needy from justice
    and to rob the poor of my people of their right,
that widows may be your spoil,
    and that you may make the orphans your prey! (10:1-2)

The villainies of villains are evil;
    they devise wicked devices
to ruin the poor with lying words,
    even when the plea of the needy is right. (32:7)

Like Amos, Isaiah viewed poverty as the creation of the wealthy. Their avarice led them to transform the judicial system into a vehicle to enhance their social position and economic power. They conspired with corrupt judges and royal officials to deprive the poor of their rights, to confiscate their land, and to reduce them to the level of hired workers. The prophet condemned the people of means as pampered and pleasure seeking, who stole from the poor to maintain their lavish lifestyle.

The prophet began his ministry during the reign of Uzziah (781–740 BCE). The forty years that Uzziah occupied the throne of David was perhaps the most prosperous period for the kingdom of Judah. But Isaiah's prophecy reveals that during this time of economic growth, Judah was becoming two societies: one made up of people of means (royal officials, wealthy traders, and owners of large estates) and the other of the poor, who paid the price for Judah's prosperity with their labor and mortgaged land. Using a familiar metaphor, the prophet compared the kingdom of Judah to a well-tended vineyard, which should have produced fine harvests but yielded only rotten grapes (Isa 5:1-7). There was little point in maintaining such an unproductive vineyard. God would abandon Judah to the "briers and thorns" of military conquest and exile. Judah would not become what it should have been through the support of and participation in the liturgy of the temple. The prophet declared that God found the rituals of the temple unacceptable and even offensive because of the crimes against the poor that were committed by the very people whose support of the cult made the liturgy the lavish and impressive affair that it was (Isa 1:10-17).

Following Amos's lead, Isaiah too announced that the day of the Lord would be a day of judgment (2:6–3:15). The moral and social chaos fostered by Judah's elite would cause it to be included among God's enemies. The prophet believed that the failure of Israel's elders, judges, and kings to defend the poor required God to take action. God could not allow the poor to remain defenseless, so the day of judgment was inevitable. That day would be a time of humiliation for the wealthy (3:16–4:1). Isaiah was convinced that divine judgment on Judah and Jerusalem was unavoidable because the nation was decaying from within and heading for ruin (6:11-12). While an insignificant remnant would survive the day of judgment, Judah would be consumed in a new catastrophe (6:13; 10:22-23). Assyria was the instrument that God chose to execute that judgment (Isa 5:25-29). The problem that the prophet faced in persuading Judah to appreciate what the "day of the Lord" would mean centered on the failure of the country's elite to recognize the gravity of the situation. Apparently they did not recognize that their economic and social policies were a breach of traditional Israelite morality that would have serious consequences. Also, they did not appreciate how serious a threat the militarist and expansionist Assyrian Empire was.

Despite Isaiah's harsh words of judgment on Judahite society, the prophet did not give up on Judah entirely. He was certain that once God's purpose was fulfilled, God would rescue Judah from the Assyrians just as God saved Israel's ancestors from the Egyptians (Isa 10:24-27). The prophet believed in a God whose purpose could not be frustrated by the avarice and injustice of the wealthy. He affirmed that the judgment that Zion would experience would purify the city from the corruption of injustice (Isa 4:2-6). What the elite of the city did to the poor will be done to them. Of course, God's purpose is not to oppress but to restore, but God's restoration of Jerusalem will not be cheap grace. There will be judgment. But once that judgment takes place, Jerusalem will be redeemed and once again be "full of justice" (1:21-28). The prophet expected a king from the Davidic dynasty to be God's instrument for the restoration of justice in Judah. The rule of this king will bring about the triumph of justice (Isa 9:7). Unlike those judges who were corrupted by the wealthy, the king whom the prophet expected will "not judge by what his eyes see, or decide by what his ears hear; but with righteousness he shall judge the poor, and decide with equity for the meek of the earth" (Isa 11:3-4). The corruption of Judah's judicial system and the consequent oppression of the poor disgusted the prophet, but he believed that God would raise up a new king for a restored Judah. The judgment that Judah will face because of the injustice done to its poor will not be God's last word. Justice will again reign in Jerusalem (Isa 28:5-6; 37:30-32). Isaiah's apparent faith in the possibilities of a renewed monarchy was misplaced. It was precisely the failure of Judah's kings to fulfill their obligations toward the powerless of Judahite society that brought divine judgment. The Judahite monarchy never became the instrument of justice that Isaiah hoped it would be.

Despite the prophet's conviction that God will not allow the poor to remain helpless, Isaiah did not idealize the poor. He even included Judah's widows and orphans among those facing judgment:

> That is why the Lord did not have pity on their young people,
>   or compassion on their orphans and widows;
> for everyone was godless and an evildoer,
>   and every mouth spoke folly.
> For all this his anger has not turned away,
>   his hand is stretched out still. (9:17)

Poverty is not a state that makes a person somehow closer to God. Poverty is the result of being denied one's fundamental rights. The corruption of Judah's political and economic system that led to the oppression of the poor and the enriching of the elite was an evil that had to be eliminated. Because Judah failed to reform its system, God would take the side of the poor to ensure the victory of justice: "The meek shall obtain fresh joy in the LORD, and the neediest people shall exult in the Holy One of Israel" (Isa 29:19). Isaiah, then, anticipated the new order in which God vindicates the poor (Isa 14:30; 26:6; 32:7). It is the prophet's confidence in the eventual triumph of justice that makes his message so engaging.

Micah

As convinced as Isaiah was about the role Judah's elite was playing in leading the country into disaster, he was certain that there was a future for Jerusalem beyond the coming judgment. The prophet's words of judgment appear to be tempered by his hope for the future. Micah's prophecy focuses much more on the judgment that Judah was going to face because of the injustice that was so endemic to its social and economic structure. Micah came from Moresheth-gath (Mic 1:1), a village in the southwestern part of Judah. His words are representative of the rural conservatives who considered the economic machinations of the rich and powerful of Jerusalem as a perversion of traditional Israelite values.

Micah's message is similar to that of Isaiah, though Micah casts his in more striking language. There is no misunderstanding what this prophet wants to say as he castigates Judah's elite for creating a two-tiered society of the wealthy and the poor. Also, like Isaiah, Micah did not consider the words of judgment he proclaimed in God's name to be the last word. He saw a future for Jerusalem, but on the way to that future, the Jerusalem of the present will come to an end so that God can reestablish the city in justice and righteousness (Mic 4). But before that can happen, the society created by perverting the justice due to the poor will have to be destroyed. Micah's declaration of that destruction is unmistakable.

According to the title of the book (1:1), Micah's ministry began during the reign of Jotham (759–744 BCE), the son and successor of Uzziah, who used a time of peace to prepare for war (2 Chr 26:9, 11-15) by strengthening the army and building fortifications. Micah also preached during the reign of the next two kings: Ahaz (743–728 BCE) and Hezekiah (727–699 BCE). Both these kings had to pay tribute to Assyria since, at Ahaz's initiative, Judah became a vassal-state of the Assyrian Empire (2 Kgs 16:7-8). Hezekiah was determined to withhold tribute from Assyria to begin a program of rearmament and fortification (2 Chr 32). The policies of these kings placed a terrible burden on the poor, who had to pay for their implementation.

In 721 BCE the Assyrian Empire ended the political existence of the kingdom of Israel, incorporating its territory into the Assyrian provincial system. One consequence of this event was that refugees from the north swelled the population of Jerusalem to three or four times what it had been.[6] This new population strained the resources of the city. It simply did not have the resources to absorb the numbers of people who came looking for protection. This likely led to an increase of prices for basic necessities. At the same time, the expanded labor market brought down wages. While this was a boon for the owners of large estates, it was another burden for the poor to bear. What Micah saw was the disintegration of Judah's social fabric (7:1-6). He believed that what was happening to the poor was contrary to the divine will. Micah was certain that Judah's unjust social and economic system made of its God a force that would bring about its destruction.

The book of Micah begins with an announcement of divine judgment against Samaria, the capital of the kingdom of Israel (1:2-7). The inclusion of Judah and Jerusalem in verse 5 appears as an afterthought, though it shows that Jerusalem should be ready to face the same judgment that is coming on Samaria. Micah's lament over Jerusalem shows that he took no joy in proclaiming its coming judgment. The prophet did not stand above the city and its people but with them. This led him to react in horror and grief to the very message that he is about to give: "I will lament and wail; I will go barefoot and naked . . . . For her wound is incurable. . . . It has come to Judah; it has reached to the gate of my people, to Jerusalem" (1:8-9). Still, the prophet was unrelenting in his criticism of those who steal the land of the poor (2:1-5). In 2:1-2, Micah identifies those he is addressing:

> Alas for those who devise wickedness
> and evil deeds on their beds!
> When the morning dawns, they perform it,
> because it is in their power.
> They covet fields, and seize them;
> houses, and take them away;
> they oppress householder and house,
> people and their inheritance.

Micah addressed the people who had economic and political power in Jerusalem and were eager to use it. He focused on the use of power to amass property, something Isaiah decried as well (see Isa 5:8). Though Micah did not provide details of how the powerful were able to seize a person's ancestral holdings, it was probably by making loans with exorbitant interest rates and then foreclosing upon default. What the prophet condemned was not simple greed, but the violation of a basic tenet of Israelite morality as found in the Decalogue. Micah even used the word "covet," which recalls the commandment (Mic 2:2; see Exod 20:17; Deut 5:21). The ideal Israelite society was not to have a class of debt-slaves, laborers, or sharecroppers: "There will, however, be no one in need among you, because the LORD is sure to bless you in the land that the LORD your God is giving you as a possession to occupy" (Deut 15:4). Everyone was to have access to the means of production, which in an agricultural economy meant the ownership of land. Jerusalem's powerful were taking the ancestral holdings of subsistence farmers by "legal" means, and thus severely limiting the economic opportunities of a whole class of people. In other words, the actions of Judah's elite were creating poverty. The prophet promised the wealthy that there would come a time when God would restore economic justice, but they and their descendants will find that they have no share in that new allotment of land (2:3-5).

So that there would be no mistaking his announcement of judgment, Micah uses a metaphor that is not merely blunt but horrific. He describes the actions of those responsible for maintaining a just society as cannibalism:

> Listen, you heads of Jacob
>> and rulers of the house of Israel!
> Should you not know justice?—
>> you who hate the good and love the evil,
> who tear their skin off my people,
>> and their flesh off their bones;
> who eat the flesh of my people,
>> flay their skin off them,
> break their bones in pieces,
>> and chop them up like meat in a kettle,
>> like flesh in a caldron.
> Then they will cry to the LORD,
>> but he will not answer them;
> he will hide his face from them at that time,
>> because they have acted wickedly. (Mic 3:1-4)

Those whom Micah addressed here were the people responsible for the administration of justice: the elders and judges. Those who should have been the guardians of traditional Israelite morality allowed themselves to be coopted by the people of means, thus abetting their theft from the poor (e.g., 1 Kgs 21). They loved bribes and this made them partners with those who were stealing the land of those who could not afford to make payoffs (see Isa 1:23 for a similar critique). The greed of these judges for bribes was so great that the prophet did not hesitate to use shocking hyperbole: these judges were guilty of nothing less than eating the innocent.[7] The priests and prophets who should have protested this corruption said nothing because they did not want to endanger their own economic status (3:5, 11). The conclusion that the prophet arrived at was obvious: because Judah's upper classes cheat the poor, they are living under a curse pronounced on them by God. (6:9-16). Of course, the country's leadership did not accept the prophet's critique and tried to silence him (2:6). Judah's elite did not want to hear where they were leading the nation. They were confident that God was with them and would protect Judah from all harm, despite what they considered overheated rhetoric from the prophet (Mic 3:1).

Micah's most bitter critique of Judah's leadership and the unjust social system over which it presides occurs in 3:9-12:

> Hear this, you rulers of the house of Jacob
>> and chiefs of the house of Israel,
> who abhor justice
>> and pervert all equity,

who build Zion with blood
            and Jerusalem with wrong!
Its rulers give judgment for a bribe,
            its priests teach for a price,
            its prophets give oracles for money;
yet they lean upon the LORD and say,
            "Surely the LORD is with us!
            No harm shall come upon us."
Therefore because of you
            Zion shall be plowed as a field;
Jerusalem shall become a heap of ruins,
            and the mountain of the house a wooded height.

This text reprises the themes of all that precedes. It begins with a general denunciation of Judah's judicial system. Abuse of power by the judges made it impossible for the people of the city to have sound relationships with each other—relationships based on the ideals of traditional Israelite morality. Micah becomes more specific when he accuses the country's leadership of building Jerusalem "with blood" (v. 10). According to the mythological perspective, building "the city of God" was God's responsibility that was transferred to the king, God's viceroy (Pss 51:18; 102:16). The prophet condemned the building of the city's fortifications, palaces, and temple as anything but a holy enterprise. Archaeology has underscored the biblical text's witness to the amount of building activity that went on in Jerusalem during Micah's ministry.[8] The work was necessary to accommodate the refugees from the north and to prepare for a probable siege by the Assyrians. Micah condemned this activity as nothing less than murder since it made the economic circumstances of ordinary folk even more precarious by consuming Judah's economic resources, which were so needed by the poor.

Micah included Judah's religious leaders in his criticism since they offered theological support for an unjust social system, providing a divine warrant for the exploitation of the poor—the very opposite of the role they should have been playing (Mic 3:11b). Jerusalem's priests and prophets sold out to the powerful and wealthy. Of particular interest is Micah's critique of the prophets. Ancient Israel had many more prophets than the few whose words are found in the Bible. Most, however, were creatures of the system that Micah hated (see 1 Kgs 22:6; Jer 28). What angered Micah most was the venality of his colleagues (Mic 3:11a). Still, the greatest folly perpetrated by Judah's leaders was the assurance that they gave the people regarding their standing before God. They counseled a naive reliance upon God and the temple when the nation was doomed because of its injustice. The prophet ended his oracle by announcing the destruction of Jerusalem—a destruction so complete that land on which the city was standing could be cultivated and the site of the temple would revert to a habitat for wild animals (3:12). The coming judgment is inescapable because it will be the outcome of a lawsuit that God has against Judah and Jerusalem (Mic 6:1-8). In that lawsuit, God will be the prosecutor, witness, and judge. Judah's response to God's call for justice was a well-functioning liturgy (Mic 6:6-7). In Micah's view, this wholly deficient response seals Judah's doom.

The prophet's message changes so abruptly in 4:1-5 that some commentators suggest that this passage was inserted into the book of Micah in the post-exilic period, when the more common prophetic form was the oracle of salvation.[9] Also, since verses 1-4 appear in Isa 2:2-4, they are hardly ever ascribed to Micah. This passage does assert that in the future, God's earthly dwelling will be changed and God will rule over all nations from Jerusalem. God's rule will bring justice and peace to the world and security to Israel:

> In days to come
>> the mountain of the LORD's house
> shall be established as the highest of the mountains,
>> and shall be raised up above the hills.
> Peoples shall stream to it,
>> and many nations shall come and say:
> "Come, let us go up to the mountain of the LORD,
>> to the house of the God of Jacob;
> that he may teach us his ways
>> and that we may walk in his paths."
> For out of Zion shall go forth instruction,
>> and the word of the LORD from Jerusalem.
> He shall judge between many peoples,
>> and shall arbitrate between strong nations far away;
> they shall beat their swords into plowshares,
>> and their spears into pruning hooks;
> nation shall not lift up sword against nation,
>> neither shall they learn war any more;
> but they shall all sit under their own vines and under their own
>> fig trees,
>> and no one shall make them afraid;
>> for the mouth of the LORD of hosts has spoken.
> For all the peoples walk,
>> each in the name of its god,

but we will walk in the name of the LORD our God
   forever and ever. (Mic 4:1-5)

The opening phrase of this text, "in days to come," is an important key to its interpretation. This prophetic formula cues the reader that what follows does not refer to the immediate future but to an ideal period that will come in God's good time. Here Micah and Isaiah agree: the Jerusalem of the present will experience severe judgment because of its unjust social system. This judgment, however, is not God's last word upon the city, for God will reestablish Jerusalem to make it what it always should have been: a city of justice. Like Isaiah, Micah appended a picture of an ideal future to his condemnation of the present. Notice that the text does not say "Jerusalem will not fall," but that at some time in the future the city will be the place from which God will rule the world with justice.

The prophet's rhetoric moves beyond the present into an ideal future, as is clear from the assertion that "in days to come" the mountain of the Lord will be higher than all other mountains. The reality is that the hill on which the temple is built is not even as high as the Mount of Olives, just across the Kidron Valley. Once the nations see the glorification of Jerusalem's temple, they will engulf the city like pilgrims, wanting to learn the Torah so that they can shape their lives according to its ideals. The problem that the prophet cites in 3:9-12 was that the priests and prophets were not teaching God's word. In his vision of Jerusalem's future, Micah affirmed that it will be God who will teach and prophesy.

The familiar words of 4:4 need no comment except to note that the line that pictures Israelite farmers relaxing under the shade of their vines and fruit trees is missing from the Isaianic parallel, but is particularly appropriate in Micah because of his complaints against the confiscation of land. Here the prophet draws a very attractive picture of the average Israelite farmer living in the security that comes from the land. The economic system of Micah's day turned the peasants of Judah into tenants and slaves, but in the ideal future they will rest on their own land. Verse 5 is an act of faith on the prophet's part. Since the nations still serve their gods, the fulfillment of this vision lies in the indeterminate future. Still, the prophet's words give hope that the unjust economic system of the present is doomed.

Micah assured his readers that God, who is responsible for the catastrophe that is coming upon Jerusalem, would restore the city and its people one day. He used the imagery of a shepherd who gathers the strays from the flock—a familiar image in his culture (4:6-8). The ideal future that the prophet described will witness God ruling from Jerusalem (4:8). Still, the people of Jerusalem worried about the difficulties that they would have to face, but

Micah assured them that God was in their midst to deliver them (4:9-10).[10] The plans of the political powers that threaten Jerusalem will ultimately be frustrated (4:11-13).

Micah's prophecy came from someone who gave up on the possibilities of the immediate present. The prophet saw injustice against the poor perpetrated by people of means and supported by Jerusalem's judges, priests, and prophets—the very people who were to uphold justice. He saw the society to which he belonged disintegrating and concluded that this was God's judgment upon Jerusalem. Still, Micah did not despair since he believed that a future was coming when the problems that dominated Jerusalem's present would be taken away. Like his contemporary, Isaiah, Micah still had some faith in the Davidic dynasty, despite its failures. He believed that a prince from this dynasty would keep Judah from total destruction and usher in an era of peace (Mic 5:1-5; ET 5:2-6). There will come a time of peace when God will reestablish Jerusalem. In that city to which the nations will come and from which God will rule the whole earth, the ordinary Israelite farmer will find security that comes from a just social order. Still, it is important to note that while Micah saw a glorification of Jerusalem in the future, the city would have to experience its judgment. The Jerusalem of the prophet's day stood under God's curse.

Micah's prophecy is so special because it reflects the perspective of the peasantry. The prophet came from a place not infected by the venality of Judah's capital. The prophetic rhetoric is extreme at times. Still, he does not make outlandish demands in the name of the poor: "they shall all sit under their own vines and under their own fig trees, and no one shall make them afraid" (Mic 4:4). Those who deny this simple pleasure to the poor stand under divine judgment, which is sure to come. Micah proclaimed that God will not allow crimes against the poor to continue with impunity.

Zephaniah

The opening verse of the book of Zephaniah dates the prophet's ministry to the reign of Josiah (641–610 BCE). A careful reading of the book leads to a bit more precision. Josiah came to the throne when he was just eight years old (2 Kgs 22:1). While the prophet severely criticized Judah's leadership, he never denounced the king, perhaps because he was still a child when the prophet preached.[11] Also, a significant concern of Zephaniah was Judah's religious syncretism (Zeph 1:4-6), which suggests a setting before Josiah began his purification of Judah's national cult in the eighteenth year of his reign (2 Kgs 22:3).

Josiah came to the throne in tragic circumstances. His father Amon (641–640 BCE) was assassinated by his own retainers (2 Kgs 21:23). During Amon's two-year reign, the pro-Assyrian policies of Manasseh's extraordinarily long rule (698–642 BCE) remained in place. Assyria's deterioration enabled Josiah to change these policies as he began to rule in his own name, but it was difficult to undo the economic and religious consequences of policies that had been in place for a half century. Manasseh was a pliant Assyrian vassal because he knew that the Assyrians would not tolerate even the hint of rebellion. Of course, someone had to pay the price for Manasseh's collaboration. While all sectors of Jerusalem's economy were adversely affected, the people with the fewest economic resources had to pay the heaviest burden. Their taxes supported Jerusalem's royal establishment and paid Judah's tribute to Assyria. The peasants of Judah and Jerusalem were conscripted for service in the Assyrian army and for work on building projects in Nineveh. But commercial contacts with the peoples of the Assyrian Empire did benefit some people. That may be why the prophet singles out Jerusalem's merchants for judgment, promising that their profits will be wiped out: "The inhabitants of the Mortar wail, for all the traders have perished; all who weigh out silver are cut off" (1:11).

Contacts with other peoples were probably also the occasion for the significant innovations in Judah's life. For example, the prophet objected to the foreign attire favored by the royal family and their retainers (Zeph 1:8) because he saw it as another example of how far the upper classes distanced themselves from the fundamental values of their ancestral religious tradition. Important consequences of this move away from these values were the "violence and fraud" that the prophet saw as characteristic of the behavior of Judah's elite (Zeph 1:9). They acted with impunity against the poor because they believed that events had shown that Yahweh was no longer an effective force in Judah's life: "At that time I will search Jerusalem with lamps, and I will punish the people...who say in their hearts, 'The LORD will not do good, nor will he do harm'" (1:12). They believed that the God of their ancestors was unable to prevent them from doing what was necessary to enrich themselves at the expense of the poor.

Zephaniah announced the harshest words of judgment that any prophet ever addressed to Jerusalem: "Ah, soiled, defiled, oppressing city! It has listened to no voice; it has accepted no correction" (Zeph 3:1-2a). The prophet continued his diatribe by criticizing the city's political and religious leadership, which he regarded as self-important and venal (3:3-4). Since the prophet singled out Jerusalem's elite for criticism, one can assume that those who were the objects of the oppression were Judah's underclass, who were exploited and even killed in the rush of the wealthy to enrich themselves.

The prophet noted that Judah's elite had heard criticism of their behavior before, but had "listened to no voice," not even that of Zephaniah's prophetic predecessors (Isa 30:8-12; Mic 2:6). The prophet cited God's promise to assemble all nations—including Judah—for judgment. Those guilty will be devoured by "the fire of [God's] passion" (3:8). But Zephaniah, like Isaiah and Micah, did not believe divine judgment was God's last word for Judah. He described the salvation of a humble remnant (3:11-13). These people will be ashamed of their past. Their behavior in both the temple and marketplace will reflect their reconciliation with God. The prophet concluded his words to Jerusalem by calling for the city and its people to rejoice. And remarkably, Zephaniah has God joining in the singing and dancing:

> The LORD, your God, is in your midst,
>   a warrior who gives victory;
> he will rejoice over you with gladness,
>   he will renew you in his love;
>   he will exult over you with loud singing. (3:17)

While the prophet had no illusions about Jerusalem's failures and the divine judgment that these will bring upon Israel, Zephaniah believed in Jerusalem's future with God—a future in which God would join the city's citizens in festive singing and dancing.

There is one feature of Zephaniah's rhetoric that deserves special comment. Zephaniah did not address the poor; he spoke only of the wealthy and powerful, describing their sin and their judgment. In two cases, however, the prophet used words that normally refer to economically and socially dependent people—'anwê hā'āreṣ ("the poor of the land"; Zeph 2:3), 'ānî (needy) and dāl (oppressed, powerless; Zeph 3:12)—to speak about those who recognize their complete dependence on God.[12] The prophet believed that the judgment coming on Jerusalem was not God's revenge or punishment on the city as much as it was God's action to transform the people of Jerusalem from being oppressive and self-sufficient to being "humble and lowly." To describe the people of Jerusalem following this transformation, the prophet borrowed the vocabulary of the poor and reinterpreted it to speak not about material poverty but a poverty of the spirit. This reinterpretation involved a positive view of "poverty of spirit," but the biblical tradition has consistently viewed material poverty as an evil that should not exist among the people of God.

The prophet insisted that the only way Judah would be able to survive "the day of the LORD" (Zeph 1:7, 14; 2:2), which would be a day of wrath, distress, and anguish, was for the elite to acknowledge their need for God's protection. Since God is the protector of the poor, Judah's elite must act like the poor to enjoy that protection. While the prophet did not call for the wealthy to embrace material poverty, he implored them to embrace the kind of faith that is nothing less than an abandonment to the divine will accompanied by an absolute confidence in divine goodness. For Zephaniah, the words that express the kind of attitude people must have toward God come from the vocabulary of the poor. If the people of Judah wish to survive the coming judgment, they must give themselves to God as the poor must always do.

Like the text in which Jeremiah identifies with the poor (Jer 20:13), Zeph 2:3 and 3:12 use words for the poor in a metaphorical sense. Albert Gelin describes Zephaniah's reinterpretation of the vocabulary of the poor as a "turning-point in history."[13] While it is true that Zephaniah's reinterpretation does spiritualize poverty, one should not conclude that the biblical tradition has reached a point when it begins to ignore poverty as a social and economic problem to be overcome—as if its "spiritual" significance makes concern for the "material" side of the question obsolete as a religious and theological issue. Zephaniah is less responsible for some sort of a "turning-point" than for simply describing the attitude of people toward God following the transforming experience of divine judgment.[14]

Zephaniah believed that Judah's political and economic institutions were leading it to a terrible and inevitable end, which he spoke of as "the day of the LORD" (Zeph 1:14-16). But he warned Judah about the approaching judgment precisely because he believed that judgment was not to be God's final word. While the Judahite state might not survive the day of the Lord, the people could if they adopted the attitude so characteristic of the poor and oppressed: absolute confidence in God. Isaiah said as much when he spoke about the remnant that God would allow to survive judgment (Isa 1:25-26; 28:5-6). Zephaniah's achievement was not introducing a new idea into the prophetic understanding of the poor. What he did was proclaim a message of hope beyond judgment, a judgment that the prophet believed was as devastating as it was deserved. He was certain, however, that Judah would survive this judgment because it would transform its people into those who, like the poor, rely completely on God alone.

Jeremiah

Jeremiah's mission to Judah and Jerusalem took place during the years immediately preceding its destruction by the Babylonians in 587 BCE. The city survived the Assyrian threat but it could not survive that posed by the Neo-Babylonian Empire. By the time Nebuchadnezzar absorbed Judah into the Babylonian provincial system, Judah was effectively reduced to Jerusalem and a few square miles surrounding the city. Still, it appears as though Jeremiah was almost alone in his assessment of the great danger that Jerusalem faced. Apparently what kept the city from appreciating its precarious political situation was a belief that somehow, some way God would find a way to save the city at the last moment—a belief that is expressed in Isa 37:33-35:

> Therefore thus says the LORD concerning the king of Assyria: He shall not come into this city, shoot an arrow there, come before it with a shield, or cast up a siege ramp against it. By the way that he came, by the same he shall return; he shall not come into this city, says the LORD. For I will defend this city to save it, for my own sake and for the sake of my servant David.

The people of Jerusalem took these words, spoken at a specific time regarding a specific crisis, and turned them into a general promise by God to save the city when it was threatened. When Jeremiah announced that the city and its temple were doomed to fall to the Babylonians (Jer 7:2-15; 26:2-6), his words sounded not only treasonous but blasphemous: "Do not trust in these deceptive words: 'This is the temple of the LORD, the temple of the LORD, the temple of the LORD'" (7:4). As was the case in Micah's time, the vibrant liturgy of the Jerusalem temple prevented the people of Judah from recognizing their true standing before God.

Jeremiah announced that Judah was under divine judgment for its crimes—idol worship (11:13; 19:4, 13), pride (13:9), and failure to keep the Sabbath (17:19-27)—for its infidelity as Yahweh's bride. But as was the case with both Isaiah and Micah, Jeremiah held that God's principal complaint against Judah was its unjust social, political, and economic system. In a passage reminiscent of Abraham's bargaining with God over the fate of Sodom (Gen 18:16-33), God asks the prophet to find a single just person so that Jerusalem could be spared (5:1-9). Jeremiah looked among both the poor and the wealthy, but did not find a single person who acted justly. The prophet implied that God had little choice but to pronounce the sentence of death on the city and its people (v. 9). The exaggerated rhetoric of this passage probably reflects the impact that the corruption that strangled Jerusalem had on the prophet from Anathoth.[15] It is important to note that Jeremiah included the poor among those who did not "know the way of . . . the law of their God" (Jer 5:4). The prophet did not idealize the poor, but he did not blame them for Judah's desperate situation. He placed all the blame on Judah's upper classes.

The prophet Jeremiah preached in Jerusalem about one hundred years after Isaiah and Micah. Isaiah was a man of the city who considered the wilderness to be a place of demons and robbers (Isa 13:21; 34:11-15). Jeremiah, however, idealized the desert as the place that witnessed the time of Israel's fidelity: "Go and proclaim in the hearing of Jerusalem, Thus says the LORD: I remember the devotion of your youth, your love as a bride, how you followed me in the wilderness, in a land not sown" (Jer 2:2). Jeremiah was not reveling in a kind of wilderness romanticism but was looking back at a time when he believed there was a certain level of equality among the Israelites. In the prophet's eyes, the wilderness period was without conflicts between rich and poor. People lived by the promise of prosperity that was to be the consequence of fidelity. They were hatching no schemes against one another. There was neither confiscation of lands nor the enslavement of poor debtors. But all this changed when Israel made the land of Canaan its own. The land that was the source of Israel's wealth and prosperity became the object of contention among the Israelites. There emerged a class of people who amassed large tracts of land for themselves. Simultaneously there was a growing number of landless peasants who became "the poor." The latter became a permanent underclass because there was little opportunity for people without land to better their economic status. Like the Deuteronomist, Jeremiah assumes that there was a serious degeneration in the social and economic conditions in Israel. Again, the prophet held Judah's elite responsible.

Discounting Jeremiah's warnings, some people asked with fatuous complacency: "Is the LORD not in Zion?" (8:19; see also 14:19). God responds with a question: "Why have they provoked me to anger with their images, with their foreign idols?" The problem with idolatry was not simply a matter of violating the exclusive claim that God had on Israel's worship. Foreign religious traditions were used as theological support for an exploitive and oppressive social system. Yahwistic religious traditions sustained an economic system that was designed to give all people access to the means of production, land. It had mechanisms such as the Sabbatical and Jubilee years to ensure, as far as possible, that ancient Israelite society would preserve this economic system (see Lev 25).[16] Non-Yahwistic religious traditions provided support for a hierarchical social system that led to the development of two distinct societies in Judah and Jerusalem: the society of the wealthy and that of the poor. What led Jeremiah to envision the fall of the city was its people's assumption that God was honor-bound to uphold the city because it was God's own: "Is the LORD not in Zion?" The prophet concluded that Jerusalem was beyond salvation (Jer 15:5-6).

What sealed Judah's doom was the unwillingness of the wealthy to admit that they were guilty of exploiting the poor:

Also on your skirts is found
 the lifeblood of the innocent poor,
though you did not catch them breaking in.
 Yet in spite of all these things
you say, "I am innocent; surely his anger has turned from me."
Now I am bringing you to judgment
 for saying, "I have not sinned." (Jer 2:34-35)

This failure of the wealthy to accept responsibility for creating poverty in Judah made any rectification of the situation unlikely. The prophet spared no words in condemning those guilty of exploiting the poor:

For scoundrels are found among my people;
 they take over the goods of others.
Like fowlers they set a trap;
 they catch human beings.
Like a cage full of birds,
 their houses are full of treachery;
therefore they have become great and rich,
 they have grown fat and sleek.
They know no limits in deeds of wickedness;
 they do not judge with justice
the cause of the orphan, to make it prosper,
 and they do not defend the rights of the needy. (Jer 5:26-28)

It is the oppression of the poor that will bring judgment on Jerusalem (Jer 6:6). What the wealthy have accumulated because of their exploitation of the poor will be taken from them and given to others (Jer 6:12). The royal family too will lose its status (Jer 13:18). This is especially fitting since it was the king's responsibility to defend the rights of the poor.

Jeremiah did not hesitate to criticize Judah's kings for their failures. For example, the prophet condemned Jehoiakim for refusing to pay the laborers who worked on the expansion of his palace (Jer 22:13-14). Rather than protecting the rights of ordinary folk, the king used his power to steal their labor. Jeremiah asserted that what makes a king is not the splendor of his palace but his administration of justice. The prophet contrasted Jehoiakim's actions with those of his father, Josiah, who "judged the cause of the poor and needy" (Jer 22:16a). In a word of judgment reminiscent of the one spoken by Elijah against Jezebel (1 Kgs 21:23), Jeremiah predicted that Jehoiakim's death and burial would be as undignified as those of a donkey (Jer 22:18-20). Jeremiah considered the king's treatment of the poor to be a barometer of his righteousness as a king (Jer 22:15). While the prophet recognized that the king had rights, he was clear that these were subordinate to the monarch's responsibility toward those who had little or no standing in Judahite society. Jeremiah condemned royal ideology that considered the poor, their labor, and their property to be available to the king without restriction. Jehoiakim should have remembered that his injustice toward his workers was inviting divine judgment: "Sing to the LORD; praise the LORD! For he has delivered the life of the needy from the hands of evildoers" (Jer 20:13).

Although Jeremiah commended Josiah for his treatment of the poor (Jer 22:15b-16), the prophet said nothing about the actions that 2 Kgs 22–23 and 2 Chr 34–35 ascribe to Josiah. According to these texts Josiah initiated a purification of non-Yahwistic features of Judah's patterns of worship. He even attempted to do the same at shrines of the former northern kingdom. Neither Kings nor Chronicles mentions Jeremiah in connection with Josiah's actions and the prophet did not discuss the reform directly. Still, there are some hints that the prophet had some misgivings about rituals that did not reflect a commitment to ancient Israel's ethical values (Jer 6:16-21). Because he was a priest and a prophet himself, Jeremiah focused his criticism on his colleagues because they proclaimed peace to the very people whose crimes against the well-being of the poor were so obvious (Jer 6:13-15; 8:10-12). The sermon Jeremiah gave at one of the gates to the temple warned the people assembling for worship that the demands of justice can become obscured behind a well-conducted liturgy (Jer 7:1-15, especially vv. 5-10). Any reform that did not include a transformation of Judah's social and economic system would be superficial at best and hypocritical at worst.

Among the unique features of the book of Jeremiah are texts in which the prophet reveals his personal reaction to his experiences as a prophet.[17] These emotion-laden texts give the prophet's readers an insight into the personal feelings of one called to proclaim impending divine judgment on Judah and Jerusalem. At the end of the fifth lament (Jer 20:7-18), the prophet proclaimed his trust in God, who delivers the life of the needy from the hands of evildoers (v. 13). The prophet identified with the poor and provided a religious connotation to the word for "poor" used in this passage (*'ebyôn*). Still, it is important that Jeremiah, like his prophetic predecessors, did not idealize the poor by maintaining that their poverty conferred on them a special religious or moral status. As we have seen, Jer 5:1-5 affirms that the poor can be as ignorant of the divine will as the wealthy. The prophet, speaking in the name of God, took the side of the poor not because poverty placed people in a special state of closeness to God but because poverty is the result of deliberate actions that unjustly deprive people of the good that God intended for them. Poverty should not exist among the people of God.

While Jeremiah's laments give a rare insight into the person of the prophet, they also testify to the conflicts going on within Judahite society. Jeremiah's inner turmoil was a consequence of his being drawn into those conflicts because of his mission to announce God's judgment on Judah (Jer 12:1-4; 15:10; 20:7-8). The conflicts that gave rise to Jeremiah's laments were fundamentally social and economic. The prophet witnessed and denounced the gross injustices that made some people very wealthy while reducing many to poverty. Jeremiah did not believe that Judah's elite were interested at all in reforming the social and political institutions that facilitated the oppression of Judah's peasant class. But the prophet was convinced that God would not allow the injustice to continue, so he concluded that God was using the expansionist policies of the Babylonian Empire to bring Judah's elite to judgment. Jeremiah announced that God was going to bring people from "the north" to punish Judah (Jer 1:15; 4:6-9; 6:1, 22-24; 10:22).[18] The prophet explicitly identified the Babylonians under Nebuchadnezzar as these "northerners" (Jer 25:1, 9; 46:26). The Babylonian victory over the Egyptians at the battle of Carchemish in 605 BCE, combined with the collapse of Assyria, left the Babylonians as the sole power in the ancient Near East. Eight years later the Babylonians laid siege to Jerusalem following an ill-advised revolt by Jehoiakim, who died during the siege. Jehoiachin succeeded his father on the throne of David. Realizing that resistance was futile, Jehoiachin surrendered to the Babylonians. Judah had to pay the price for its rebellion. The temple was looted and the country's elite, including the king, were taken to Babylon (2 Kgs 24:14).

Not everyone in Judah agreed with Jeremiah in identifying Babylon as God's instrument of judgment on a corrupt and oppressive society. Some saw Babylon as rebelling against God's rule. Judah's defeat was only a temporary setback in a battle that God would win for Judah. Such were the views of the prophet Hananiah, who announced Babylon's imminent defeat and the return of Judah's exiles within two years (Jer 28:2-4). While Jeremiah wished that Hananiah's words were true, he knew better (28:6). Jeremiah accused Hananiah of leading Judah to believe in a lie (28:15). Jeremiah then wrote to the exiles in Babylon, telling them to expect an exile of at least seventy years (Jer 29:10). Hananiah's prophecy was founded on his belief that the principal conflict of his day was between Judah and Babylon—or more correctly, between Yahweh, Judah's patron, and Marduk, Babylon's patron. The conclusion that Hananiah came to regarding Babylon's imminent defeat flowed from Israelite tradition: Yahweh always defeats the enemies arrayed against Israel. Yahweh would prove more powerful than Marduk just as Yahweh proved to be stronger than the gods of Egypt and Canaan.

Jeremiah's analysis of Judah's situation saw that the principal conflict was not between Judah and Babylon but between the rich and the poor in Judah. In that conflict, God always takes the side of the oppressed, just as God did when the Hebrew slaves were led to freedom from the oppression of their Egyptian taskmasters. Babylon was simply the instrument of liberation. Once the elite were led off into exile, the poor came to repossess the land that was unjustly taken from them.

Nowhere is the conflict between the rich and poor in Judahite society more dramatically demonstrated than in Jer 34. In verses 1-7 Jeremiah recounts Nebuchadnezzar's final siege of Jerusalem. As a desperate move during the height of the siege, King Zedekiah convinced the wealthy to free their bond slaves even if they had not completed their six years of service (see Deut 15:1-6). Perhaps the king thought that he could then call on the freed slaves to defend the city. When the immediate threat to Jerusalem subsided, the wealthy reenslaved their debtors. The prophet's condemnation of this outrage turns on a wordplay that is lost in translation: "You yourselves recently *repented* and did what was right in my sight by proclaiming liberty to one another . . . but then you *turned around* and profaned my name when each of you took back your male and female slaves, whom you had set free according to their desire" (vv. 15-16). The prophet points out the irony in the actions of the wealthy by using the same Hebrew verb to describe their actions in setting their slaves free and then reenslaving them. The oracle of judgment that the prophet announces in response to the reenslavement of the poor seals the doom of Zedekiah and Judah's elite. They "shall be handed over to their enemies" (v. 20).

Included in the book of Jeremiah as it has come down to us are several sections that are summaries of passages from 2 Kings.[19] Those summaries assert that following the Babylonian conquest of Judah and Jerusalem and the exile of the upper classes, only the poor were left behind to care for the land (Jer 39:10; 40:7; 52:15-16). The irony is obvious. The wealthy, who spent so much of their energy in acquiring land from the peasants and thereby creating poverty in Judah, were exiled from that land, which they unjustly acquired. Instead of Judah's kings ensuring that the land was returned to its rightful owners, it was a Babylonian officer acting in the name of Nebuchadnezzar, king of Babylon, who returned the land stolen from the poor.

Habakkuk

By the time Jeremiah had identified Babylon as the instrument of divine judgment on Judah's unjust economic system, the notion that God would use the nations to punish Israel had become a prophetic commonplace. Amos believed that God had chosen the Assyrians to punish Israel for its oppressive economic system (Amos 6:12-14). Isaiah made the same assertion about the Assyrians, though he used different language (Isa 5:26-30; 9:9-10 [ET 10-11]; 10:5-6). While Habakkuk agreed with his contemporary Jeremiah that Babylon was God's chosen instrument of judgment on a corrupt society, he recognized that more must be said about this. God's dealing with injustice through the use of militaristic empires raised as many problems as it solved. Habakkuk attempted to deal with those problems.

Habakkuk was appalled by the injustice of Judahite society. Some of his oracles may date to the reign of Jehoiakim (608–598 BCE) whom Jeremiah criticized for not only tolerating but also perpetrating injustice upon the poor (Jer 22:13-15a).[20] While Habakkuk did not name names, he was clear about his reaction to the injustice of Judahite society. His book opens by lamenting those injustices:

> O LORD, how long shall I cry for help,
>   and you will not listen?
> Or cry to you "Violence!"
>   and you will not save?
> Why do you make me see wrongdoing
>   and look at trouble?
> Destruction and violence are before me;
>   strife and contention arise.
> So the law becomes slack
>   and justice never prevails.
> The wicked surround the righteous—
>   therefore judgment comes forth perverted. (Hab 1:2-4)

The prophet begins boldly by complaining not only about the injustice he witnesses but especially about God's failure to deal with it. While all the prophets assume that God demands justice of Israel, Habakkuk here demands justice of God. Especially significant is verse 4, which states the problem succinctly: God's failure to end the oppression of the poor undermines the ethical basis of Judahite society as much as the crimes of the wicked. The Hebrew verb that the NRSV renders as "becomes slacked" means "to be numb from the cold" or "to be feeble." The Torah included the notion that God rewards the just and punishes the wicked. Because God has failed to punish the wicked, people lose faith in the Torah's promises and Judah is caught in a downward spiral of infidelity. God's reply to the prophet assures him that God will take action against a society that perverts justice: "I am rousing the Chaldeans,[21] that fierce and impetuous nation" (Hab 1:6). The prophet recognized the Chaldeans as God's instruments, but he was perplexed by God's choice since the Chaldeans were themselves guilty of great oppression (1:12-17). It appears as though God is substituting one oppressor for another. The lot of the poor will likely not improve. Those God commissioned to punish Judah's elite were a scourge to the poor as well (Hab 3:14).

Habakkuk wanted a glimpse of Judah's future beyond judgment. He refused to believe that judgment was God's final word to Judah. The prophet believed that Babylon was God's instrument of judgment. But he also looked forward to another intervention that would result in Babylon's destruction and the preservation of the faithful in Judah (Hab 2:1-5). Habakkuk revived ancient Israelite imagery, which depicted God doing battle with the powers arrayed against Israel (3:1-19). The prophet believed that his vision of Judah's ultimate destiny could help believers deal with the dislocations and contradictions of the present. He portrayed God not only as a righteous judge avenging the injustices done to the poor but also as a mighty warrior who will ultimately save Judah from total destruction.

Habakkuk firmly believed that despite Judah's perversion of justice and oppression of the poor, God would not abandon Judah to its fate. The prophet attempts to broaden Judah's horizons beyond the sight of its immediate future. He wants Judah to envision God's ultimate salvation, for he is certain that it is coming. Yahweh will be victorious over the powers of evil that oppress Judah—all the powers of evil. In the meantime, the just ought to live with complete confidence in God's final victory.

Ezekiel

This prophet was a younger contemporary of Jeremiah; however, the setting for his prophetic activity was not Judah but Babylon. Ezekiel was among those whom the Babylonians led into exile following the surrender of Jerusalem to Nebuchadnezzar in 597 BCE. While some Judahites like Hananiah (see Jer 28) believed that the Babylonian hegemony over Judah was only temporary, Ezekiel was not one of them. He insisted that Jerusalem was headed for an even more tragic destiny. Of course, Ezekiel also insisted that it was the people's own failures that led to their defeat and exile. The prophet spoke of the fall of Jerusalem and the exile of its citizens as God's judgment on Judah's sins (Ezek 14:21-23).

In chapter 18, Ezekiel mentions some of the traditional Israelite moral values. The prophet lists the righteous person who "does not oppress anyone, but restores to the debtor his pledge...gives his bread to the hungry and covers the naked with a garment, does not take...accrued interest...executes true justice between contending parties..." (vv. 7-8). But the prophet equated oppression of the poor, the failure to restore a garment taken in pledge, and the taking of interest with idolatry (see Ezek 18:12-14). These were capital crimes that called for a sentence of death upon Judah and Jerusalem.

What led the prophet to equate the oppression of the poor with idolatry was Judah's failure to deal with the social and economic evils that turned God against Jerusalem. The people sought comfort and security in the worship of other gods. They set up images of foreign deities in the temple (8:3-6). They decorated the walls of the temple's forecourt with relief work depicting unclean animals (8:7-12). The elders excused this departure from tradition by asserting: "The LORD does not see us, the LORD has forsaken the land" (8:12). In the temple precincts, women are lamenting for the god Tammuz (8:14-15). Finally, in the very sanctuary of Yahweh, the priests are worshiping the sun (8:16).

The principal blame for all this falls upon Judah's leaders: its royal family, civil administrators, priests, and prophets (Ezek 22:12, 23-31). Instead of protecting the rights of the poor, the members of Judah's leadership classes committed acts of extortion and bribery, confiscated property, and oppressed the poor and needy. The prophet asserted that these were the very crimes for which Sodom had to pay the ultimate penalty and claimed that the crimes committed in that proverbial city of sin were no match for those committed in Jerusalem (Ezek 16:48-49). Similarly, Samaria, which was destroyed because of its sins, appeared righteous when compared with Jerusalem (Ezek 16:51). The prophet, then, saw poverty and wealth as interconnected phenomena. Judah's leaders were prosperous and wealthy because they extorted and bribed their way to prosperity. Their wealth was built up through robbing and oppressing the poor. Ezekiel did not believe that poverty was a chance occurrence or that it was something that befell people because of their foolishness. The prophet alleged that poverty in Judah came about because of the actions of the wealthy, whom the prophet compares unfavorably with the people of Sodom and Samaria, both of which were destroyed because of their sinfulness. Poverty, for the prophet, was no accident; it was the consequence of decisions made by the rich to deprive the poor of what little they had.

On January 19, 586 BCE, Ezekiel's prophecy underwent a profound transformation. It was on this day, according to Ezek 33:21, that a fugitive who escaped from the second Babylonian siege of Jerusalem informed the prophet that the city had fallen and its temple destroyed. Ezekiel was right about Jerusalem's fate. But like his prophetic predecessors, he did not believe that judgment was God's final word to Judah. Once he heard that the full measure of divine judgment had come upon Jerusalem, the prophet felt free to offer the city hope. Ezekiel 33–39 contains oracles of salvation for all Israel. They promise restoration: a return to their land and a renewal of their relationship with God. When describing a restored Israel, the prophet sends a very pointed warning to Israel's leaders: "Thus says the Lord GOD: Enough, O princes of Israel! Put away violence and oppression, and do what is just and right. Cease your evictions of my people, says the Lord GOD" (Ezek 45:9). In the prophet's vision of a restored Jerusalem, justice and righteousness were to replace violence and oppression.

Isaiah 40–55

Ezekiel spoke to the exiles of Judah in the first years of their stay in Babylon. His purpose was to enable his fellow exiles to understand what was happening to them and why. Many of these Judean exiles took Jeremiah's advice (Jer 29) and established roots in Babylon. Most of the exiles were sent to agriculturally marginal regions in Mesopotamia, though some rose to important positions in Babylon's civil service. After some years, another prophet arose among the exiles, reminding them that they belonged somewhere else and promising them that God was about to lead them back to Jerusalem. It is ironic that this prophet, whose words are among the most stirring of all prophetic oracles, chose to remain anonymous, completely subordinating his person to his message. Because the oracles of this anonymous prophet became associated with those of the eighth-century prophet named Isaiah, they have become known as "Second Isaiah."

Because of a succession of incompetent and unpopular rulers, the Babylonian Empire was beginning to unravel. A new imperial power was beginning to assert itself: Persia. Its armies were led by a vigorous and successful general named Cyrus. The prophet took these events as his cue and began to speak about Yahweh's return to center stage. Judah's God was not hidden or powerless before Babylon. In fact, the new political events that were stirring things up were directed by Yahweh for one purpose: the restoration of Judah and Jerusalem. "[Yahweh] says of Cyrus: 'He is my shepherd, and he shall carry out all my purpose'; and [he] says of Jerusalem, 'It shall be rebuilt,' and of the temple, 'Your foundation shall be laid'" (Isa 44:28). In his enthusiasm at the rise of Cyrus and the inevitable fall of Babylon, the prophet called Cyrus Yahweh's "messiah" (45:1), a title once reserved for kings of Judah's own Davidic dynasty. Certainly the use of this word had to astonish the prophet's fellow exiles. Choosing this word for its shock value, the prophet spoke in the name of a God who was about to use every resource and set aside hallowed traditions in order to answer the exiles' laments. Since there was no descendant of David to lead them, God chose a Persian general—but not to be an instrument of judgment, as God used Sennacherib and Nebuchadnezzar. Cyrus the Persian, "the anointed one," was to be an instrument of salvation, fulfilling a role once reserved for Judah's own kings.

The prophet's fellow exiles were skeptical about his message. The loss of Jerusalem, its temple, and the Davidic dynasty left the exiles with the feeling that Yahweh's action in the world was something that belonged to the past—or at best that Yahweh had forgotten them: "But Zion said, 'The LORD has forsaken me, my Lord has forgotten me' " (Isa 49:14). To the exiles it appeared that Marduk, the god of Babylon, was the one who was controlling events. Could the prophet convince his fellow exiles otherwise? His strategy was to boldly assert that God could never forget the exiles of Jerusalem:

> Can a woman forget her nursing child,
> > or show no compassion for the child of her womb?
> Even these may forget,
> > yet I will not forget you.
> See, I have inscribed you on the palms of my hands;
> > your walls are continually before me. (Isa 49:15-16)

Second Isaiah was certain that a new exodus was on the horizon—one so spectacular that it would eclipse the escape of the Hebrew slaves from Egypt:

> Thus says the LORD,
> > who makes a way in the sea,
> > a path in the mighty waters,
> who brings out chariot and horse,
> > army and warrior;
> they lie down, they cannot rise,
> > they are extinguished, quenched like a wick:
> Do not remember the former things,
> > or consider the things of old.
> I am about to do a new thing;
> > now it springs forth, do you not perceive it? (Isa 43:16-19*a*)

The prophet's strategy for restoring the exiles' hope was to lead them to identify with their ancestors, whom God freed from slavery in Egypt. What God had done once, God would do again with an even greater manifestation of power and authority. The proper response to this new act of liberation was trustful surrender. The prophet uses the vocabulary of the poor to speak of what God is doing for the exiles: "Sing for joy, O heavens, and exult, O earth; break forth, O mountains, into singing! For the LORD has comforted his people, and will have compassion on his suffering ones" (Isa 49:13).

The poor, then, become a metaphor for the exiles who wait with faith and confidence for the coming day of their salvation. The prophet emphasized that God is the one who takes action on behalf of "the poor" and "the afflicted" (41:17; 51:13-16; 54:11). Indeed, Second Isaiah begins with a divine decree to console the exiles of Jerusalem with the news that their suffering is about to end: "Comfort, O comfort my people, says your God. Speak tenderly to Jerusalem, and cry to her that she has served her term, that her penalty is paid, that she has received from the LORD's hand double for all her sins" (Isa 40:1-2). With hyperbole born of his desire to convince his fellow exiles the prophet implies that Jerusalem's punishment exceeded its crimes, so the time of its restoration must be imminent. The prophet's goal was to strengthen his people's commitment to their ancestral religion, so he sought to be more persuasive than threatening. He did not announce divine judgment but proclaimed God's forgiveness and the nearness of Jerusalem's restoration. In one notable exception, the prophet spoke of the wicked and the rich in the same breath: "They made his grave with the wicked and his tomb with the rich" (Isa 53:9*a*).

A recurring motif in Second Isaiah is the "servant of the LORD" (Isa 42:1-7; 49:1-6; 50:4-11 and 52:13–53:12). The first of these passages identifies the mission of the servant as the establishment of justice—not just in Israel but also throughout the world (Isa 42:1, 4). But this mission will not be achieved easily. The servant will be "cut off from the land of the living" by a "perversion of justice" (Isa 53:8), although in the end his mission will be successful and he will "make many righteous" (Isa 53:11). With justice restored, all people can look forward to a world in which oppression and poverty do not exist. Of course, Second Isaiah's prophetic predecessors accused Israel of failing to live up to these ideals. It was the abandonment of justice and the oppression of the poor that led to the divine judgment on Israel. It was the mission of the servant to establish justice that would transform Israel and the world.

Haggai and Zechariah

The picture that Second Isaiah painted of Israel's future was resplendent indeed. Yahweh, the Sovereign Lord and Creator, was on the verge of restoring Israel to its glory. But this restoration was to involve more than the return of the exiles to Judah and a revival of the national state. It was to be nothing less than the universal triumph of the divine will. Israel was to be restored, of course, but Yahweh's rule was to extend over all the nations of the world. But the restoration did not proceed according to Second Isaiah's vision. First, only a minority of the exiles returned to Judah, though the Persian authorities not only permitted but encouraged their return (see 2 Chr 36:23).[22] Second, the early years of the Persian period were marked by disappointment, frustration, and discouragement.[23] Certainly a succession of poor agricultural yields contributed to the sense of frustration (Hag 1:9-11; 2:15-17). The crop failures left many farmers without adequate food and clothing (Hag 1:6).

What compounded the problems of the restoration period was the conflict between those who returned from exile and those who had never been in exile. First, there were the Samaritans, who lived in the highlands north of Jerusalem. They considered Judah an adjunct to their territory and sought to exercise control over it. They regarded the returnees as illegal interlopers and tried to frustrate their plans to rebuild Jerusalem and its temple (Ezra 4:1-23). Similarly, the people of Judah who did not go into exile regarded the land as their own (Ezek 11:15; 33:23-33) and did not readily acquiesce to the claims that the returnees were making. Finally, the returned exiles regarded themselves as the purified remnant of the true Israel and regarded both the Samaritans and the people of the land as unclean. The tensions may even have led to violent confrontations (see Zech 8:10).[24]

Still, there were voices calling Judah to lift itself out of the doldrums caused by unfulfilled expectations. The prophets Haggai and Zechariah suggested that Judah's circumstances would improve following the rebuilding of the temple (Hag 1:1-11; Zech 1:16).[25] The connection that these prophets saw between economic progress and the rebuilding of the temple is not just a flight of pious fancy. It is necessary to recognize the function that a temple played in ancient Near Eastern societies. Temples were more than simply places of sacrificial worship. They were administrative institutions dealing with political, economic, and judicial matters along with the religious and liturgical. Ancient Near Eastern temples and their priesthoods had very significant economic functions. It is estimated that Egyptian temples controlled 80 percent of the country's arable land. They were Egypt's principal employers and the main producers of its food. This gave Egypt's priests immense political and economic power—power that even the pharaohs had to recognize. Also, from an ancient Near Eastern perspective, the building of a temple brings economic prosperity. One purpose of its rituals was to ensure the fertility of the land. People brought the firstfruits of their harvest to the temple with the expectation that, in exchange for their gifts, the gods would make their land productive during the next growing season. Ancient Near Eastern temples were pivotal centers for the management of a country's economic resources. In the agricultural economies of the region, this meant that the temples controlled the agricultural surpluses. Temples served as communal storehouses for produce and as clearinghouses in its distribution.

The people of Judah did bring sacrificial offerings to the site of the ruined first temple, but Haggai announced that God "blew them away" (1:9). The benefit of these gifts for the community was lost because, as verse 9 notes, the temple was not rebuilt; in other words, there was no central administration of the community's economic output. In addition to the lack of a temple building, their administrative structure was gone as well. Before the exile, the monarchic system supplied the necessary administrative apparatus, but now there was no Judahite monarchy. While there were, of course, the Persian bureaucrats, their main concern was the collection of taxes, not the economic welfare of Jerusalem and its people. But the reconstruction of the temple had stalled despite the imperial support for the project. Finally, the new temple was finished in 516 BCE, almost twenty-five years after the first group of exiles returned to Jerusalem. Still, the promises made by Haggai and Zechariah were not fulfilled. Judah remained a minor subprovince of the Persian Empire, although it enjoyed limited local autonomy while the Persians controlled its economic resources. The national state had not been reestablished and the native dynasty was not restored. Instead the community was ruled by high priests. Certainly the small Jewish community was disappointed that the restoration did not proceed as they were led to expect. All this set the scene for the emergence of other prophetic voices known collectively as Third Isaiah.

Isaiah 56–66

The last eleven chapters of the book of Isaiah contain oracles given by prophetic voices raised both before and after the rebuilding of the temple and reflect tensions within the Jewish community during that time (56:9–57:13; 59:1-8; 66:1-16; 65:1-6). Isaiah 59:9 aptly reflects the mood of the community because of these conflicts and unfulfilled expectations: "justice is far from us, and righteousness does not reach us; we wait for light, and lo! there is darkness; and for brightness, but we walk in gloom." The reason for this gulf between expectation and reality lies not with God but with the people of Judah (Isa 59:1-2). The prophet directs his criticism primarily at the community's leadership, the priests, whom he characterizes as "dogs [who] have a mighty appetite" (Isa 56:9-12).

The question that the Jewish community faced was exactly how to bridge the gulf between its frustrated expectations and the harsh reality of its daily existence. The priests suggested a special fast accompanied by appropriate rituals (Isa 58:1-2). The response to this suggestion comes in words that mirror the passion of Amos:

> Is such the fast that I choose,
>> a day to humble oneself?
> Is it to bow down the head like a bulrush,
>> and to lie in sackcloth and ashes?
> Will you call this a fast,
>> a day acceptable to the LORD?
> Is not this the fast that I choose:
>> to loose the bonds of injustice,
>> to undo the thongs of the yoke,
> to let the oppressed go free,
>> and to break every yoke?
> Is it not to share your bread with the hungry,
>> and bring the homeless poor into your house;
> when you see the naked, to cover them,
>> and not to hide yourself from your own kin? (Isa 58:5-7)

This text is evidence of conditions that developed within the Jewish community that allowed a privileged few to become wealthy while the majority of the people were reduced to economic dependency because of the exploitative practices of the people of means. The careful observance of practices like fasting and prayer provided these people with a veneer of religiosity. The foundation of Judah's life with God was just relationships within Judahite society. If those relationships were askew, there was really no possibility of maintaining a positive relationship with God. The prophet expected that there would be a correspondence between piety and justice. In itself, fasting is without value. The renunciation that the prophet expected but did not find is the renunciation of one's well-being for the sake of a fellow Israelite in need.

The prophet did not see justice revered as a value in his society, so he expected that God was going to raise up someone to transform the community—to reorganize its social, political, and economic life in a way that would make it possible for those on the margins to share in the blessings promised to all:

> The Spirit of the Lord GOD is upon me,
>> because the LORD has anointed me;

he has sent me to bring good news to the oppressed,
to bind up the brokenhearted,
to proclaim liberty to the captives,
and release to the prisoners;
to proclaim the year of the LORD's favor,
and the day of vengeance of our God;
to comfort all who mourn.... (Isa 61:1-2)

The immediate context of these words is the poverty caused by the difficult times of the restoration period and the profiteering of the wealthy. The text is a prophetic protest against the conditions within the community that allowed poverty to flourish again. Because the people of means continue to exploit their position of power, God will raise up someone to set things right. These verses signal the need for a complete reorganization of Judah's social structure. It is likely that the prophet's words evoked a response similar to that given to Jesus when he used these words to describe his mission (see Luke 4:18-19). People who have a stake in maintaining the status quo resist any reordering of the social system, especially the type of reordering called for by the prophet.

Third Isaiah uses the temple and its worship as a means to focus attention on social and economic divisions within the Jewish community. Unlike Haggai and Zechariah, who believed the reconstruction of the temple was a most profound expression of Jewish hope for the future, Third Isaiah concluded with a bitter critique of the temple's liturgy, a critique that is without equal in the Bible (Isa 66:1-6). The prophet proclaimed that God was not looking for worshipers but for people who are "humble and contrite in spirit" and who tremble at God's word (Isa 66:2). But this characterization of those whom God seeks does not spiritualize poverty since the prophet did not see poverty as a permanent state of the pious. He wanted it to end; he did not want to exalt it to some sort of a spiritual plane. He looked forward to a time when the peasants would enjoy the fruits of their labor: "I will not again give your grain to be food for your enemies, and foreigners shall not drink the wine for which you have labored" (Isa 62:8). In fact, he expected that one day the wealth of the nations would support the poor (Isa 60:5; 61:5-6; 66:12).

The words of Third Isaiah reflect a genuine conflict within postexilic Judah. This conflict was not about theological perceptions or liturgical practices. The conflict was over the just distribution of the few material resources that were available to the community. Like other prophets, Third Isaiah saw poverty in the community as the consequence of decisions that people make to steal from the poor and then mask that theft with a cloak of religiosity. The prophet was certain that God would not remain passive because God hates injustice and will come to the aid of the faithful poor (Isa 61:8). He invites the community to wait with him for the day of jubilee, when God's own agent will put an end to injustice and oppression (Isa 61:1-4).

Finally, the city of Jerusalem became the metaphor for the new world of justice that God's agent was to bring into existence (Isa 66:7-16). Jerusalem will be like a "river of peace" (Isa 66:12). Of course, this "river of peace" will bring the people of Jerusalem security not only from military conflict but also from economic exploitation. Jerusalem will no longer be home to the poor but an international center of commerce and wealth. This economic transformation will be resisted by those who want to maintain the status quo, but God will ensure that justice comes for the poor (Isa 66:15-16).

Conclusion

The prophets supposedly took the traditional Israelite belief that God was the protector of the poor and transformed it into seeing poverty as entitling people to God's favor. According to this view, the poor were led to accept their condition by the prophetic tradition that eventually came to call for "a submission in faith, an accepted smallness, a religious humility."[26] While there are indeed several prophetic texts that call for the poor to have confidence in God, ancient Israel's prophets do not idealize poverty. They see poverty as an evil created by Israel's elite classes, who engage in immoral practices to enrich themselves at the expense of those without power and influence. The prophets see this as a principal reason for the divine judgment that Israel experienced. The prophets do not portray the poor as people who are especially close to God because of their exploitation. The poor are victims. They are victims of the wealthy who violate the most fundamental stipulations of the covenant. There is only one proper response to these circumstances and that is protest. And the prophets do protest against the people who maintain a social and economic system built on injustice.

Believers today can bring the biblical tradition to bear on social problems if they hear again the prophetic protest against poverty and the people who cause it. Spiritualizing poverty leads to an acceptance of injustice—something the prophets never did. Ancient Israel's prophets presented poverty as a terrible evil that could only bring divine judgment upon Israel. They longed for the day when God would end such injustice and bring the blessings of peace and prosperity to all Israel.

Questions for Reflection

1. What was the social conflict that moved ancient Israel's prophets to announce that divine judgment was coming on Israel?

2. How did the prophets like Amos and Isaiah reinterpret the motif of "the day of the Lord"?

3. Who were the principal objects of prophetic criticism? Why did the prophets criticize these people so severely?

4. What was the prophetic vision of Israel's immediate future?

5. Why did the prophets equate the oppression of the poor with idolatry?

6. How did the prophets use the "vocabulary of the poor"?

7. According to the prophets, what will be God's final word to Judah and Jerusalem?

WISDOM LITERATURE

The wisdom tradition differs markedly from those traditions preserved in the Torah and prophets. Among the more significant differences is the world of the wisdom tradition. Jeremiah reports that his enemies assured themselves that there would be little fallout from their plots against him with the words: "instruction shall not perish from the priest, nor counsel from the wise, nor the word from the prophet" (Jer 18:18). This text suggests that the "wise" formed a recognizable leadership class analogous to the priests and prophets.[1] Profiling this leadership class, however, is not a simple matter. Some may have served as advisors and scribes in the royal courts; the reference to "the officials of Hezekiah" in Prov 25:1 has led to the suggestion that royal scribes were responsible for much of the material in the book of Proverbs. Reading this book makes it clear that the concerns of these scribes transcended those of the royal court. If "the wise" were royal counselors and one of their achievements was the collecting of proverbs that corresponded with their point of view, they must have belonged to an elite group. Sirach's comparison of the learned scribe with other people (Sir 38:24–39:11) certainly reflects an elitist perspective.

One feature of the wisdom literature of the Hebrew Bible (Proverbs, Job, and Ecclesiastes) is the absence of motifs that are central to both the Torah and the Prophets—for example, the Exodus and covenant. Though such motifs do appear in the wisdom literature from early Judaism (Sirach and the Wisdom of Solomon), their absence from the wisdom tradition of ancient Israel has led some to consider these books as foreign to the "biblical tradition."[2] The aim of "the wise" is not to hand on the ancient Israelite traditions found in the Torah and Prophets but to show how people can master life rather than be mastered by it.

While the wisdom literature does deal with the themes of the poor and poverty, its way of approaching these two motifs differs markedly from that of the Torah and the Prophets because of the wisdom tradition's elitist origins and its special concerns. For example, one does not find the moral outrage at the oppression of the poor that one finds in prophetic literature. "The wise" approach the question of poverty from an angle that is quite different from the rest of the Old Testament canon. This is shown in the vocabulary of the wisdom tradition when it speaks of the poor. For example, a word for the poor that occurs frequently in the prophetic corpus is *'ebyôn*. This word appears seventeen times in prophetic literature and usually refers to those without the security that wealth gives (Isa 14:30; 25:4; Amos 8:4), those who are exploited by the powerful (Amos 2:6; 8:6), those whom the judicial system oppressed (Isa 32:7; Jer 20:13), and those mistreated by officials (Isa 32:6-7). But this word occurs only four times in Proverbs (14:31; 30:14; 31:9, 20). When speaking of the poor, wisdom texts prefer the word *rāš*, which is used to speak about someone who has little economic or political status, usually because of laziness. This word occurs twenty-two times in the Hebrew Bible, with seventeen of those occurrences in wisdom texts (e.g., Prov 10:4; Eccl 5:8). A synonym is *mahsôr*, which occurs almost always in wisdom texts (e.g., Prov 6:11).

Finally, a word needs to be said about the claims made by "the wise." Both the Torah and the Prophets claim divine authority for their texts. The wise make no such claims. The authority of the wisdom tradition derives from the ability of the wise to persuade. In Proverbs, for example, persuasion is a result of the sages' ability to encapsulate the experience of the past in aesthetically pleasing ways. The artful character of the sages' formulations guaranteed their value. Unfortunately, the aesthetic features of the ancient Israelite proverb cannot always survive translation. The wise were convinced that the action of God was beyond calculation, so they acknowledged the relativity of their insights into the human condition. They considered their teaching as the result of careful observation about "the way things work." But they always recognized that their conclusions were subject to revision. Indeed, the books of Job and Ecclesiastes are best understood as attempts to suggest the need for some revision. It is important for the contemporary reader to remember that ancient Israel's sages were not rehearsing theses about the immutable order of reality. They recognized that whatever conclusions they arrived at were always subject to alteration, if only because the ways of God always remain beyond human comprehension.

Proverbs

Modern readers of the book of Proverbs usually have a difficult time with the book's apparent lack of organization. Certainly the book does not treat poverty and the poor in a systematic way. Of course, it still is possible to extract from Proverbs some idea of the sages' attitude toward the poor, but we need to remember that this will be the result of our efforts rather than those of the sages themselves.

The Deuteronomic tradition presents poverty as the result of Israel's disobedience. If Israel were to obey the Torah, poverty would not exist. The prophets see poverty as the result of the greed of the wealthy who oppress the poor. Proverbs, however, offers another explanation. Poverty is a consequence of laziness and negligence: "A slack hand causes poverty" (Prov 10:4); "Do not love sleep, or else you will come to poverty" (Prov 20:13); "Whoever loves pleasure will suffer want" (Prov 21:17). Proverbs seems to be heartless in its approach to poverty, appearing to blame those whom the prophets regard as victims. But it is important to remember that Proverbs is not engaging in a sociological analysis of poverty nor even in theological reflection on its significance for the community of believers. The book addresses itself not to the poor but to the sons of the wealthy, who must realize that poverty is a threat to their social and economic standing if they are lazy (Prov 10:4) or waste their resources foolishly (Prov 21:17).

The sages wrote for people who were in control of their destiny. These were young men from the upper classes, destined for important roles in Israelite society.[3] The choices that such people made determined their lot in life. Numerous sayings in the book of Proverbs denounce both drunkenness and laziness as the cause of serious problems. If people neglect their responsibilities because of sloth and excessive drinking, what other result can they expect but poverty? Success is the result of a disciplined life. People who choose to live otherwise will lose the advantages that their social standing gives them. Israelite peasants would find much of the advice given in Proverbs to be irrelevant to their lives. The poor did not control their destiny. The people of means were able to use their political and economic power to control the lives of ordinary Israelites. But Proverbs makes no connection between the problems faced by the poor and the actions of the wealthy because this book looks at the question of poverty, not as a social or moral problem in Israelite society, but as a potential threat to the well-being of Judah's elite.

The sages assume that people "choose" poverty, albeit indirectly. A fundamental assumption of the wisdom tradition is that actions have consequences and that these consequences are quite predictable. If experience has taught people anything, it is that poverty comes to those who live an undisciplined life. But this does not mean that the book of Proverbs writes off every poor person as lazy and shiftless. The book uses the specter of poverty to persuade its readers to be very careful to follow the advice given in it: "Poverty and disgrace are for the one who ignores instruction, but one who heeds reproof is honored" (Prov 13:18). The sages do not assume that the poor can "pick themselves up by their bootstraps," nor do they blame the victims of social injustice. They warn the young against "choosing" poverty because they believe that such a state is completely avoidable. Those who do not take care to avoid poverty are despised even by those who should be most sympathetic to them: "If the poor are hated even by their kin, how much more are they shunned by their friends!" (Prov 19:7). By choosing to lead a life of dissipation, a person chooses to be poor and such a choice cannot bring admiration, only derision.

Though the book of Proverbs looks upon poverty as an inevitable consequence of leading a dissipated life, it is clear that this does not represent the totality of the sages' reflections on poverty. If poverty were, in fact, purely and simply the result of personal choice, the sages' sympathy for the poor would be hard to explain. The sages, though, consider concern for and assistance to the poor as values (Prov 21:13; 22:9). Following a familiar ancient Near Eastern pattern, the sages see the assurance of justice for the poor as a fundamental duty of the king (Prov 29:14).[4] But like the Torah and the Prophets, the wisdom tradition extends this duty to all Israelites, describing an act of compassion to the poor as an act of kindness done to God (Prov 19:17) and neglect of the poor as an insult to God (Prov 14:31; 17:5a), a perspective echoed by Jesus in Matt 25:31-46. Finally, the sages assert that God defends the poor so that any crimes against them call for divine retribution: "Do not rob the poor because they are poor, or crush the afflicted at the gate; for the LORD pleads their cause and despoils of life those who despoil them" (Prov 22:22-23). This is as strong an identification of God's concern for the cause of the poor as one finds in the biblical tradition. Proverbs 22:22-23 comes from a section of the book (22:17–24:22) that found much of its inspiration in an Egyptian wisdom text, the *Instruction of Amen-em-opet*. In the Egyptian text, the moon-god Thoth, the jurist among the gods, is described as pleading the cause of the poor against their oppressors. It is clear, then, that the sages did not despise the poor. While Proverbs had nothing good to say about those whose foolish and undisciplined life led them into poverty, the sages nonetheless recognized that God regarded every act of oppression against the poor as a personal insult.

Too many people dismiss Proverbs as being concerned for little more than success, prosperity, and happiness for the elite of society. Such a characterization of Proverbs oversimplifies the book. Ancient Israel's sages spent their lives looking for effective ways to cope with the problems of life. They did not find the solution to those problems in wealth. They were realistic enough to know that wealth brings with it a set of problems just like poverty does. Just as the sages did not despise the poor, they did not idolize the rich (Prov 29:13). The sages prayed that God would protect them from the pitfalls that come with both poverty *and* wealth:

> Two things I ask of you;
>> do not deny them to me before I die:
> Remove far from me falsehood and lying;
>> give me neither poverty nor riches;
>> feed me with the food that I need,
> or I shall be full, and deny you,
>> and say, "Who is the LORD?"
> or I shall be poor, and steal,
>> and profane the name of my God. (Prov 30:7-9)

Wealth can blind people to the real source of their prosperity. They can believe that their success was the result of effective planning and careful judgments when, in fact, it was due to the goodness of God (Prov 19:21). Similarly, the privations of poverty can lead people to take the kind of drastic steps that lead them away from God. The sages held that there were things in life worse than poverty (Prov 19:1, 22; 28:6). Poverty and wealth are the kinds of extremes that are dangerous because they both can lead people to be forgetful of God.

Finally, the book of Proverbs closes with a poem that lauds the ideal wife (Prov 31:10-31). The poem actually describes the figure of Wisdom to whom the sage is "married" after becoming imbued with the ethos and values presented in the rest of the book.[5] One of the virtues of the ideal wife (Wisdom) is that she "opens her hand to the poor, and reaches out her hands to the needy" (v. 20). Thus the book of Proverbs closes with a text that presents generosity toward the poor as the kind of behavior that embodies true wisdom. No matter what the reason for a person's poverty, generosity toward the poor is the response that should be characteristic of a true sage.

Job

The book of Job is the ancient Israelite variation on a common ancient Near Eastern story of an innocent sufferer. The long poetic section of the book (chs. 3–41) contains the speeches of Job's friends as well as Job's replies. The friends attempt to convince Job that there is no suffering without sin, while Job asserts that his case must be an exception to this general rule. Job challenges God to prove him wrong. The poetic section ends with the speeches of God, who reminds Job that he is incapable of understanding the ways of God. In marshaling arguments to persuade Job of God's justice, the friends recite traditional Israelite beliefs, one of which declares that God saves the poor and gives them reason to hope: "But [God] saves the needy from the sword of their mouth, from the hand of the mighty. So the poor have hope, and injustice shuts its mouth" (Job 5:15-16). Elihu, one of the friends, makes essentially the same point in his speeches (34:19, 28; 36:6, 15). One basic assumption of the traditional Israelite notion of God is that God must be just. A second assumption is that sinner and suffering are connected, so that it is safe to assume that Job's suffering ultimately has its roots in his behavior. Zophar suggests that Job may have failed in the area of proper concern for the poor. The righteous "give back [the poor] their wealth" (Job 20:10), while sinners "have crushed and abandoned the poor, they have seized a house that they did not build" (Job 20:19).

In the course of his replies to the friends, Job uses a variety of approaches to show that there are exceptions to the doctrine of "no suffering without sin." He finds the experience of the poor as an appropriate parallel to his own since their suffering is caused not by their sins but by the greed of the wealthy. Job 24:1-14 is a powerful indictment of the way people of means treated the peasants, reducing them to poverty. Job offers a whole litany of crimes and their consequences: the wealthy cheat the poor—even the widow and orphan—out of their land and livestock (vv. 2-3); the poor are subjected to physical abuse to intimidate them (v. 4); the poor must hunt and glean to feed their children (vv. 5-6); they are left without adequate clothing or housing (vv. 7-8, 10); and the wealthy take infants as collateral for loans to the poor (v. 9). While the author does not intend to provide a socioeconomic analysis of Israelite society, the passage's argument loses all cogency if these kinds of circumstances did not exist. The text asserts that the plight of the poor is completely undeserved and asks why God does nothing to end their oppression; the defenseless poor were precisely the people who supposedly were protected by God. Israel's poor, then, offers another example of innocent suffering. Job is not the only exception to the doctrine of "no suffering without sin."

In asserting his innocence, Job also takes a positive approach by claiming that he has done all that he could to assist the poor (Job 29:12-20). Job maintains that he championed the cause of the poor and responded to their pleas for help (v. 12). Specifically, he helped the disabled (v. 15), comforted the widows (v. 13*b*), stood with the aliens (v. 16*b*), and stopped the expropriation of property (v. 17). Job calls himself "a father to the needy" (v. 16*a*). Job used his power and wealth to benefit the poor, not harm them. Though Job states that he sympathized with the poor (30:25), his compassion was not a matter of feelings alone. He is quite explicit about the specific actions he took on behalf of the poor. Job presents himself as a model of the kind of behavior that the prophets called for and that they found completely lacking in Israel.

In attempting to convince God and his friends of his innocence, Job engages in another review of this past (31:1-40). This chapter is made up of sixteen oaths that Job takes regarding different aspects of his moral and religious behavior.[6] As part of his assertion of innocence, Job maintains that he did not withhold anything from the poor, that he cared for widows, that he shared his food with orphans, and that he gave clothing to those in need of it (31:16-21). In short, Job calls for vindication by God because he has fulfilled his responsibilities to the poor. Job claims that he has been more than just—he has responded to every need of the poor. Job goes on to challenge God to prove him wrong and show what aspect of his life shows moral failure. Job is certain that it cannot be in the way he has dealt with those in need.

The book of Job offers a bleak picture of the treatment that the poor usually received at the hands of their oppressors. But it also describes the kind of treatment they should receive from people of means. Job's arguments imply that poverty is caused by the callousness of the wealthy. It is the result of actions that the wealthy take, not of actions that the poor do or do not take, since the poor are not masters of their fate. The book also assumes that the wealthy are to take actions that benefit the poor rather than harm them. God will judge their actions in this area.

Ecclesiastes (Qoheleth)

Ecclesiastes is like no other book in the Bible. Some readers find its insights fresh and relevant while others are put off by its skepticism and cynicism. The author's burden centers on his inability to find meaning and value in life (Eccl 1:16-18). The best he can do is suggest that his readers enjoy life as best they can (Eccl 9:7-10). Like Proverbs and Job, Ecclesiastes reflects the experience of Israel's elite.[7] The book does not deal with poverty and wealth in any systematic way, but poverty and the injustice that causes it are topics that the author does not avoid. He just does not know if anything can be done about the pervasiveness of injustice in society (Eccl 3:16-18; 4:1). But his fundamental assumption about the lack of any connection between an act and its consequences undermines the belief of the wealthy that they "worked" for their prosperity while the poor have only themselves to blame for their condition.[8] For example, Ecclesiastes notes that official corruption abetted the oppression of the poor:

> If you see in a province the oppression of the poor and the violation of justice and right, do not be amazed at the matter; for the high official is

watched by a higher, and there are yet higher ones over them. But all things considered, this is an advantage for a land: a king for a plowed field. (Eccl 5:8-9)

Ecclesiastes considered official corruption to be endemic in ancient Israel. The very system that was to protect the poor had been perverted to disenfranchise them. The hierarchic organization of the state breeds injustice. Qoheleth calls for no revolution, he makes no protest. He simply advises his readers not to be surprised by injustice in the world. It is difficult to be sure whether the writer is being ironic or just cynical here when he asserts in an almost offhanded way that oppression of the poor, which the government is to prevent, is actually promoted by a hierarchy of officials who are in collusion to defraud the poor. Qoheleth does not try to persuade his readers to take action to end injustice because he believes that such action would be ineffectual. The oppression of the poor is simply the way the world works: the strong exploit the weak.

Another interesting insight into the status of the poor is given in a short parable that Ecclesiastes tells:

There was a little city with few people in it. A great king came against it and besieged it, building great siegeworks against it. Now there was found in it a poor wise man, and he by his wisdom delivered the city. Yet no one remembered that poor man. So I said, "Wisdom is better than might; yet the poor man's wisdom is despised, and his words are not heeded." (Eccl 9:14-16)

This story shows the effects of a social system based on economic status. Even when a poor man does something quite out of the ordinary, he is forgotten because poor people are not supposed to distinguish themselves—or at least that is what the wealthy tell themselves to rationalize the existence of poverty in their society. The poor man is trapped; he cannot extricate himself from his poverty even by saving his city. Even wisdom does not help the poor, for the sage who lacks wealth goes unremembered. This little story can help people of means understand how trapped the poor feel. No achievement of theirs—no matter how great—can bring them out of their poverty. Despite this, Ecclesiastes still believes that poverty and wisdom are better than wealth and position joined to folly (4:13).

Because Ecclesiastes speaks from his experience as a man of wealth, he is able to point out the foolishness of greed (Eccl 5:10-6:9). He begins by asserting that the lust for wealth can never really be satisfied. The more money one has the more money one spends and the more money one needs. He goes on to describe the loss of wealth in bad business ventures that deprives one's children of their inheritance. But he also points out the futility of working and saving one's entire life just to pass one's wealth onto others. For Ecclesiastes diligence and thrift are simply subtle forms of greed. There are really no advantages to a life of greed (Eccl 6:7-9). Without words of judgment and condemnation like the prophets, Ecclesiastes just as effectively points out the folly of greed that has moved so many to rob from the poor.

Of course, it is greed that leads to avarice, and the insatiable desire for wealth leads to the subjection of the poor. Ecclesiastes saw what evil resulted from the avarice of the wealthy: "Again I saw all the oppressions that are practiced under the sun. Look, the tears of the oppressed—with no one to comfort them! On the side of their oppressors there was power—with no one to comfort them" (Eccl 4:1). This is as touching a description of the lot of the poor as one can find in the Bible.

Ecclesiastes' words give an insight into the social situation of his day, which was probably in the third century BCE. It was a time of great economic insecurity and social stratification.[9] Ecclesiastes manifests a skepticism that assumes that there is no way out of the economic and social problems of Judah. They are simply too formidable to be overcome. They illustrate the futility of human existence, which Ecclesiastes describes as *hebel*, a breath of air. The book of Ecclesiastes testifies that the interests of the wealthy and those of the poor inevitably clash. He finds this frustrating but inevitable. He offers no advice on how to improve the lot of the poor because he does not see how any such action could really change anything. His only advice is for people to enjoy the simple pleasures of life before it is too late. These simple pleasures are available to rich and poor alike:

> Go, eat your bread with enjoyment, and drink your wine with a merry heart; for God has long ago approved what you do. Let your garments be always white; do not let oil be lacking on your head. Enjoy life with the wife whom you love, all the days of your vain life that are given you under the sun, because that is your portion in life and in your toil at which you toil under the sun. Whatever your hand finds to do, do with your might; for there is no work or thought or knowledge or wisdom in Sheol, to which you are going. (Eccl 9:7-10)

Sirach (Ben Sira, Ecclesiasticus)

While Job and Ecclesiastes are at odds with some of the assumptions of conventional Israelite wisdom as exemplified in the book of Proverbs,

Sirach's polemics are directed at what he considered a dangerous development of his day: the inroads that Hellenism was making in the Jewish community, especially its upper class.[10] Sirach composed his book about 180 BCE, shortly after the province of Judah passed from Ptolemaic to Seleucid rule. To help support the military adventures of the Greek empires, the state began to control Judah's economy more directly in order to extract taxes more efficiently.[11] The policies of the Hellenistic states led to severe economic problems that exacerbated social conflict in Judahite society. On the one side was the relatively small but wealthy upper class; on the other was the much larger lower class that was much more conservative theologically and culturally. The former had more dealings with their Greek masters and the nearby states that also were subject to Hellenistic influence. The conservatives were not really *one* group but were made up of the lower ranks of the clergy (whose values are reflected in the books of Chronicles, Ezra, and Nehemiah), those who considered themselves the heirs of the prophetic tradition, and those who were giving birth to the apocalyptic tradition. What united these disparate conservative groups was their distaste for any accommodation with Hellenism and their precarious economic circumstances. These groups regarded any accommodation with the Greeks as the product of a desire to win the favor of Judah's overlords by compromising traditional values.[12] Sirach is one example of Judah's elite who wanted to preserve traditional values. He believed that ancient Israel's wisdom tradition was a tool to withstand the temptation to abandon the ancestral religion of the Jews through accommodation with Hellenism.

In assessing Sirach's views regarding poverty and the poor, it is important to remember the author's background and that of his intended audience. The book of Sirach is the work of a member of the upper class who wished to communicate to those with a similar background what experience had taught him. The purpose of his writing was to ensure that his readers would not be so mesmerized by the allurement of Hellenistic culture that they would come to regard their religious traditions as outmoded relics. In his treatment of poverty and the poor, Sirach, for the most part, reaffirms the perspectives of conventional Israelite wisdom as found in the book of Proverbs. But he also includes insights of the prophetic tradition to counteract Hellenistic views that were not sympathetic to the poor. The Greeks did not recognize any responsibility to the poor, while ancient Near Eastern and Israelite tradition always held that people of means were to respond to the cries of the poor because God is their protector.[13]

Because Sirach is addressing the sons of Judah's elite, he cautions them against behaving in a way that will bring poverty upon themselves: "Do not revel in great luxury, or you may become impoverished by its expense. Do not become a beggar by feasting with borrowed money, when you have nothing in your purse" (Sir 18:32-33; see also 25:3). This advice, given to his students who were born into wealth, should not be extrapolated into a general rule that the poor brought their poverty upon themselves. Sirach adamantly underscores the responsibilities that people of means have toward the poor. In fact, at times his criticism of the wealthy is quite similar to that of the prophets. In a sense that is to be expected of a person who saw himself as a successor to the prophets: "I will again pour out teaching like prophecy, and leave it to all future generations" (Sir 24:33).

Like the prophets, Sirach engages in a very striking polemic against feverish attempts to amass wealth:

> A merchant can hardly keep from wrongdoing,
>> nor is a tradesman innocent of sin.
> Many have committed sin for gain,
>> and those who seek to get rich will avert their eyes.
> As a stake is driven firmly into a fissure between stones,
>> so sin is wedged in between selling and buying.
> If a person is not steadfast in the fear of the Lord,
>> his house will be quickly overthrown. (Sir 26:29–27:3)

Sirach probably considered traditional agricultural pursuits to be the more acceptable way of earning a living (7:15; 20:28). He evidently had a problem with the merchant class, which certainly had more occasions to deal with foreigners and consequently more opportunities to compromise Yahwistic traditions than those who followed agrarian occupations. More serious is the author's intimation that the rich take advantage of the poor to enrich themselves. He condemns those who use what they have stolen from the poor to provide material for sacrificial worship, those who deprive the poor of their most basic needs, and those who withhold the wages of the poor (34:21-27). He graphically describes how the poor are at the mercy of the rich: "Wild asses in the wilderness are the prey of lions; likewise the poor are feeding grounds for the rich" (Sir 13:19).

The words of Sirach reflect a social climate characterized by observable social conflict between the rich and the poor: "What peace is there between a hyena and a dog? And what peace between the rich and the poor?" (Sir 13:18; see also 13:20).[14] What made this conflict so acute was the perception by the poor and those who sympathized with them that the rich were ready to compromise or ignore traditional Israelite morality for economic gain. Evidence of this is the unequal treatment that the poor had to endure in society (Sir 13:3, 21-23) and the penchant the rich had for exploiting the poor

(Sir 13:4a). People of means feign interest in the plight of the poor, only to manipulate them for selfish gain.[15] Of course, Sirach urges his readers to take action to relieve the suffering of the poor:

> Give a hearing to the poor,
>> and return their greeting politely.
> Rescue the oppressed from the oppressor;
>> and do not be hesitant in giving a verdict.
> Be a father to orphans,
>> and be like a husband to their mother;
> you will then be like a son of the Most High,
>> and he will love you more than does your mother. (Sir 4:8-10)

The familial ethos of Israelite society as envisioned by the Deuteronomist was certainly not operative in Sirach's day. That is precisely why Sirach engages in the level of social criticism that he does. He encourages his readers to pay attention to what the poor have to say and to treat them with respect (10:22-23). When the poor are in need, people of means should not hesitate to be of assistance (Sir 29:2). Though some borrowers may be unprincipled (Sir 29:4-7), this should not be an excuse to avoid helping the poor in their need (Sir 29:8-9).

Despite the social tensions and economic conflict within Judahite society, Sirach does not condemn riches as such. He values wealth that has been gained honestly because it guarantees a secure life (10:27; 13:24a; 40:18a). But Sirach also warns against the dangers of riches (8:2; 13:15-24), condemns ill-gotten gains (Sir 4:1-3; 5:8; 21:8), and warns that it is difficult for the rich to remain honest and faithful to God (Sir 26:29–27:2; 31:1-11). He reminds the wealthy of their responsibilities toward the poor (Sir 4:1-6) and advises them to be generous in helping the needy (Sir 7:32-36; 29:9-13). Because the poor need loans to survive at times, he asks the wealthy to be forthcoming even though there are many problems connected with making loans (29:14-20). To motivate his students Sirach reminds them of the judgment that awaits those who oppress the poor and the blessing that will come to the generous (Sir 4:6; see also 7:32; 10:14; 21:5; 22:23).

While Sirach appears to equate the poor with the righteous (Sir 12:1-5), he does not spiritualize poverty: "My child, do not lead the life of a beggar; it is better to die than to beg. When one looks to the table of another, one's way of life cannot be considered a life" (Sir 40:28-29). Sirach considered poverty to be an aberration that can and should be eliminated if people would live in accord with the divine will. He condemns those who oppress the poor and calls the wealthy to be generous to the needy. But Sirach recognizes that the basic equality of rich and poor lies in their relationship to God: "The rich, and the eminent, and the poor—their glory is the fear of the Lord" (Sir 10:22). He therefore recognizes and praises those poor whose understanding brings them closer to God (Sir 10:23; 11:1). Finally, Sirach suggests that his upper-class readers adopt the attitude of the poor since it is the key to experiencing divine mercy (Sir 3:17-19). He notes that Moses was chosen by God precisely because he was humble (Sir 45:4).

Sirach considers wealth only a relative good. The sage should be "content with little or much" (Sir 29:23a). Though he praises those who have gained their wealth honestly, he recognizes the social problems that the quest for wealth brought to Judah (Sir 13:4) and he criticizes with the intensity of a prophet those who exploit the poor. Sirach is critical of the people of means because many were enjoying prosperity as a result of their collaboration with Judah's Greek masters. Underlying the entire book of Sirach are the author's fears about the dark side of this collaboration. He is afraid that the young people of early Jewish society will be beguiled into abandoning traditional Israelite values—one of which is justice for the poor and oppressed.

The Wisdom of Solomon

Though written a little more than one hundred years apart, Sirach and the Wisdom of Solomon had a similar purpose: to promote fidelity to the ancestral religious traditions of the Jews. The book of Wisdom, however, was written to encourage Jews in Egypt. In that milieu, it was impossible for Jews to isolate themselves from the dominant Hellenistic culture, which looked upon Judaism with suspicion if not disdain. Relations between the Greeks and Jews of Alexandria, for example, were often marked with tension. These tensions erupted into anti-Jewish riots during the early Roman period. In such a setting, the book of Wisdom calls Jews to be proud of their ancestral faith. Still, this book is among the most Hellenized works found among Jewish religious texts. Having been written in Greek rather than Hebrew, the book of Wisdom expresses traditional Jewish belief by using Greek literary and philosophical conventions.

The book's treatment of the poor and poverty is quite traditional. Indeed the book begins with an exhortation to love justice as the way to immortality (Wis 1:1-15). The rest of the book simply reinforces this fundamental idea. The term "justice" that frames the opening exhortation of the book (Wis 1:1, 15) is a synonym for several other terms that appear in that exhortation: "goodness" (v. 1), "power" (v. 3), "wisdom" (v. 4), "a holy spirit"

(v. 5), "the spirit of the Lord" (v. 7).[16] All these are characteristics of God, who does not countenance injustice. Of course, the wicked choose to ignore this advice and in Wis 1:16–2:24 the book characterizes their behavior as the way to death. The book allows the wicked to explain their actions and motivation. What they describe are plots against the "righteous poor man" and his widow (Wis 2:10-20). The wicked describe living a just life as "strange" (Wis 2:15). Though the wicked do not hesitate to condemn the honest poor to "a shameful death" (Wis 2:20), the poor who remain faithful will become immortal and will eventually "govern nations and rule over peoples" (Wis 3:4, 6-9).

The book of Wisdom presents the Exodus as the paradigmatic act of God's will in which justice triumphed, for it was wisdom (= justice) that delivered the Hebrew slaves from oppression (10:15). And God will continue to act to deliver the oppressed "at all times and in all places" (19:22).[17] The book illustrates its thesis about the triumph of justice and the vindication of the poor with an elaborate contrast between the punishment of the Egyptians and the liberation of the Hebrew slaves (chs. 11–19). Of course, the book of Wisdom has to defend itself against the complaints of those Jews who point to their experience of oppression under the Romans as evidence that its teaching about the vindication of the poor must be wrong. The book counters that the final vindication of the poor will take place after death. The death of the poor only looks as though it is their final defeat, but the gift of immortality, which God grants to the just, enables them to arise in judgment over their former tormentors (Wis 3:1-9).

Tobit

Another work designed to provide guidance to Jews living in the Diaspora is the book of Tobit. Though it is not a wisdom text like the others in this chapter, it does resemble the story of Joseph (Gen 37–50), a novella from the Hebrew Bible that reflects the perspectives of the wisdom tradition. Like Joseph, Tobit was tested by God. Tobit was an observer of the Torah (Tob 1:5-8) and was generous to the poor (2:2). But his wife questioned the value of his almsgiving and other acts of charity (2:14); her criticism seemed to ring true since Tobit's piety and generosity did not prevent him from being stricken with blindness. Being blind is a severe impairment at any time but was especially so in antiquity, when the blind could do little to support themselves. Because of his disability, Tobit's family faced poverty. But he advised his son not to worry about this extreme change in their economic status: "Do not be afraid, my son, because we have become poor. You have great wealth if you fear God and flee from every sin and do what is good in the sight of the Lord your God" (4:21). In addition, he advised his son that both the rich and the poor should give alms. One's own poverty should not prevent a person from helping another poor person:

> [G]ive alms from your possessions, and do not let your eye begrudge the gift when you make it. Do not turn your face away from anyone who is poor, and the face of God will not be turned away from you. If you have many possessions, make your gift from them in proportion; if few, do not be afraid to give according to the little you have. (4:7-8)

Tobit believed that generosity toward the poor "saves from death and purges away every sin" (12:9). With his final breath Tobit advised his family to "do what is right and to give alms" (14:8-9).

The book of Tobit does not denigrate the poor as responsible for their plight, and it underscores the importance of being charitable to the poor. It praises Tobit as a model of such charity (1:3; 14:2). Though Tobit and his family become poor, the book does not idealize or spiritualize their poverty. In fact, the book shows that Tobit's fidelity to the Torah and his charity toward the poor are rewarded when he is restored to economic prosperity. The centrality of acts of charity toward those in need in Tobit probably owes more to the Deuteronomic than to the wisdom tradition. Tobit illustrates the effects that obedience to the Deuteronomic laws regarding the needy produced in the life of one person who was careful to observe these laws. Though Tobit does suffer the loss of his sight, the book is not really a discourse about the suffering of the innocent as is the book of Job. The book is really concerned to show how Jews ought to remain faithful to their religious traditions, even in the face of personal tragedy, for God will not forget any kindness shown to the poor.

The *Testaments of the Twelve Patriarchs*

Though the *Testaments of the Twelve Patriarchs* are not canonical, they illustrate how giving to the poor—despite one's own economic situation—became an important concern in early Judaism. They bridge the gap between texts like Tob 4:8 and Luke 21:1-4. Tobit 4 and 14 are both examples of testaments, in other words, moral exhortations given to children by their father in view of his impending death. In the book of Tobit, these testaments are components of a short narrative about events in Tobit's life. But the *Testaments of the*

Twelve Patriarchs are presented as the last words of Jacob's sons to their children. These testaments contain the kind of practical advice and reflect traditional ethical values that characterize wisdom literature, although they are not wisdom texts themselves. Each of the testaments focuses on specific ethical concerns.

The *Testament of Issachar* focuses on the virtue of integrity, or wholehearted obedience to God's commandments. Its opposite is duplicity (see *T. Asher* 3:1-2). Issachar asserts that his generosity to the "poor and oppressed" is evidence of his integrity (*T. Issachar* 3:8). He admonishes his children to follow his example by loving God and neighbor and being compassionate toward the poor (*T. Issachar* 5:2), anticipating the connection Jesus saw between the two great commandments (see Matt 22:34-40). Like conventional wisdom, the *Testament of Issachar* implies that there is a connection between hard work and prosperity (*T. Issachar* 5:3-5), but it also notes that the person of integrity does not seek great wealth; such a desire sometimes leads people to defraud their neighbors (*T. Issachar* 4:2). In his final confession before death, Issachar calls attention to his identification with and compassion for the poor. He joined them in lamenting their oppression and shared his bread with them (*T. Issachar* 6:5).

The *Testament of Asher* shows that life can be a bit more complicated than the *Testament of Issachar* assumes. Asher speaks about the contradictory behavior of those who steal and cheat but have "pity on the poor" (*T. Asher* 2:5-7). In such cases, charity toward the poor is little more than a mask for injustice. The behavior that Asher describes is similar to that of a multinational corporation that pays slave wages in one country and supports charities in another. Asher calls for his children to act with integrity. He does not allow "conscience money" to release people from acting justly in all circumstances. Unjust actions will invariably lead to death (*T. Asher* 5:2).

The *Testament of Judah* takes the traditional route as it notes that greed prevents people from showing mercy to those in need (17:1; 18:3), but it also embraces the perspectives of apocalyptic, which became popular during the persecution by Antiochus.[18] The *Testament of Judah* ends with a description of the resurrection and notes that "those who died in poverty for the Lord's sake shall be made rich" (25:4). Fidelity to traditional Israelite morality often carried with it economic consequences. Judah encourages his sons to remain faithful because there will be a reversal of fortunes at the time of the resurrection. Of course, poverty will not exist in the world to come and those who accepted impoverishment as the price of their fidelity to the Torah in this age will be enriched in the age to come. The *Testament of Judah* does not spiritualize poverty, for it speaks to real people who have experienced privation because of their loyalty to their ancestral religious traditions. It also does not idealize poverty since it recognizes it as the result of decisions made by evil men—decisions that will be reversed in the world to come.

4QInstruction

The Qumran community produced several works on wisdom, but the fragmentary character of what remains of them makes these texts difficult to understand. There is, however, one such work that has survived in seven fragmentary copies, which may indicate its significance for the people of Qumran: 4QInstruction.[19] Poverty, wealth, and financial matters are prominent topics in this work, which is addressed not to the sons of the wealthy as Sirach is but to an individual that J. Strugnell and D.J. Harrington call "the maven."[20] The instruction shows no concern for the wealthy as a social class, but concentrates on giving advice to the maven in avoiding destitution. It also does not admonish the maven to care for the economically disadvantaged, presumably because he is in no position to do so. The instruction reminds the maven that he is among the poor (4Q415 6, 2; 4Q416 iii 12; 4Q418 177, 6) and warns him that he must not further endanger his economic status by remaining in debt: "As much as a man's creditor has lent him in money, hastily pay it back. And thou wilt be on an equal footing with him [sc. the creditor]" (4Q416 ii 4-6).

The maven is to be content with the social status that comes with his poverty, but, if he receives a position of power and authority that elevates him to a higher status, he should remember the coming judgment and act accordingly (4Q416 2 iii 9-15). The proper response for the advancement in social rank should be gratitude to God. Though advancement may be a possibility, the instruction provides the maven with more advice on how to deal with continuing poverty. First, poverty should not be used as an excuse to avoid study (4Q416 2 iii 12). The instruction implies that the quest for knowledge should not be left to the elite. Second, the instruction warns the maven that the poor will have no special status before God on the day of judgment (4Q417 2 i 11-16). The maven must not consider his poverty as a means to avoid divine judgment. The poor who sin require God's forgiveness.

4QInstruction is one wisdom text that approaches the problem of poverty from the perspective of a poor person. It provides practical advice to the maven to help him avoid sinking deeper into destitution. It does not idealize poverty, but warns the maven to devote himself to study and to prepare himself for judgment. His poverty does not exempt him from either.

Conclusion

The wisdom tradition finds the origins of poverty in laziness and folly as well as in oppression and injustice. This stands in contrast with the prophets, who condemn the avarice of the wealthy for creating the social and economic conditions that lead to the impoverishment of the Israelite peasant. But the wisdom tradition never "blames the victim." When it speaks about laziness as a cause of poverty, it is not excoriating the peasant farmer but it is warning the sons of the upper class that they can lose their social standing if they are not careful. The wisdom tradition does recognize the responsibility of the people of means for creating and perpetuating poverty and calls for the wealthy to accept their responsibility toward the poor. The poverty of the peasants calls for action from the wealthy to alleviate the burdens that their fellow Israelites must bear. It calls for generosity toward those in need, something that became a hallmark of Jewish religious observance.

Questions for Reflection

1. How does the attitude of Proverbs toward the poor and poverty differ from that in the Torah and Prophets?

2. How did Job find the situation of the poor to be parallel to his own circumstances?

3. What did Ecclesiastes think of the possibility that the poor might be able to rise above their circumstances? Why?

4. How did Hellenism affect Sirach's approach to the poor and poverty?

5. What action does the wisdom tradition suggest as one response to poverty in the Jewish community?

CHAPTER FIVE

THE PSALMS

The oppression of the poor is a frequent subject of ancient Israel's prayers, which are preserved in the book of Psalms. The psalms of lament, in particular, describe the suffering of the poor and call upon God to judge those responsible for it and thereby end the oppression of the poor. The psalms are poetry and part of the beauty of poetry is found in its use of metaphor. Sometimes the psalms do use the vocabulary about the poor metaphorically, especially as it describes the marginalization of the pious by those who did not take their ancestral religion seriously. But the use of metaphor must not be confused with the spiritualization or idealization of poverty as a state that places one in a closer relationship with God. The biblical tradition looks at poverty and its effects in ancient Israel as a tragic evil. It calls upon God to end that evil, which was destroying Israel. In reading and praying the psalms, one certainly should be sensitive to the metaphorical use of language. Still, using the psalms to support a spiritualization of poverty and the poor is an unauthentic way to appropriate these ancient prayers today. It is still necessary to hear the cries of the poor as articulated in the psalms. These are cries for justice. They call for a social and economic system based on justice. They rely on God to take action in order to bring about the triumph of justice.

If good liturgy reflects life, then the book of Psalms shows that ancient Israel's liturgy did not ignore the harsh realities of life for the poor. The Psalter is replete with references to the poor. But it is necessary to recognize the function that the Psalter had in Israel's life. It was the hymnbook of the temple, so it served the community's liturgy. At the same time, it was to nourish the spirituality of the individual. It was not legislation like that found in the Torah, nor was it a collection of prophetic oracles, nor advice from Israel's sages. Still, this does not mean that it was detached from the experience of believers, rich or poor. If it were, the book would not have survived to the present. The challenge for contemporary believers as they read the psalms is to keep in check the tendency to spiritualize its references to the poor in the attempt to appropriate these texts. But some interpreters insist that a spiritualization of poverty is evident in the psalms themselves. In his commentary on the Psalter, Artur Weiser maintains that the terms "poor" and "needy" designate those who are faithful to Yahweh and this terminology is simply liturgical metaphor. It does not arise from any existential experience of material deprivation. He asserts, for example, that the Hebrew words *'ānî* and *'ānāwîm* often translated as "the poor," actually mean "bent low" and refer to the external and internal posture of those who stand before God in submission and adoration. Weiser considered the use of these words to describe social or economic status to be secondary.[1] Like Weiser, Albert Gelin was certain that the psalms, when referring to the poor, were speaking not of people's "mere sociological status" but of a spiritual quality of those who were obedient to the Lord.[2] Gelin finds in the Psalter a source for profiling what he considers the spirituality of "the poor." Poverty in the psalms, according to Gelin, does not refer to economic status but to an inner attitude, a spiritual value, a moral ideal.

The basic question of interpretation related to the psalms is the identification of "the poor and needy." Are the poor of the psalms the economically poor? Has the language of social and economic stratification and conflict become simply a convention in these prayers to speak about the community of Israel as a whole or about a group of the pious within the community? Does the word "poor," when it appears in the psalms, represent a spiritual quality? Have the poor become the pious in the psalms, as Weiser and Gelin suggest? Has God, who according to common ancient Near Eastern usage was the protector of the poor, become the protector only of the righteous?

Psalm 72

An important place to begin formulating an answer to these questions is Ps 72, a prayer for the king. The twenty verses of this psalm mention the poor nine times (vv. 2, 4[2x], 12[2x], 13[3x], 14[2x]). But in speaking of the poor, Ps 72 focuses on their powerlessness rather than on their deprivation. The psalm asks God to empower the king to perform one of his most fundamental duties: the defense of the poor against those who exploited them. The people of means corrupted the judicial system through bribery, as is evident by the frequent reference to bribery in ancient Israel's legal, prophetic, and wisdom traditions (see Exod 18:21; 23:8; Deut 16:19; Isa 1:23; 5:23; 10:1-2; Amos 5:12; 6:12; Mic 3:11; 7:3; Prov 6:19; 12:17; 18:16). The wealthy were able to preserve their interests at the expense of the rights of the poor, who did not have the resources to protect themselves. Even if outright bribery did not take place, judges were surely tempted to give greater credence to the word of the powerful and influential in society rather than to someone with little or no social standing or economic resources (see Lev 19:15). It was the subversion of the legal system that maintained poverty and ensured the division of the Israelite community into a creditor and a debtor class. The only recourse the powerless had was an appeal to the king. Kings throughout the ancient Near East styled themselves as protectors of the powerless and Ps 72 reflects that common cultural assumption about the responsibilities of the monarch. The powerless had to depend upon the king since they had no avenues to find justice in their claims against the powerful.

Psalm 72:2, as it prays for the king to be endowed with God's justice, speaks of "your [God's] poor." The king is the protector of the poor because he stands in God's place. Unlike the prophets, the Psalter only rarely speaks of the king's responsibility toward the poor as Ps 72 does. Perhaps this reflects the function of ancient Israel's temple worship, which tended to support rather than challenge the national state. The Psalter consistently portrays God as *the* protector of the poor. Psalm 113 calls Israel to praise God precisely because the one who is "high above all nations" (v. 4) uses the divine power to reverse the fortunes of the poor, who are forced to scavenge for food among the garbage (v. 7). The person who had no social standing now has access to the places of power. The psalm, then, lends divine authority to every attempt to halt and reverse the process whereby Israel becomes a nation permanently divided into two economic classes. The psalm makes sense only against the backdrop of the real social conflict that Israel's prophets railed against. The psalm asserts that in this conflict God will take the side of the poor.

Psalm 72 presents the king as the instrument by which God's justice and righteousness come to the people, especially the poor (vv. 1-2). The very basis of the king's legitimacy rests on his taking the side of the poor as the instrument of divine justice (vv. 12-16). The psalm concludes by acknowledging that God is the source of justice no matter who the human agent may be (vv. 17-19). There is no spiritualization of the poor here. When Ps 72 speaks about the poor and needy, it is speaking about those people whose lack of material resources makes their exploitation a simple matter for the wealthy. Clearly this psalm makes sense only against the backdrop of social conflict in ancient Israel.

Lament Psalms

It is important to read several of the psalms of lament against the social conflict that took place in ancient Israel during the monarchic period, when ancient Israel's agrarian economy was being transformed into a commercial one. More and more family holdings were being swallowed up into the large estates of wealthy landowners, who grew crops such as olives and grapes not to feed themselves and their families, but to produce by-products that could be easily transported and sold. With less land available for the growing of food staples such as grains, the pressure on the peasants grew. While the owners of large estates became wealthier through the export of olive oil and wine, the peasants became poorer because of the dwindling supply and consequent higher price of basic foodstuffs. The frustration of the poor finds expression in the laments that speak of the damage done by the "enemies." Clearly the "enemies" of Ps 35:19, for example, are those who oppress the poor, exploit the needy, subvert the judicial process, and profit at the expense of the poor (Ps 35:10-26). The psalm asks God to join in the lawsuit of the poor in order for justice to triumph (Ps 35:23-24). Failing to read this psalm against the social and economic conflicts in ancient Israelite society is to misread it. Other lament psalms may use vague terms such as "the wicked" to describe those who oppress the poor (e.g., Pss 10:4; 12:8; 140:4, 8) but Ps 109 also makes obvious the economic origins of the social conflict when it speaks of the enemies of the poor as "plunderers" and "creditors" (v. 11) and describes the psalmist's immediate problem as malnutrition (v. 24). The only way to see this conflict as a metaphor for a spiritual conflict between good and evil is to ignore the concrete meaning of the psalm's vocabulary and phraseology.

Lienhard Delekat has suggested that several lament psalms reflect one way that the poor coped with the social and economic conflict, which they were clearly losing: they sought refuge from their creditors in the temple.[3] According to this suggestion, Ps 86 is a prayer expecting an oracle of protection against overzealous creditors:

> Incline your ear, O LORD, and answer me,
>   for I am poor and needy....
> O God, the insolent rise up against me;
>   a band of ruffians seeks my life,
>   and they do not set you before them....
> Turn to me and be gracious to me;
>   give your strength to your servant;
>   save the child of your serving girl.
> Show me a sign of your favor,
>   so that those who hate me may
>   see it and be put to shame,
>   because you, LORD, have helped
>   me and comforted me. (Ps 86:1, 14, 16-17)

125

Delekat asserts that terms like "refuge," "stronghold," and "protection," which occur frequently in psalms of lament, refer to sanctuaries where the poor found relief from the hounding of their creditors. It was only as a result of later spiritualization that these words came to be understood as metaphors for communion with God. Certainly the poor did find the temple to be a place where they could pray for legal aid and righteous judgment (10:13-14).

The language of the psalms of lament, then, is not at all metaphorical. It is the one opportunity to hear the authentic voice of the poor. The Torah, while it seeks to eliminate social and economic stratification, speaks about the poor. The books of the prophets contain the words of charismatic spokesmen for Israel's ancient religious traditions and values, but they do not contain the words of the poor. The wisdom literature contains the reflections of the intellectual class about the poor. But the psalms of lament give voice to the complaints of ancient Israel's poor. To spiritualize these complaints is to blunt their force and render them mute in speaking to social and economic conflicts today.

Yahweh's action on behalf of the poor stands in marked contrast to that of others gods, which Ps 82 condemns for ignoring their responsibilities to the most vulnerable in human society. The psalmist portrays the world as governed by a council of gods who meet in a divine assembly. The God of Israel asserts that the members of this council have been governing the world unjustly (v. 2). The sentence God pronounces on the members of the divine council for their failure is death because God fully expects that the powerless in society be accorded justice and that the weak be delivered from their oppressors (vv. 3-5). The use of five synonyms for the poor in verses 3-4 is an effective technique to ensure that readers understand that the psalm is speaking about people with real material needs.

The psalm is not simply an expression of ancient Near Eastern imagery and metaphor. Religion then, as it often does now, supported a particular socio-economic system. Yahwism supported a society of equals. All Israelites were to think of themselves as descendants of the slaves whom God freed and gave an equal share of the promised land. Baalism, the principal competitor for the loyalty of the Israelites, supported a political and economic system based on dominance. The king was the viceroy of the gods, who had a hierarchy among themselves. He presided over an economic system in which the labor of many supported the luxury of a few. Ancient Israel emerged in the central highlands of Canaan as people began withdrawing their loyalty from a system in which they did not enjoy the fruits of their labor. Taxation and internecine warfare drove the peasant farmers to give their allegiance to a nonhuman lord, Yahweh, who provided them with a bountiful land and rest from their enemies. Unfortunately, the establishment of the two Israelite national states turned the Israelite social and economic system around, making it like that of the nations. It is little wonder, then, that Israel's kings tolerated and some-times promoted the worship of Baal and other non-Israelite gods. The injustice of the Israelite economic system and the infidelity expressed by the worship of foreign deities, condemned by the prophets, were just two sides of the same coin.

The stratification of Israelite society, which the introduction of the monarchy made inevitable, led to conflict between the rich and the poor. The psalms reflect this conflict as they describe the poor as victims of the "wicked" (see Pss 10:4; 12:8; 109:6, 16; 140:4, 8). The terms used to describe the wealthy who take advantage of the poor include "despoilers" (Ps 35:10), "plunderers" and "creditors" (Ps 109:11), and "malicious witnesses" (Ps 35:11). The poor are hounded by their oppressors (Pss 10:2, 9; 14:6; 35:10; 37:14; 109:16). This conflict involves the very survival of the poor: "The wicked draw the sword and bend their bows to bring down the poor and needy, to kill those who walk uprightly" (Ps 37:14; see also 109:16). The social conflict within Israelite society was real, as is clear from the prophetic corpus. The words of the psalms, then, are not merely metaphors but reflect the real struggles of people who were materially poor, and were often made so by deliberate actions of the wealthy.

Another lament that depends upon the belief that God takes the side of the poor against their oppressors is Ps 12. Here there is no description of the problems of the poor. The psalmist decries the effects of malicious speech of friends who have proven false. God interrupts the lament by assuring the one making it that God will act on behalf of the poor and needy (v. 5). Again, there is no hint of any humble acceptance of oppression. In fact, the assurance made to the suppliant is based on the belief that God does not allow the suffering of the poor to go on indefinitely. Many of the references to the poor in the psalms assert that God will bring an end to their suffering, for example, 14:7; 22:26; 34:7; 35:10; 69:33; 70:5; 74:19, 21; 76:9; 86:1. There is not a single instance in the psalms in which the poor or those who identify with them appear to accept their oppression.

Indeed there would be more of a problem had the psalms expressed a kind of resignation to the experience of oppression. Israel's initial encounter with God, which is celebrated by ancient Israel's liturgy, is remembered as an experience of Israel's dire need and God's gracious response. Israel lamented its oppression under the pharaohs and God freed them from that oppression. In the wilderness, the freed slaves complained of their hunger and thirst and God provided them with manna from heaven and water from the rock. In Canaan, Israel faced a much stronger indigenous population, and God gave them victory over all who were arrayed against them. Where these stories are recounted, the distress of the Israelites is graphically described, their cry of distress is recalled, God's promise of deliverance is rehearsed, their triumph is celebrated, and the people respond with praise.[4] Ancient Israel experienced and celebrated God as one who saves from oppression, not one who requires humble submission to oppression. A significant element in the process of deliverance is the cry for help. The psalms, then, are to be understood not so much as idealizations of poverty but as components of a process that will lead to liberation. The psalms show that cries to God for help were a substantial component of the interchange that went on between God and Israel.

Because the psalms of lament are complaints about oppression, it is unlikely that those who made these complaints regarded their suffering as something that was to be accepted submissively. These psalms take seriously the human failure to maintain a just society, but they do not believe that God's actions on behalf of the poor ought to be hampered by human failure. The reason believers brought their complaints to God is that they were convinced their prayers would be heard. Were it otherwise the laments of the Psalter would be nothing more than an exercise in self-pity. Since the poor address their laments to the One who can remove their oppression, the laments are much more. They affirm that oppression is not something that is to be endured with patience but is something that is to be brought before God.

The ʿānāwîm

Attempts to understand the nature of this social conflict have focused on the word ʿānāwîm, one of the Bible's several terms for "the poor."[5] It is not the most common word for "the poor," appearing only twenty-four times in the Hebrew Bible. But thirteen of those occurrences are in the book of Psalms, principally in lament psalms. These psalms call upon God to remember the ʿānāwîm (Ps 10:12, 18). Indeed, God does guide the ʿānāwîm and rescues them from their difficulties (Pss 25:9; 34:6; 69:33; 76:9; 147:6; 149:4). Their problems are concrete enough: they need food and land on which to produce it (Pss 22:26; 37:11).[6] Gelin read the images of the poor in these psalms as metaphor. Religious Jews, no matter what their economic status, spoke of themselves as "the poor." The word ʿānāwîm became a self-designation that made this term functionally equivalent to "pious" or "humble" and the opposite of "evil" and "wicked." The ʿānāwîm were the faithful in contrast to those who were ready to abandon their ancestral religion. The conflict that the poor had with the wealthy had been overshadowed by a conflict between the observant and nonobservant. The oppressors of the ʿānāwîm were those who no longer believed. Though this usage may reflect a certain "spiritualization" of poverty and the poor in some of the psalms, these prayers still do not detach themselves completely from the economically poor and they certainly do not idealize poverty. The intensity of the language in the lament psalms clearly shows that the *'ănāwîm* did not accept their social position as the divine will. They beg for deliverance. They ask for a hearing. They long for the defeat of their enemies. By no means are they resigned to a situation that they experience as oppressive. Indeed, those who pray these psalms fully expect that God will vindicate them. The "humility" of the *'ănāwîm* expresses itself in the acknowledgment of God as their only savior and in absolute confidence that their deliverance is assured. By identifying with the materially poor, those who feel marginalized by the nonobservant do not idealize poverty as a state that brings one closer to God. Adopting this metaphor serves to express confidence in God, who will move against the oppressor and vindicate "the poor."

Gelin suggested that Pss 9 and 10 reflected the ideology of the *'ănāwîm* most clearly.[7] Those who offered this prayer called themselves the *'ānî* (10:2, 9) and *'ănāwîm* (10:17). Because the so-called *'ănāwîm* were on the margins of ancient Israelite society and oppressed by their adversaries, they saw themselves in a situation similar to that of the economically poor and adopted their identity. Still, the psalms do not idealize poverty as leading a person to a closer relationship with God nor do they suggest a humble acceptance of oppression in obedience to the divine will. The psalms describe the evil of the oppressors in great detail in order to move God to take the side of the poor (10:1-15). As king and judge, God not only judges the nations aligned against Israel (9:7-8, 19; 10:16), but also vindicates those who oppress the poor (9:3-4). The *'ănāwîm* offer this prayer with the confidence of being heard because they are convinced of the righteousness of their cause. They call upon God to move against their oppressors. The use of imagery related to the plight of the materially poor reflects the attempt to identify with the poor. Like the poor who wish to escape the oppression of the powerful, so the *'ănāwîm* hope for deliverance from the wicked, who have abandoned the service of God. The psalm ends with a statement of confidence in God, who hears the laments of the *'ănāwîm* and stops their oppression (10:17-18). There is no hint whatsoever in this psalm that the *'ănāwîm* accept their oppression. What the poor accept is their complete dependence on God.

Conclusion

The psalms consistently portray God as the protector and deliverer of the poor (e.g., Pss 9:12, 18; 10:14; 35:1; 68:10; 69:33; 107:41; 109:31; 113:7;

140:12; 147:6; 149:4). Those who experience exploitation ask for God's protection and strength in their conflict with the rich (Pss 12:1; 69:33) for the poor are those who depend upon God (Pss 10; 25; 34; 37; 82). The poor turn to prayer in the midst of their oppression because they believe in God's love and fidelity (Pss 69:13-15; 86:5, 15). They pray that God will vindicate them, establishing justice according to God's righteousness (35:23-24; 140:12).

It is only because the Bible considers material poverty as an evil that the book of Psalms has been able to reinterpret the vocabulary of poverty to speak about the oppression of the pious. The problem with spiritualizing the vocabulary of poverty as representing "the ability to welcome God, an openness to God, a willingness to be used by God, a humility before God"[8] is that it can lead to "canonizing" the poor, as though material poverty gives people a special access to God. There is, of course, no socioeconomic path to salvation. A second problem with spiritualizing the poor and their oppression is that it mutes the Bible's serious and consistent criticism of those responsible for creating a social and economic system that creates poverty and divides humanity into the rich and the poor, the possessors and the dispossessed, the oppressors and the oppressed. The psalms of lament call for God to judge those who create poverty and thereby end the oppression of the poor.

Questions for Reflection

1. To what extent can the language of the psalms be described as metaphorical when speaking of the poor?

2. How do the psalms portray God's relationship with the poor?

3. What is the best way to describe the response of the poor to their oppression as reflected in the psalms?

4. What problems arise with "spiritualizing" the psalms' sentiments about the poor and their oppression?

CHAPTER SIX

APOCALYPTIC LITERATURE

The *Testament of Judah* 25:4 asserted that those who become poor "for the Lord" in this age will become rich at the time of the resurrection. The Jewish religious ideology that makes such a statement possible has been called "apocalyptic." As a way of coping with reality, apocalyptic has been defined as "a Judeo-Christian world-view which located the believer in a minority community and gave his life meaning by relating it to the end, soon to come, which would reverse his present status."[1] The impulse behind such a perspective on human experience is a genuine restlessness and total dissatisfaction with the evils of the present and the desire for a new and total solution to the human problem. Such a perspective on life gave rise to a body of literature with a characteristic literary form that has been defined as "a genre of revelatory literature with a narrative framework, in which a revelation is mediated by an otherworldly being to a human recipient, disclosing a transcendent reality which is both temporary, insofar as it envisages eschatological salvation, and spatial insofar as it involves another, supernatural world."[2]

Though the origins of apocalyptic are still a controverted question, apocalyptic's way of making sense of human experience has its basis in the collapse of a previously accepted worldview. Certainly the persecution of the Jews by Antiochus IV called into question the well-defined structures of the Torah as interpreted by the prophets. The Law and the Prophets spoke to people who were in control of their own destiny, who were free to make decisions about their future, who were able to shape events. For the most part, from the sixth century BCE, the Jews were not that kind of people. By the second century, some Jews no longer felt there were any prospects for changing the political and economic status quo. They gave up on the possibilities of the present and began to look for change that would come with a new world. They looked for another world in which their unpleasant circumstances would be reversed. The texts that reflect these views reveal to the faithful a vision of a new world—a world in which justice and right triumph. In other words, it will be a world unlike that of the present age. The basic assumption of all apocalypses is that this world is disordered. It is controlled by the power of evil. There will come a day when God will vindicate the just, who will then be victorious over their enemies. By relegating the final and complete victory of divine justice to another age, apocalyptic handled some very difficult theological problems, for example, the suffering of the innocent, the reality of divine justice, and the nature of reward and punishment. It provided some measure of solace for the oppressed because they do not experience divine justice in this world. But it did so at a price—by asserting that there can be no justice in *this* world. At the same time, however, apocalyptic texts assure their readers that the triumph of justice is coming very soon.

Daniel

The book of Daniel mentions the poor only once, in an admonition to Nebuchadnezzar (Dan 4:24; ET 4:27). The Babylonian king is advised that compassion toward the poor may atone for his sins. This solitary reference to the vocabulary of the poor, however, should not leave the impression that Daniel was not concerned about the poor and the oppressed. Quite the opposite is true, since the book's central concern is to help Jews remain faithful to their ancestral religious traditions despite the oppression they experienced from the Greeks and the elite of the Jewish community, who cooperated with their Greek masters. The book of Daniel is a product of the Maccabean period (167–164 BCE). The purpose of the book is to make it possible for the Jews to benefit from the teaching of "the wise [*maśkîlîm*] among the people" (Dan 11:33).[3] While some Jews began a violent revolution against the Seleucids, the *maśkîlîm* suggest a stance of passive resistance.[4] Of course, such a stance will lead to the death of some Jews but there will be a resurrection that will be the vindication of the righteous (Dan 12:1-4).

The principal concern of the first six chapters of Daniel is to demonstrate that God does not abandon those who remain faithful to the Torah. The setting for the narratives in Dan 1–6, like that of Tobit, is in the Diaspora. The stories show that while Jews may be tolerated by their Gentile masters, they experience immense social, economic, and political pressures to abandon their religion. The point of the narratives is that God does not abandon those who continue to observe the Torah even in the most difficult circumstances. The questions of justice, social conflict, and the exploitation of those on the margins seemed less important than affirming God's concern for those who continue to be loyal to Judaism despite the pressures to abandon their religion.

In Dan 7–12, the attitude of the Gentile rulers toward the Jews clearly changes from tolerance and even sympathy to opposition and persecution. The Jewish community was divided on how to respond to this persecution. The elite endorsed a thoroughgoing Hellenization of Judah (e.g., 1 Macc 1:11-15), while the majority of the largely poor population opposed this development. At this time, the office of high priest was sold to the highest bidder by the Seleucids, who used the money to finance their wars. During one of these wars waged by the Seleucids against their rivals, the Ptolemies, traditionalists in Jerusalem revolted against Seleucid rule (2 Macc 5:5). The success of this revolution was short-lived and Antiochus retook Jerusalem and exacted heavy tribute from the people. The high priest, who was in league with Antiochus, even helped strip the temple of its gold (1 Macc 1:21-28). Two years later Antiochus began a full-scale persecution of the traditionalists among the Jews, whom he saw as disloyal and troublesome.[5] Complicating matters for the Jews of Palestine were the divisions within the Jewish community. For the most part, the book of Daniel ignores these divisions and defines the conflict as though it were a purely religious one between the Jewish faithful and the faithless king. But Dan 11 does shed some light on the cultural and social conflict within the Jewish community as it distinguishes three groups among the Jews: those "who forsake the holy covenant" (v. 30), "the people who are loyal to their God" (v. 32), and the "many" (v. 34). The fate of the last group mentioned is apparently determined by whether they join those who violate the covenant or those who remain loyal to it.

Daniel 7–12, true to the perspective of apocalyptic, sees the final triumph of those who are faithful as the result of God's action through the archangel Michael (Dan 10–12). It rejects the revolutionary perspective that pervades 1–2 Maccabees because this world is passing away. Though the passive resistance promoted by Daniel may mean that some of the faithful will lose their lives in the course of the persecution, the book's ideology will be proven correct when the just are raised to everlasting life (12:2). The book of Daniel, however, does not offer any practical solutions to the problems that the Jewish community was experiencing, either because of internal social conflict or external political and religious persecution.

Daniel deals with questions of justice from an apocalyptic perspective, one that looks for the imminent intervention of God to reverse the fortunes of the faithful. It does not suggest ways that people can overcome injustice since it regarded human actions as genuinely ineffective against the powers of evil that control this age. Oppression, persecution, and poverty are only passing phenomena, as are the kingdoms of this world (Dan 7). In the end, the "holy ones" will receive the kingdom and possess it forever (Dan 7:18), not because of actions they take but because of God's determination to take control of the world from the powers that hold it in subjection. The faithful need to remain loyal to their religious traditions in spite of the pressures to do otherwise. The book's faith in the power of God to control the future enabled those who accepted its message to defy the forces of oppression.

A materialist reading of Daniel regards the book's approach to the problem of oppression as impractical and even illusory. Those who first heard its message, however, experienced the book as life-giving and liberating. Still, one cannot transform the book's perspectives into an ethic that is universally valid. There were striking differences of approach to the persecution of Antiochus among Jews who had to face that persecution.[6] The book of Daniel represents one view. Though it offers no "practical" advice on overcoming oppression, it obviously regards it as an evil that calls forth divine judgment. Again, oppression is not spiritualized or idealized. The "people who are loyal to their God" (11:32) are praised not because they are persecuted but because they remain faithful to their God despite the political, social, and economic consequences of their fidelity. Daniel, however, affirms that the suffering of the faithful is not in vain. God will overcome every power arrayed against the faithful—including death—and raise them up to be like the stars (Dan 12:3).

Sibylline Oracles Book 3

The third book of the *Sibylline Oracles* (*Sib. Or.*) is a Jewish propagandistic work from the second century BCE. In the course of this anti-Roman and pro-Ptolemaic tract, the Jews are praised for how they live their social ideals by being generous, not avaricious, especially toward those in need. Also, the text praises them for the justice of their economic practices (see *Sib. Or.* 3:234-47). Of course, all this is meant to underscore the injustice that characterizes the social and economic practices of other nations. The vision that this third book of the *Oracles* has of the future is an idealistic one in which justice will triumph and there will be material prosperity and, above all, an end to the exploitation of the poor: "Bad government, blame, envy, anger, folly, poverty will flee from men" (*Sib. Or.* 3:377-78).[7] The focus in these oracles is not on the economic exploitation taking place within the Jewish community but that which is a consequence of Roman rule. Like other texts with an apocalyptic perspective, however, the *Sibylline Oracles* Book 3 looks forward to the day when justice will triumph and poverty will be no more.

1 Enoch

While the book of Daniel and the *Sybilline Oracles* 3 focus on the oppression that religious Jews experienced at the hands of foreign rulers, *1 Enoch* provides a closer look into the social conflict within the Jewish community. Coopted by the Seleucids, Judah's elite prospered because of their collaboration with the Greeks. Judah's lower class tended toward religious conservatism and paid a high economic price for holding on to their religious traditions. A principal affirmation of the book is that those who engage in economic exploitation and political oppression are sinners. The guilty are not only the Gentiles who occupy Judah but also the Jewish aristocracy that benefits because of their cooperation with the Gentile oppressors. The book demonstrates the depth of resentment that Judah's lower class felt toward their society's elite.

Chapters 92–105 of *1 Enoch* contain a letter written by Enoch to his children.[8] The purpose of this letter is to provide the assurance that God is coming to reward the righteous and punish sinners. Such assurance encouraged Jews to be faithful to the Torah in troubled times. The heart of the letter is a series of woes directed at the wicked. The contents of these woes give a clear idea of what Judah's lower class suffered at the hands of the Jewish aristocracy. Some of the crimes for which the wicked are indicted are religious: idolatry (99:7), blasphemy (94:9; 96:7), false teaching (98:15), and the perversion of the Torah (99:2). The bulk of the charges made against the sinners, however, are social and economic:

> Woe unto you, O rich people!
> . . . .
> In the days of your affluence, you committed oppression. . . . (94:8-9)[9]

> Woe unto you, witnesses of falsehood!
> And unto those who prepare oppression! (95:6)

> Woe unto you who eat the best bread!
> And drink wine in large bowls,
> trampling upon the weak people with your might. (96:5)

> Woe unto you, O powerful people!
> You who coerce the righteous with your power,
> the day of your destruction is coming! (96:8)

> Woe unto you who gain silver and gold by unjust means. (97:8)

Woe unto you who build your houses through the hard toil of others,
and your building materials are bricks and stones of sin. . . . (99:13)

Woe unto you, sinners, when you oppress
the righteous ones. . . . (100:7)

The context makes it clear that these are eschatological woes, in other
words, the curse they invoke upon the wicked will come to fulfillment as God
brings an end to this age. Enoch assures his children that while sinners are
prospering now, a severe punishment awaits them. Like other apocalypses,
1 Enoch gives up on the possibilities of the present. One reason for such pes-
simism about any triumph of justice in this age is the experience of the pious.
They are not receiving the rewards that should come to them because of their
righteousness. In fact, they are experiencing the curses of Deut 28, which
should be inflicted upon those who ignore the Torah. What makes matters
even worse is that the righteous are receiving these curses at the hands of sinners (*1 En* 103:9-15). Justice is turned inside out. Sinners flaunt the will of
God, yet their rebellion goes unpunished. The righteous are not rewarded for
their goodness but are oppressed by the wicked.

It is interesting to compare the woes found in Sirach (2:12-14; 41:8-9)
with those in *1 En* 92–105. Both texts reflect a similar tension between the
rich and the poor in Judahite society. Sirach, however, appears to be addressing himself to the rich. He advises them to be concerned about the poor and
to use their wealth responsibly by responding to the cries of the needy. Enoch
addresses the poor. He does not foresee any way that the Judahite aristocracy
can reform itself, so Enoch simply curses the wealthy. To the poor he promises an imminent reversal of fortunes in which the injustice and oppression
of the present will be eliminated. He consoles the poor by revealing to them
that already in the present angels are interceding for them with God, that
their names are inscribed in the register of the righteous in heaven, and that
their salvation is guaranteed (*1 En* 102:4–104:8).

The book of *1 Enoch* does not spiritualize poverty. The author speaks about
people who have experienced the real effects of the Greek domination of
Judah's economy. The poor, however, are righteous not because of their economic status but because they are faithful to the Torah. Similarly, the wicked
do stand under judgment not because of their wealth but because they have
abandoned their ancestral traditions for the sake of advancing their social
and economic status. They have collaborated with the Seleucids in oppressing the righteous and so they will experience divine judgment, while the
poor will enjoy the reward that belongs to the just.

The Dead Sea Scrolls

The discovery of the Dead Sea Scrolls and the excavation of the settlement used by those who produced these texts have made available the physical setting, the literature, and some idea of the history of a group of Jews who were imbued with apocalyptic perspectives. The existence of the Qumran community in the Judean wilderness and the analysis of the texts that this community valued, produced, and transmitted provide another insight into the internal debates and social conflicts within Judaism to which texts like *1 Enoch* witness. It is clear that these conflicts gave rise to a number of diverse groupings within early Judaism. The content and tone of portions of the literature produced at Qumran allow the inference of serious social conflicts within the Jewish community. Of course, the Qumran community understood these conflicts in religious terms for the most part. Still, the conflicts had genuine social and economic consequences. They were serious enough for members of the community to leave the population centers of Palestine and establish a settlement for themselves in the uninviting Judean desert near the Dead Sea. They did not make this move for ascetical but for practical reasons. The people of Qumran experienced persecution—perhaps even the murder of the Teacher of Righteousness—from the priestly aristocracy. The community moved to the desert, hoping to avoid further persecution. Of course, they expected to return to Jerusalem once God had executed judgment on the wicked priests.

The Damascus Document (CD), one of the rules followed by the Qumran community, urges the members of that community to remain faithful and assures them that God always rewards fidelity. They are to demonstrate their fidelity by scrupulous observance of the Torah in an "age of wickedness." Among the sins the faithful are to avoid is exploitation of the poor (see CD 6: 1 8; *DSSE*, 103). In a more positive tone, the members of the community are told that: "They shall love each man his brother as himself; they shall succour the poor, the needy, and the stranger" (CD 6:21-22; *DSSE*, 103). The same rule lists "the poor and the needy" among the groups that the community is to support (CD 14:14). In these texts, "the poor" refers to a socioeconomic class. It is not a technical term for the community itself.

This is not the case in the War Rule (1QM), which deals with the eschatological war that was to usher in the new age expected by the Qumran community. The War Rule is not a military text as much as it is a theological reflection on the continuing struggle between good and evil. This struggle will end only when God steps in to fight on the side of "the poor," in other words, those who appear to be unlikely to prevail in the war but who do win by the power of God: "For Thou wilt deliver into the hands of the poor the enemies from all the lands, to humble the mighty of the peoples by the hand of those bent to the dust" (lQM 11:13; *DSSE*, 138). Here "the poor" are those without the ability to gain a military victory but who are triumphant because of God's power (see also 1QM 13:12-14; *DSSE*, 141; 1QM 14:17; *DSSE*, 142). The term "the poor" represents the weakness and vulnerability of the faithful.

Included among the distinctive texts of the Qumran community is a collection of exegetical writings that comment on individual books of the Bible. In the commentary on the book of Habakkuk (1QpHab), the first two chapters of the prophetic book are applied to the history of the community itself. The comment on Hab 2:17 reads: "this saying concerns the Wicked Priest, inasmuch as he shall be paid the reward which he himself tendered to the Poor" (1QpHab 12:2, *DSSE*, 242). The commentary uses familiar imagery to describe the oppression that the community experienced at the hands of their principal opponent, the Wicked Priest. The exploitation of the powerless by the powerful is a familiar enough theme in the Bible for the commentary to describe the persecution of the Qumran community in precisely that fashion. In the commentary on Ps 37 (4Q171; also 4QpPs 37), the focus is again on the conflict between the community and the Wicked Priest. The comment on verses 10-11 and 22 uses the term "the congregation of the poor" (4Q171 2:9; 3:10; *DSSE*, 243-45). Psalm 37 refers to the poor and the needy as those who are persecuted by the wicked who are wealthy (Ps 37:14, 16). The Qumran commentary sees this psalm as a prophetic description of the community's persecution by the priests of Jerusalem. The term "poor" does not so much speak of Qumran's economic status but of its place on the margins of the Jewish community.

The Qumran community followed the practice of renouncing private property. This is clear enough from the community rule sometimes known as the Manual of Discipline (lQS): "They shall separate from the congregation of the men of falsehood and shall unite, with respect to the Law and possessions, under the authority of the sons of Zadok.... Every decision concerning doctrine, property, and justice shall be determined by them" (1QS 5:2; *DSSE*, 78). Those who entered the community were required to transfer their wealth to the common fund (lQS 1:1-3; 6:17-23; *DSSE*, 72, 82). There were penalties for lying about one's property (6:25; *DSSE*, 82) and for failing to care for the community's property (7:6; *DSSE*, 83). It is important to note that such texts do not exhibit a negative attitude toward possessions as such, but attempt to eliminate distinctions between the wealthy and the poor because no such distinctions would exist in the world that the Qumran people were expecting.

Among the texts produced by the community is a collection of poems called the *Hodayot* (1QH), prayers modeled on the biblical thanksgiving psalms. Those who experienced salvation through their inclusion in the community expressed their gratitude through these prayers that praised God for the knowledge and salvation granted to them. The use of the term "poor" in these prayers is quite similar to its usage in the canonical psalms. The speaker of the *Hodayot* identifies himself as a "poor one" whom God has rescued from the wicked, in other words, the opponents of the Qumran community:

> I thank Thee, O Lord,
>> for Thou hast [fastened] Thine eye upon me.
> Thou hast saved me from the zeal
>> of lying interpreters. . . .
> Thou hast redeemed the soul of the poor one
>> whom they planned to destroy. . . . (1QH 2:31-33; see also 5:1, 13-18)[10]

In another hymn, the community as a whole is referred to as the *ʿănāwîm* ("humble," i.e., "the poor"):

> I thank Thee . . . O Lord,
>> for Thou hast not abandoned the fatherless
>> or despised the poor . . . .
> yet [hast Thou done marvels] among the humble
>> in the mire underfoot,
>> and among those eager for righteousness,
> causing all the well-loved poor
>> to rise up together from the trampling. (1QH 5:20-22)[11]

> Thou didst open [his fountain] . . .
> [that he might be], according to Thy truth,
>> a messenger [in the season] of Thy goodness;
> that to the humble he might bring
>> glad tidings of Thy great mercy. . . . (1QH 18:14-16)[12]

This usage has led some interpreters to conclude that *ʿănāwîm* is a technical term in the *Hodayot*, referring to a specific group.[13] In fact, some suggest that the Qumran people used the word *ʿănāwîm* as a self-designation, though there is serious doubt that this was the case.[14] It is likely that the *Hodayot* uses the term "poor" to speak of those whom God has predestined for salvation but who are not yet members of the community outside, of which there is no salvation.[15] The deliverance that the people of Qumran experienced following their entrance into the community was a harbinger of the decisive and final victory over evil that God will make possible and an impetus driving them to enlighten "the poor" who still stand outside the community.[16]

The community of Qumran readily identified itself with the poor because in the biblical tradition the poor are the objects of unjust oppression. The Qumran community saw itself in just those circumstances. It was not the wealthy who exploited them but the priests of Jerusalem who opposed their religious reforms. There is not enough conclusive evidence, however, that this community ever referred to itself as "the Poor," as though this term was a self-designation. At most, some Qumran texts use the term metaphorically to refer to the community as the object of persecution and recipient of salvation. The community's rules made it clear that members of the community were not to take advantage of the poor as the Wicked Priest did. In addition, they were to contribute to the welfare of the poor with a portion of their income. Finally, the community attempted to develop a lifestyle that did not differentiate between the rich and poor among its membership because of its belief that no such distinction would be characteristic of the coming age.

The *Psalms of Solomon*

While the Dead Sea Scrolls regulate the life of a community that lived in the Judean desert, the *Psalms of Solomon* reflect an urban setting: Jerusalem in the years just before the time of Jesus. They contain repeated but veiled references to events connected with the Roman occupation of Jerusalem in 63 BCE. The perspectives of the *Psalms of Solomon* and the Dead Sea Scrolls, however, are similar. The texts produced by the Qumran community and the *Psalms of Solomon* are didactic and polemical works with a clear apocalyptic character. Though these eighteen poems ascribed to Solomon are termed "psalms," it is unlikely that they were used in the liturgy of the temple, as were their biblical exemplars. A prominent feature of the *Psalms* is their interest in the poor and their criticism of those who created the social and economic evils that afflicted the Jewish community. The *Psalms* imply that the desire for wealth and power corrupted the Hasmonean kings and the priests of Jerusalem. It was this corruption that brought divine judgment on Jerusalem in the form of the Roman conquest of the city.

The *Psalms* present God as the defender of the poor (*Pss. Sol.* 5:2,11; 10:6; 15:1; 18:2) in accord with the biblical tradition. God's concern for the poor gives the psalmist hope. The deplorable circumstances of the poor result from decisions made by those who were not observant, who were not pious, who were not concerned about the Torah. The wealthy are sinners, so the psalmist prays for "moderate sufficiency," in other words, neither excessive wealth nor abject poverty (*Pss. Sol.* 5:16). He prays for strength to deal with his poverty, which he regards as a test from God (*Pss. Sol.* 16:13-14). Still, the *Psalms* are less concerned with the economic circumstances of the poor than they are with the moral qualities that set them apart from the wealthy. The psalmist speaks of the poor and the pious in the same breath: "And the devout shall give thanks in the assembly of the people, and God will be merciful to the poor to the joy of Israel" (*Pss. Sol.* 10:6).[17] The psalmist looked forward to when the circumstances of the rich and the poor would be reversed (*Pss. Sol.* 17:21-34).

It may appear as though the *Psalms* spiritualized poverty. But this results from the psalmist's decision to speak less about the economic circumstances of "the poor" than about their fidelity to their ancestral religious traditions. The wealthy are sinners who are responsible for the devastation of Jerusalem. The psalmist prays for the day when Jerusalem will experience a reversal of its fortunes, when God will take the side of the poor against their oppressors. God's actions on behalf of the poor become an important metaphor that helps the psalmist assert that Israel remains God's people despite the fall of Jerusalem to the Romans. The psalmist expected a messiah to come and "purge Jerusalem (and make it) holy as it was even from the beginning" (*Pss. Sol.* 17:30).

Conclusion

Apocalyptic literature reflects a continuing social and economic conflict between the poor and the wealthy within the Jewish community as well as the problems the Jewish community faced as a result of its political impotence. It may very well have been that apocalyptic emerged as one response of the dispossessed to deal with their experience of oppression. Apocalyptic literature exhibited a point of continuity with earlier biblical tradition when it presented God as the defender of the oppressed. The characteristic contribution that apocalyptic made to the elaboration of this motif was its assertion that God's final intervention on behalf of the poor was imminent and that this intervention will usher in a new world. In that new world God's justice will be triumphant and the poor will experience a reversal of fortunes and thereby finally receive the reward that belongs to those who remain faithful even in the midst of oppression.

In the book of Daniel, Gentile rulers are responsible for the oppression of the pious. The book assures its readers that the power of these rulers is going to come to an end very soon and the faithful will be rewarded with everlasting life. *First Enoch* condemns those within the Jewish community who oppress the poor. The people of the Qumran community looked forward to a world in which distinctions between rich and poor no longer exist. Similarly, the *Psalms of Solomon* and the *Sibylline Oracles* await the day when the poor will be vindicated and justice will triumph.

At times apocalyptic texts use "the poor" as metaphors for the pious, but most often these texts speak about genuine oppression that causes all sorts of problems for the righteous, including material poverty. The texts promise speedy vindication for those who remain faithful, for God remains the protector of the oppressed. There is no spiritualization of poverty as a state that brings one closer to God. Vindication comes to those who are faithful to their religious traditions. This fidelity often has social and economic consequences, so when God moves to end the oppression of the pious, this move will be an economic boon to the faithful. Poverty is an evil that will be overcome very soon with a marvelous display of power. Poverty is not a mark of holiness, but a scandal that will not exist in the new world that God's power will call into existence. In that new world there will be no rich or poor, no oppressors or oppressed. God's justice will rule.

Questions for Reflection

1. How do the views of apocalyptic texts on the poor and poverty differ from those of the prophetic tradition?

2. What were the causes of the social and economic conflict in the Jewish community reflected in apocalyptic texts?

3. According to apocalyptic texts how will the poor finally experience vindication?

4. How will the poor ensure that they will be vindicated in the world to come?

CHAPTER SEVEN

THE NEW TESTAMENT

The Hebrew Scriptures and the writings from early Judaism exhibit a wide variety of attitudes toward the poor. The existence of the poor is a sign of Israel's infidelity to the covenant. God is the protector of the poor. The wealthy oppress the poor and cause poverty. In the age to come the poor and the rich will have their roles reversed. People ought to be kind to the poor. Poverty is the result of foolish decisions people make. The poor are those who have an attitude of total dependence upon God. In most of the texts that have been considered, the poor in question are the materially poor. Even in the texts in which "the poor" becomes a metaphor of a religious reality, the socioeconomic meanings of this term are never excluded. This should be evident because these ancient Israelite and early Jewish texts do not speak very often about "poverty." They almost always speak about the poor, the oppressed, the exploited, the widow. This anchor in socioeconomic reality is a key to seeing the context in which the Bible does speak about the so-called ʿănāwîm. There is no idealization of the poor in the Bible. The poor are blessed not because they are poor but because God is their protector. Both the poor and the wealthy are to observe the law. The latter are condemned not because they are wealthy but because they do not observe the law and thereby call divine judgment upon themselves. These perspectives also undergird much of what the New Testament says about the poor.

The New Testament both exhibits strong lines of continuity with ancient Israelite and early Jewish traditions and reflects the Greco-Roman cultural environment in which those who first heard and read these texts lived. Sometimes the Greco-Roman world is presented as completely devoid of concern for the poor.[1] It is perhaps more accurate to say that such concern was rather narrowly defined as limited by an attitude of exclusivism. Concern for the needs of others was expressed by care for one's relatives, friends, fellow citizens, and allies rather than by a liberality toward all who may be in need.[2] The Stoics, who believed that humanity was one, taught that benevolence was to be extended to all people. They also taught that wealth was to be shared and poverty endured. A question that still needs to be answered is the extent of the Stoics' influence in the Hellenistic world. Even so, benevolence in the Greco-Roman world was not directed at the causes but the symptoms of economic oppression and exploitation and, therefore, benevolence was not effective in eliminating poverty from the Greco-Roman world. The New Testament speaks to that world and offers a more inclusive perspective that had its foundation in the religion of ancient Israel.

The Gospels

While the Gospels make some significant statements about the poor, it is important to be certain of the perspective from which these statements are made. It is necessary that interpreters know whether sayings such as "Blessed are you who are poor" (Luke 6:20) and "What will it profit them to gain the whole world and forfeit their life?" (Mark 8:36) were made by someone who was rich or poor. Were those statements made as a subtle attempt to preserve privileges of the rich or were they authentic attempts to encourage the poor? Were they calls to justice or were they content to leave the poor in their misery while conferring on them a certain aura of holiness? The significance of such sayings depends, in part, on the one who uttered them.

Jesus and his disciples were not among the elite of Roman Palestine. They shared the lot of the poor. Though the disciples worked as fisherman, their labor barely provided enough to keep them from destitution. Their profits were diminished substantially by Roman taxes and Jewish tithes. The Gospels portray Jesus of Nazareth as a poor man. Jesus, however, belonged to a family that was not poor. His legal father, Joseph, was a *tektōn*—a builder, a contractor, a skilled laborer. But Jesus left his family and occupation. He asked the same of those who wished to follow him. In Jesus' inaugural sermon, Luke has Jesus proclaim a Year of Jubilee (4:18), when the poor have their debts forgiven. During his ministry he had no place where he could lay his head (Matt 8:20; Luke 9:58). Throughout his life Jesus was able to dissociate himself from possessions because they accounted for nothing in terms of the reign of God that he was called to announce. He challenged his followers to trust in God implicitly (Matt 6:25-34). His solidarity with the poor became complete during his passion, when he died the death of a criminal. Paul called this act of solidarity the taking on of the form of a slave (Phil 2:7). It is among the least important and neediest members of the Christian community that Jesus is to be found (Matt 25:31-36). Because of his own poverty, Jesus' call for detachment from every care and for complete trust in God (Matt 6:25-34; Luke 12:22-32) has an air of authenticity about it.

That Jesus himself was poor ought to be evident since his approach to poverty and wealth was not marked by asceticism or vague idealism. It exhibited the realism of the genuinely poor. Jesus allowed himself to be supported by generous women of means (Luke 8:1-3). He had no problem with the wealthy as long as they used their wealth for good, such as the support of parents (Mark 7:9-13) or lending to those in need without expecting a profit (Matt 5:42). Evidently Jesus enjoyed a good meal since he was criticized for being a glutton and a drunkard (Matt 11:19). Jesus denounced riches when they became the dominating force in a person's life, but he did not approach the issue of poverty and wealth like a fanatical ascetic or even like the people of Qumran. The Gospels present Jesus as materially poor and his statements about the poor and the wealthy need to be heard from that perspective, marked as it is by authenticity and realism.

Mark

The Gospel of Mark is not directly concerned with the poor. They do not play as central a role in Mark as they do in Luke. But there are three pericopes in which "the poor" make an appearance in the Gospel of Mark. None of the three is unique to Mark though the Markan context does suggest a specific spin on each.

The first passage is the story of a rich man whose wealth stands in the way of his acceptance of the invitation to discipleship that Jesus offers him (10:17-22). The story begins with a question: "Good Teacher, what must I do to inherit eternal life?" Such a question would not have occurred to most Pharisees. They believed that eternal life was to be their reward for faithful observance of the Torah. Evidently, the person posing the question did not think that Torah observance was enough. Jesus answered the query in a way that showed that he understood the man's feeling of uneasiness. The inquirer's heightened religious sensitivity led Jesus to love the unnamed rich man—the only person about whom this is said in Mark's Gospel. Jesus declared that there is indeed more to a person's relationship with God than the behaviors that are the subject of the Torah's legislation. The way to eternal life, Jesus affirmed, is to cast one's lot with him by becoming a disciple (v. 21b). But the way to discipleship is costly, for it will involve making oneself share the lot of the poor (v. 21a). The story ends sadly for the rich man since he was unwilling to part with his wealth.

Just as most of Jesus' contemporaries would not have identified with the rich man's question, most would not have appreciated Jesus' answer since wealth and prosperity were considered to be blessings from God that come to the righteous. Why should one reject such a blessing? Indeed, Jesus' own disciples find it hard to accept Jesus' teaching (vv. 24*a*, 26). Mark appends verses 23-27 to the story of the rich man to provide an explanation for a demand that was so difficult and apparently out of line with traditional Jewish perspectives. This exchange between Jesus and his perplexed disciples fits very well into the larger context of 9:30–10:31. In that larger unit, Jesus describes the cost of discipleship. After the second prediction of the passion (9:30-32), Jesus wants his disciples to understand that they too will have to sacrifice and suffer as he will. Jesus' request that the disciples make themselves poor, then, is not an idealization of poverty as such. Divesting themselves of their possessions prepares the disciples to share the renunciation and suffering of their Master.

Next is the incident in which Jesus comments on the action of the poor widow who donates the last of her money to the temple (12:41-44). She serves as the perfect foil to the scribes who "devour widows' houses" (12:40*a*) because of their greed. Of course, there were many conscientious scribes, but Jesus points to the crimes of a few. He contrasts their avarice with the widow's generosity. The parallels to this story in Jewish sources make it clear that the economic and social cleavage reflected in Mark 12 was real.[3] These parallels praise the generosity of the poor widow. Here precisely is the difficulty for some contemporary readers of this story. They find any implication that the widow's action is commendable to be an act of exploiting the poor to support a wealthy religious institution. Indeed, the widow gave the temple "all she had to live on" (v. 44). But that, of course, is precisely the point. The widow's actions prefigure those of Jesus himself, who will shortly give his life as a ransom for many (see Mark 10:45). When Jesus spoke about what he was facing in Jerusalem, Peter "rebuked" Jesus for being prepared to embark on a course of action that Peter thought was simply unreasonable (Mark 8:31-33). The story of the poor widow in Mark 12, then, makes a christological point, not a social or economic one. Like the poor widow and Jesus, the disciples will have to learn self-denial in order to be authentic followers of Jesus. Elizabeth Struthers Malbon sees the poor widow, along with two other women in Mark's Gospel (the hemorrhaging woman [Mark 5:25-34] and the Syrophoenician woman [Mark 7:24-30]), as taking "decisive action to which Jesus makes a significant reaction."[4] The way these women exemplify authentic discipleship stands in contrast to their social location. Their lower social status makes their actions even more significant.

The most difficult Markan passage mentioning the poor is the incident of an unnamed woman anointing Jesus while he was having dinner at the house of Simon the leper in Bethany a few days before the crucifixion (14:3-9). Anointing with oil was a common practice of refreshment before a meal. Guests expected their hosts to provide them with such refreshment (see Luke 7:44-47). A woman performed this service for Jesus and she used an expensive imported oil. Nard was made from the root of a plant from Nepal. The reaction over the use of an alabaster jar of this perfumed oil to anoint Jesus' feet is understandable. It was made even more expensive (300 denarii was the equivalent of a common worker's pay for half a year) by its costly container and the distance from which it had come. Jesus deflects the criticism of the woman by stating, "For you always have the poor with you, and you can show kindness to them whenever you wish; but you will not always have me" (14:7). Unfortunately, some have read this text as asserting the futility of any social action. Of course, generosity toward those in need should not impede a person from an act of kindness like the one the woman performed for Jesus. The biblical tradition as a whole does not regard poverty as a "normal" part of life, but as an evil exception to the divine plan. What is to be "normal" is the concern that moves people to be kind to those in need. Mark does not attempt a thoroughgoing discussion of poverty. Again, he is likely making a christological point. He likely sees that the anointing is a token of Jesus' messiahship—something that will become evident at his death (Mark 15:39). The service that the woman performed for Jesus must not become an excuse to evade responsibility to the poor because a poor man spoke these words.

It is important to note that in each of these three passages, the word "poor" refers to the destitute. Also, there is no evidence in Mark of the spiritualization of poverty as a state that places one closer to God. The poor here are objects of charity. Though someone like the poor widow may be praised, the texts do not provide the poor with a special aura of holiness because of their poverty.

Matthew

There are parallels in Matthew to two of the Markan passages that mention the poor: Matt 19:16-21 reprises the story of the rich man (Mark 10:17-22) and Matt 26:6-11 the anointing in Bethany (Mark 14:3-9). In neither case does Matthew appreciably alter the fundamental thrust of these stories as they relate to the poor. Matthew's Gospel does not have a parallel to the story of the poor widow (Mark 12:41-44). Two texts concerning the poor in Matthew that are not found in Mark are the beatitude about the poor in spirit (Matt 5:3) and Jesus' reply to the Baptist's inquiry (Matt 11:5).

Much has been made of the difference between the beatitude about the poor in Matthew and Luke. The latter simply states "Blessed are you who are poor" (Luke 6:20) while the former has "Blessed are the poor *in spirit*" (Matt 5:3; emphasis added). Supposedly Matthew's formula represents a kind of "spiritualization" of poverty.[5] A closer look at his Gospel makes that conclusion questionable. Matthew underscores the mindset of the poor and oppressed. These are people who have not had recourse in the face of oppression because their lack of power and influence has left them completely vulnerable. The poor had to rely on God, and Jesus' proclamation of the imminence of God's reign gave the poor hope for the future. Matthew, then, does not "spiritualize" the term "poor." When he uses this term, he refers to the destitute and working poor of first-century Roman Palestine—people who were on the margins of social and economic life.

Focusing on the broader context of this beatitude can help one evaluate the validity of the view that Matthew commended "spiritual poverty" to his readers. It is important to recognize that the people who are called "blessed" by Jesus are people in distress, in other words, those who mourn, those who are deprived of justice, and those who are persecuted (Matt 5:4, 6, 10). Jesus asserts that the fortunes of these people will be reversed when God's reign on earth begins. The behaviors that bring unhappiness and suffering in the present will be revealed as those that will bring status and salvation when the reign of God begins. The Beatitudes exhibit, then, an apocalyptic approach to the poor and poverty, one that involves a reversal of fortunes. The assumption of such a perspective is that, in the present, the power of evil has perverted the designs that God had for the world. The reign of God, however, will be a new age that will witness the rectification of the distressful circumstances of the present age. The circumstances confronting both the working poor and the destitute would have immediately suggested themselves as symptoms of the hold that evil has on this age. This beatitude does not so much spiritualize poverty as much as it uses the distress felt by the poor to describe a much more comprehensive reality: the new age in which God's justice will triumph over the powers of evil.

It is likely that Matt 5:3 ought to be read in tandem with 5:5: "Blessed are the meek, for they will inherit the earth." No doubt the Semitic word that lies behind the Greek word *praeis* ("meek") is *ʿănāwîm* ("afflicted, poor, bowed down"). Verse 5, then, does not commend a submissive and nonassertive attitude toward others. Here the "meek" are those bowed down by those who exploit their lack of power and influence in society. Jesus, however, asserts that being among the "meek" in the present means that in the future, when God's reign begins, one will "inherit the earth"—in other words, one's poverty will end. Matthew 5:3 also speaks to the poor and asserts that in the future they will have a place in God's reign. Matthew—no matter what "in spirit" may mean—insists that those who follow Jesus in the present will have a place in the world to come. The apocalyptic tenor of the Beatitudes, however, implies more than a readjustment of this world's social and economic system. In the future, those who are poor and oppressed now will gain the greatest possession of all. Matthew 5:3 and 5 make the same assertion.

It is also important to remember that the Beatitudes speak to people who lived in a world that prized wealth, power, and social status. In such a world the poor are at a great disadvantage, for they have no access to these things. Still, the Beatitudes affirm that the poverty and oppression that the disciples experienced in the present indicate that they have found God's favor and so they are "blessed." The Beatitudes promise that the distress, poverty, and oppression that people experienced because of the political, social, and economic realities of Roman Palestine will come to an end once God's reign on earth begins. Indeed, this great reversal has already begun through the ministry of Jesus. God's victory and that of the disciples is assured.

A distinctive Matthean passage that mentions the poor is 11:2-5. The imprisoned John the Baptist sent emissaries to Jesus to inquire about his identity. John wished to know if Jesus was "the one who is to come" (v. 3). Instead of answering John's inquiry directly, Jesus invited the Baptist's messengers to consider what they have seen and heard. Jesus summarized the effects of his ministry in a verbal montage (v. 5) of texts from Isaiah: 26:19; 29:18-19; 35:5-6; 42:7; and 61:1. With these allusions to the book of Isaiah, Jesus characterized his ministry as a movement toward those on the margins. Of course, the poor are among these people, included in this montage with the assertion that "the poor have good news brought to them." Coming at the end of the list, this assertion bears a certain significance as Jesus implies that he was indeed "the one who is to come." Since the biblical tradition sees God as the protector of the poor, the one who hears their cries and brings them deliverance, Jesus' proclamation of "good news" to the poor is a clear sign that God is the power behind the words and deeds of Jesus.

Matthew does not spiritualize the word "poor." When he uses this word, he is speaking about one of the groups whose existence was on the margin of Jewish society in first-century Palestine. Their lack of power and influence left them particularly vulnerable to exploitation by the Roman occupiers but also to their Jewish collaborators and other people of means. Matthew's eschatological vision sees that the circumstances of the poor and others on the margins will be reversed soon because Jesus is inaugurating the reign of God on earth. One certain sign of this is Jesus' ministry that proclaims good news to the poor.

Luke-Acts

The poor have a privileged place in Luke-Acts. Luke addresses his two-volume work to a person he calls "most excellent Theophilus" (Luke 1:3; Acts 1:1), and this has led some to conclude that Luke wrote for the wealthy and influential.[6] Still, the Third Gospel makes the poor a special concern. In it there are ten pericopes that specifically deal with the poor, with six of these being unique to Luke.[7] An obvious place to begin is Mary's Song, also known by its Latin name: the Magnificat (1:46-55). Luke's Infancy Narrative (chs. 1–2), in which Mary's Song appears, serves as the prologue to his Gospel. In it the evangelist introduces all of the themes that he will develop in the rest of this two-volume work.[8] The Magnificat is part of the prologue's third scene (1:39-45), which describes the meeting between Mary and Elizabeth while both were pregnant. Though the term "poor" does not appear in this text, W. D. Davies has detected in this hymn allusions to three social evils experienced by the people of Judah in the first century: 1) foreign domination, 2) the Diaspora of the Jews, and 3) the oppression of the poor by the wealthy.[9] Allusions to ancient Israelite and early Jewish texts abound in the Magnificat.[10] This passage deals with the oppression of the poor by calling upon a common biblical motif: God's salvation of the lowly and the associated rejection of the mighty.

In verse 48 ("for [God] has looked with favor on the lowliness of his servant") Luke marks out an important theme of his Gospel: the poor, the hungry, and the oppressed have received God's favor, while God has disregarded the rich and powerful. The most dramatic illustration of this truth is that a peasant maiden has been chosen to bear the Messiah. Mary's "lowliness" is not simply a pious expression of humility. It reflects the social differentiation in first-century society that set Mary not among the powerful and influential but among those without social position and prestige. While this expression reflects material poverty, it is much more comprehensive. Mary numbers herself among those who were on the margins of the Jewish social and religious world because of their gender, age, cultic impurity, illness, or economic status. According to the biblical tradition it is just such as these who can expect God to deliver them. The hymn praises God, who will remove the mighty from their positions of power and have the poor replace them (v. 52). Not only are the powerful superseded but they are sent away empty, while the hungry poor are satisfied (v. 53). In using this imagery, Luke presents the economically poor as recipients of God's benevolence. Still, he casts his net beyond them to include all those in need of salvation. The poor are representative of the wider circle of humanity that stands in need of salvation. That salvation is forthcoming because God responds to those in need.

Another programmatic text is Luke 4:16-30, the story of Jesus' initial attempt at public ministry. By weaving together texts from Isa 58:6 and 61:1-2, Luke has Jesus characterize his mission as fulfilling the hopes for Israel's restoration as envisioned in the Isaianic tradition. According to this tradition, the restoration of Judah will be inclusive. Participating in it will be all those who were usually considered to be excluded. For example, Isa 56:3-8 mentions eunuchs and Gentiles. Jesus underscored this by pointing to the ministries of the prophets Elijah and Elisha in Luke 4:25-29. These prophets helped those on the margins: a childless and poor widow and a Gentile leper. While Luke presents Jesus' mission as preaching "good news to the poor" (Luke 4:18), the evangelist's notion of "the poor" is quite comprehensive, including those who were left behind by Jewish society without necessarily being among the destitute. Jesus asserts that one can authenticate his message by simply observing the benefits that "the poor" enjoy because of it.

In Luke's "Sermon on the Plain" (6:17-49), Jesus calls the poor "blessed" because the kingdom of God is theirs (v. 20). In comparison with Matthew's version of this beatitude (Matt 5:3), it is much easier to claim that Luke was not speaking about some sort of "spiritual poverty" but the actual experience of life on the margins that was the fate of the poor. Of course, here the poor serve as a particularly apt metaphor for those who had no hope except in God. Because they were so far removed from most people's concerns, they were in a position to hear and respond to the claim of God. Their very marginalization places them in circumstances that make responsiveness to Jesus less of a problem. The woe that Jesus pronounces against the rich (Luke 6:24-26) brings this out clearly. People of means are at risk precisely because their social, religious, and economic circumstances can make them unresponsive to Jesus' proclamation of the kingdom. Still, this does not necessarily mean that the poor actually recognized the nature of Jesus' mission any better than did the wealthy. Luke is simply describing the kind of attitude that helped people accept Jesus and his message.

The poor are blessed because the coming kingdom of God will put an end to their poverty. According to ancient Near Eastern tradition, the poor enjoyed special divine protection, which was guaranteed by the king. By establishing God's reign on earth, Jesus is bringing that special protection to those in need of it. Both the Matthean and Lukan versions of the beatitude of the poor reflect the perspective of apocalyptic, which gives meaning to the experience of the poor by relating it to the coming of God's kingdom that will reverse the fortunes of the poor. It is only in view of the world to come that the experience of the poor makes them blessed.

In this world, however, social and economic status mattered. In Jesus' day, practices surrounding the sharing of food became the barometer of this status.

Luke tells the story of an occasion when Jesus was a dinner guest of someone with significant standing in the community: a leader of the Pharisees (14:1-24). Jesus' admonition to his host speaks for itself:

> When you give a luncheon or a dinner, do not invite your friends or your brothers or your relatives or rich neighbors, in case they may invite you in return, and you would be repaid. But when you give a banquet, invite the poor, the crippled, the lame, and the blind. And you will be blessed, because they cannot repay you, for you will be repaid at the resurrection of the righteous. (vv. 12-14)

In a burst of eschatological enthusiasm, one of the guests at table responded to Jesus' admonition by asserting: "Blessed is anyone who will eat bread in the kingdom of God!" (v. 15). This gave Jesus another opening to affirm the inclusive character of his vision of the kingdom through his parable of the great supper (vv. 16-24). It is a story of a banquet given by a person of means. The invited guests, who presumably included people of a social status similar to that of their host, declined the invitation. In Matthew's version of the parable (22:2-10), servants are told to invite as many others as they could find to take the place of those who were not going to come (Matt 22:9). Luke is more specific by having the servants ordered to bring in "the poor, the crippled, the blind, and the lame" (Luke 14:21).

The sharing of a meal in common to remember the Lord became the central social and religious activity of the early Christian community. While people of means within the community might provide the meal, the "guest list" was to be inclusive. No special places of honor were to be reserved for the elite. On the contrary, the host ought to provide a special welcome for the poor. Certainly, the comments that Jesus makes to his host spoke to the well-off members of the Christian community and urged them to include the poor in their community meals, no matter how much this violated the usual practices of hospitality. Paul criticized the Christian community at Corinth for its failure in this area (see 1 Cor 11).

The parable of the great supper originally spoke to the failure of Jesus' mission among the religious elite of his day. Luke's version implies that the negative response of these people does not disqualify Jesus as the one sent from God. On the contrary, the invitation that goes out to those on the margins of Jewish society confirms the authenticity of Jesus' mission. Once again this reflects the vision of Judah's restoration characteristic of the Isaianic tradition, which describes Judah's future as a banquet for the poor (Isa 55:1-3). The presence of the poor at a great banquet is another metaphor for the inclusive nature of the salvation that comes through Jesus. But the kind of people who will be saved are those who see themselves as dependent on the generosity of God, just as the poor are dependent for their survival on the generosity of the rich.

In the parable of the rich man and Lazarus (Luke 16:19-31), another pericope unique to Luke, the evangelist again exploits the economic and social differentiation between the rich and poor. The parable is addressed to those who "love money" (Luke 16:14) and concentrates its attention on the fate of the rich man, who, in death, was suffering in hell. The parable offers no suggestion of any special failures that could explain such a fate, except his failure to care for Lazarus. Similarly, the parable does not attach any particular merit to Lazarus, except that he was destitute (vv. 20-21). But Lazarus's very name, a Hellenized form of the Hebrew name Eliezer ("my God helps"), reminds the hearers of the biblical tradition that God is the helper of the poor. The parable implies that the kingdom belongs to the poor, while the rich may share in it if they treat the poor with kindness. Also, Abraham's words to the rich man (v. 29) affirm that the requirement to act justly and mercifully toward all, especially the poor, comes from the Torah and the prophets, in other words, from sacred Scripture. Though the parable is set in the afterlife, its purpose is to describe how the rich ought to lead their lives in this life.[11]

The last uniquely Lukan passage to mention the poor is the story of Zacchaeus (19:1-10). The principal character is a "chief tax collector" (v. 2). Luke adds the unnecessary detail that he was rich. The Romans contracted the collecting of taxes to individuals by requiring contractors to pay the taxes that were due. These contractors or "tax collectors" were then free to use appropriate means to collect money to reimburse themselves at a profit.[12] Most people assumed that the contractors enriched themselves at the expense of their fellow Jews (see Luke 3:12-13). The unexpected attention that Jesus paid to Zacchaeus as he was passing through Jericho on his way to Jerusalem led Zacchaeus to make a surprising announcement: "Look, half of my possessions, Lord, I will give to the poor; and if I have defrauded anyone of anything, I will pay back four times as much" (Luke 19:8). Jesus replied: "Today salvation has come to this [Zacchaeus's] house" (v. 9a). Zacchaeus is the only rich person about whom Jesus makes such a statement in Luke's Gospel, and the evangelist clearly presents him as an example of those who also want to experience salvation. Earlier in the Gospel, Jesus tells the disciples to give alms with the expectation that this will bring "treasure in heaven" (Luke 12:32-33). In both of these texts, the poor are those who are economically destitute.

Zacchaeus was willing to forgo the profits he made from collecting taxes for the sake of the reign of God. Luke, however, knew the story of another man who was not so willing to give up wealth. The story of the rich ruler is common to the Synoptics (Mark 10:17-31; Matt 19:16-30; Luke 18:18-30). Luke, then, was not the only evangelist to point out the dangers to salvation that wealth brought. He, however, accentuated the warning regarding the proper use of wealth. Indeed, Luke's potential disciple is someone who had social standing and the wealth that accompanied it, but decided not to surrender everything in order to follow Jesus. But Luke also tells the story of Levi, who did leave *everything* and followed Jesus (5:28). Luke has Jesus say that those who are unwilling to do the same cannot be a disciple (14:33). Furthermore, those who make this total renunciation have no special merit; they have only done their duty (17:10).

Jesus called the rich ruler to make the kind of renunciation made by Levi, but with one additional specification. The rich ruler was to sell his possessions and give the proceeds to the poor. Jesus was not merely expecting his disciples to have a proper *attitude* toward wealth and social position. Like John the Baptist, Jesus was looking for *action* as a sign of repentance—for concrete acts of benevolence toward the poor (Luke 18:22; see also 3:10-14). In explaining the failure of the rich ruler to pick up on the challenge offered by Jesus, Luke simply notes that he was "very rich" (v. 23). Disciples are to repent, let go of their possessions, and follow Jesus without reservation. Because the rich ruler was unwilling to let go of his possessions, he was not numbered among Jesus' disciples.

Luke contrasts the rich ruler with the poor widow, whose gift of two copper coins to the temple left her with nothing to live on (Luke 21:1-4). If the rich ruler is the negative example that Luke presents to his readers, the poor widow is the person Luke wishes his readers to emulate. Luke has Jesus simply observe and report her actions; he does not have Jesus speak any specific words commending her behavior.[13] Tobit 4:8 suggests that poverty does not exempt one from giving alms. Still, one may suggest that a religious tradition that extracts donations from someone who cannot afford them is itself bankrupt. But Luke is not speaking about fundraising. He is contrasting two patterns of response to Jesus. The rich ruler's unwillingness to let go of his wealth shows that he is not willing to trust God, while the widow's decisive and risky action is just the kind of response that Luke is trying to evoke from his readers.

The command that the rich ruler give to the poor (18:22) and the donation of the poor widow to the temple (21:1-2) do not idealize the poor. The command to give one's wealth to the poor makes no sense if poverty was to be regarded as somehow virtuous in itself. The gift of the widow shows that even the poor must respond to the gospel with generosity, though they do not have much to leave behind. That the rich ruler was unwilling to surrender his wealth for the sake of the kingdom provides ample testimony to the danger.

The readiness of the poor widow to surrender her last two coins suggests that the poor do not have automatic access to the kingdom. They too have to let go of everything and place all their trust in God. The poor widow did just that. Jesus expects every disciple to leave behind *everything* in order to follow him. The contrast between the response of the wealthy and that of the poor serves to dramatize people's attitudes toward Jesus and his message.[14] The poor respond; the wealthy do not. While it is true that most often Luke presents people like the poor widow as objects of charity, here he presents the woman as a giver of charity.

Luke's insistence on generosity to the poor will not allow people of means to excuse themselves by claiming that poverty cannot be effectively eliminated no matter how much a society tries to achieve this goal. Each of the four Gospels has a story about a woman who anoints Jesus with expensive ointment (Matt 26:6-13; Mark 14:3-9; Luke 7:36-50; John 12:1-8). Except for Luke, these similar though not parallel accounts have someone criticize the anointing of Jesus with expensive ointment as an inappropriate extravagance given the needs of the poor. Jesus defends the woman by asserting, "You always have the poor with you, but you will not always have me" (Matt 26:11; Mark 14:7; John 12:8). Luke omits this because he does not wish to introduce a tension between generosity toward the poor and toward God. For the evangelist, generosity toward the poor is generosity toward God. Luke has Simon the Pharisee look disdainfully on Jesus for allowing a sinful woman to touch him (Luke 7:39), thus making the story of the anointing into an account of the transforming power of forgiveness.

The absence of references to the poor in the book of Acts appears, at first, to be anomalous since "the poor" are so central to the Gospel of Luke. But Luke's use of "the poor" as a metaphor for those awaiting salvation offers an explanation. For the evangelist, "the poor" need not wait for salvation any longer, for it has come through Jesus. The reversal of fortunes between the rich and the poor that the Magnificat spoke of has already occurred in Acts. Luke, of course, does not forget the destitute; he mentions almsgiving several times (Acts 3:2, 3, 10; 10:2, 4, 31; 24:17). He also gives widows, one of the traditional categories of the poor, special treatment in Acts 6:1-6. In Acts 4:34, Luke observes that the problem of destitution did not exist in the first Christian community of Jerusalem since the members of that community shared their food and possessions. Later circumstances did make it necessary for the Jerusalem community to receive help. Acts 24:16-17 may refer to the collection that Paul writes about in 1 Cor 16:1-4.

In Acts, then, Luke does not focus on the destitute who need charity, but he describes the actions of the first Christians that eliminated poverty from their community:

All who believed were together and had all things in common; they would sell their possessions and goods and distribute the proceeds to all, as any had need. (Acts 2:44-45)

Now the whole group of those who believed were of one heart and soul, and no one claimed private ownership of any possessions, but everything they owned was held in common.... There was not a needy person among them, for as many as owned lands or houses sold them and brought the proceeds of what was sold. They laid it at the apostles' feet, and it was distributed to each as any had need. (Acts 4:32, 34-35)

Some Gentiles of Luke's day found this Christian practice attractive. Greek philosophers, including Plato and Aristotle, spoke highly of friends who shared their goods with each other.[15] But the portrait Luke paints of the first Christian community is not made up of colors taken from the Greco-Roman culture of the day. Acts 4:34 ("There was not a needy person among them") reproduces the Septuagint rendering of Deut 15:4, which implies that poverty should not exist in the Israelite community if that community observes the Torah. Luke presents the church as the true Israel living in the final times and, therefore, he does not hesitate to apply this text to the community in Jerusalem. That no one in that community was suffering from poverty was a clear sign that Moses' promise had been fulfilled.

If it is true that Luke directs his two-volume work to the influential and wealthy members of the early church, his insistence on generosity toward the poor is indeed significant. For Luke, the true disciple is to be compassionate and generous toward those in need. Such compassion and generosity will break down the social and economic barriers that separated members of the Christian community, just as the gospel that Luke proclaimed was to break down the barriers between Jew and Gentile. The example of the rich giving away their wealth to the poor is a dramatic witness to the world of the repentance that leads to salvation. Once the wealthy become disciples, they give expression to their new life by sharing their goods with people in need. The poor also serve as powerful metaphors for the inclusion of the Gentiles into the new Israel that Jesus called into existence. People who had been excluded or considered unworthy for admittance into the community of believers because of their economic standing, ethnic background, health, or ritual impurity were to be included. The Acts of the Apostles shows how the ideals of Jesus were implemented in the first Christian community. The members of that community shared their goods and eliminated poverty. Finally, Luke portrays the poor as one of the central concerns of Jesus, as is evident from the first words that Jesus says as he begins his ministry: "The Spirit of the Lord is upon me, because he has anointed me to bring good news to the poor" (Luke 4:18a).

John

The poor are mentioned only twice in the Gospel: in the story of the anointing at Bethany (12:1-8) and in the story of Judas's dismissal from the Last Supper (13:21-30). The latter reveals an interesting detail about Jesus and his circle of disciples: they had a common purse, which was used to cover communal expenses and to supply the needs of others (see John 6:5-8). Judas Iscariot administered that purse. When Jesus sent Judas away from the Last Supper with the words, "Do quickly what you are going to do" (13:27b), the other disciples misunderstood Jesus' command. They thought that Judas was going to pay for expenses connected with the meal or to "give something to the poor" (13:29b) as was customary on Passover night.[16] The disciples' misunderstanding, however, tells us quite a lot about the attitude of Jesus and the disciples toward the poor. Clearly, Jesus and the disciples thought of almsgiving as a normal activity expected of every person, even those who were not wealthy. The recognition that Jesus and his disciples kept a common purse also helps clarify the seemingly insensitive retort made by Jesus when Judas criticized Mary of Bethany for anointing Jesus' feet with expensive perfume (12:4). Judas suggested that the perfume could have been sold for the benefit of the poor, but Jesus, defending Mary, replied, "You always have the poor with you" (12:8a). One important use of the funds kept in the common purse was to give alms to the poor. Jesus assures the disciples that the poor would not be deprived of help because of Mary's extravagance. To ensure that the reader would not misunderstand Jesus' remark, the evangelist comments that Judas was not thinking of the poor but of himself (12:6).

Statistics alone do not reveal the importance that "the poor" have in the Fourth Gospel. The poor are a subgroup of the marginalized, who are of primary importance in the Fourth Gospel.[17] The Fourth Gospel portrays Jesus as actively seeking out those people who found themselves outside the "norm" in first-century Jewish society. In addition to the poor, such groups included those uneducated in Torah, Gentiles, women, the sick, and the ritually unclean. Because these people lived on the margins of Jewish society, they were particularly vulnerable to oppression, exploitation, and exclusion. But it is precisely such people whom Jesus sought to include in his circle of followers. A case in point is the story of the man born blind (9:1-41). Leviticus 21:20 disqualified a blind man from serving as a priest, but in Jesus' day, the exclusion of the blind from religious practice was more comprehensive.[18] Because he could not fully participate in the life of the community, the blind man was reduced to begging to support himself (9:8). He was then numbered not simply among the "working poor" but among the destitute, dependent on the charity of others. This served to push the blind man further out on the margins of society. The disdain with which the Pharisees respond to the blind man's comments about Jesus indicates that they regarded his testimony as worthless since it did not come from a person instructed in Torah as they were. Because the Pharisees could not disprove the authenticity of the healing (vv. 18-27), they disavowed the blind man's testimony by expelling him from the Jewish community (vv. 34-35). The blind man does not even enjoy a position on the margins of the community. But it is precisely to such a person that Jesus reaches out (vv. 35-39).

Over the years, the Christian movement began to develop an identity separate from that of Judaism. Achieving that identity sometimes meant abandoning certain Jewish observances, such as circumcision and the dietary laws, and the reinterpretation of others, such as the Sabbath and sacrificial practice. But one Jewish practice that the Johannine community obviously maintained was the care for the poor through almsgiving, because Jesus and his disciples themselves observed this practice. In addition, Jesus consistently reached out to the poor and marginalized in his society in order to include them among his disciples. The church, then, is not an association of the socially and religiously elite. Those who live on the margins of society are to find a home in the community of believers.

Paul

Paul's attitude toward the poor was probably colored by his expectations regarding the imminent return of Christ. The apostle's belief that Christ's return was near made dealing with socioeconomic problems at any great length unnecessary. If people work, the lack of a comfortable life will at least be tolerable. Paul sets himself up as a model:

> For you yourselves know how you ought to imitate us; we were not idle when we were with you, and we did not eat anyone's bread without paying for it; but with toil and labor we worked night and day, so that we might not burden any of you. This was not because we do not have that right, but in order to give you an example to imitate. (2 Thess 3:7-9)

Also, Paul did not urge people to work for social change. On the contrary, he advised maintaining the social status quo. For example, in 1 Cor 7, Paul addressed matters raised by the Corinthians. One of the issues apparently had to do with slaves who wished to obtain their freedom. Perhaps Paul's views of social equality (e.g., Gal 3:28) led the Corinthians to ask about maintaining a social system that included slavery. The general principle that Paul used to formulate his answer implies that a person's social standing is fixed by God and that people ought to retain their place without seeking to rise higher or allowing themselves to fall to a lower place: "[L]et each of you lead the life that the Lord has assigned, to which God called you. This is my rule in all the churches.... In whatever condition you were called, brothers and sisters, there remain with God" (1 Cor 7:17, 24). Because Paul believed that one's social and economic status was ultimately irrelevant (1 Cor 7:22), he advised the Corinthians not to bother with trying to change the status that had been assigned by God—even if it meant remaining in slavery or presumably in poverty.[19] Apparently in the case of Onesimus, Paul followed his own advice and did not call upon Philemon to free his runaway slave.

In his own case, Paul embraced downward social mobility for the sake of Christ. As a Roman citizen and as an educated person (Acts 22:3), Paul belonged to the socially elite. As such, Paul enjoyed access to the high priest (Acts 9:1-2) and was able to invoke the privileges of Roman citizenship (Acts 16:37; 22:25). Still, Paul chose to work with his hands, something the elite of Roman society would never do, though the rabbis thought it important to have a trade for support. Paul lived the life of an itinerant artisan and teacher, accepting the dangers, humiliations, and poverty that such a life entailed. Paul did not become a "resident theologian" but a missionary who accepted the dangers and difficulties of that life and refused to be a financial burden to anyone. Paul described himself as having no social status (1 Cor 4:10-12) and as being well acquainted with the burdens that flow from the life he chose: hunger, oppression, and marginalization (1 Cor 4:11-13; 2 Cor 4:8-9; 6:4-10; 11:23-28; 12:10). Paul, then, was a person of high social status who took up a life of poverty for the sake of his mission. This enabled him to speak with integrity to Christians who were people of means as he urged them to be content with what they had (Phil 4:4, 11), to be generous to those in need (2 Cor 8:7-15), and to live more simply (1 Cor 7:30-31). He also could speak with authority to Christians of lower social status, urging them to work (1 Thess 4:11), to avoid covetousness (Eph 5:3; Col 3:5), and to give alms to other poor people (Eph 4:28).

While Paul believed that Christ's return was going to happen sooner rather than later, this did not lead him to ignore the needs of the poor. Paul called upon Christian communities that had the resources to share those resources with the Christian community of Jerusalem. Many members of the Jerusalem Christian community were destitute. Paul's appeals to the church of Corinth have been preserved in the New Testament (1 Cor 16; 2 Cor 8–9). Presumably, he made similar appeals to other Christian communities as well (see Rom 15:26; Gal 2:10). Paul based his appeal to the Corinthians on the assumption that they could not be authentic brothers and sisters to the Christians of Jerusalem without sharing their money with them. Christians who have more money are to help those who have less.[20] Paul asserted that the goal of Christians in the money economy is not the amassing of wealth but the sharing of wealth. Paul taught that Christians ought not to consider money something that they need to gather for themselves. It is something that they ought to give away—to the poor among their brothers and sisters in Christ.

Paul could make this appeal to the Christians of Corinth because the church there included not just those of low status (1 Cor 1:26-31) but also people of means such as Crispus (1 Cor 1:14; Acts 18:8), an influential and well-to-do member of the Jewish community, and Erastus, the city treasurer of Corinth (Rom 16:23). Paul believed that the willingness of such wealthy people to share with the poor testified to their belief that a new world is coming, a world whose values turn those of this world inside out. Though the precise sum Paul was able to collect for the poor of Jerusalem is not known, it is very likely that the sum was considerable. Certainly a paltry amount would have been considered an insult. The generosity of the Gentile Christians toward the Jewish Christian community certainly helped to ease the tensions between the two communities (Rom 15:27).

Paul not only considered concern for the poor as part of his responsibility as an apostle (Gal 2:10), he also saw the example of Christ as providing its theological basis: "For you know the generous act of our Lord Jesus Christ, that though he was rich, yet for your sakes he became poor, so that by his poverty you might become rich" (2 Cor 8:9). The wealth that the Gentile Christians shared with the poor of Jerusalem, then, was not an act of "benevolence" that was common in Greco-Roman culture. In that system, benevolence was usually shown to the most prosperous rather than to the poor. Benefactors simply assumed that they would receive something in exchange for their gifts. Paul saw the donation of one's monetary resources without the expectation of a material return as an act modeled after Christ's gift of his life. For Paul, to follow Christ was to establish a community of sharing.

It is important to note that the apostle does not seem to promote any "spirituality" of the poor. For Paul, the poor were the economically destitute, those of low status, the hungry, and widows and orphans. He does not idealize the poor as being pious nor does he spiritualize poverty as spiritual need. When Paul mentioned the poor, he was speaking of those with serious material needs. Paul, however, did refer to himself as "poor" (see 2 Cor 6:10). But this self-designation is a part of a highly rhetorical and emotional defense of his ministry. In using the term "poor," Paul was not describing his personal circumstances. He was reluctant to live off the charity of others (2 Thess 3:7-9). Paul asserted that his economic independence was important to him (Phil 4:11) so he had to learn how to be content with a little.[21] The apostle was willing to make the necessary renunciations not because he valued poverty in itself but because he valued self-sufficiency more than a comfortable existence.

There is one instance in which Paul sounds like a revolutionary. This is when he was speaking to a particularly disturbing aspect of the community life of the church at Corinth. Evidently there were social differences among the members of that community. The Greco-Roman world was quite class-conscious and the divisions within Corinthian society spilled over into the community of faith: "when you come together as a church, I hear that there are divisions among you" (1 Cor 11:18). Wealthy members of the church of Corinth kept to themselves, feasted on their own food at the Lord's Supper, and neglected the hungry. Paul condemned such behavior because it undermined the unity of the body of Christ (1 Cor 11:22, 29). The wealthy Corinthians were introducing an unjust social system into the church. This Paul rejected by describing how God acts toward the poor: "God chose what is low and despised in the world, things that are not, to reduce to nothing things that are, so that no one might boast in the presence of God" (1 Cor 1:28-29). Paul stated that the community of faith represents God's intervention to overturn the existing unjust social order. The social tensions of Corinthian society must not be allowed to spill over into the church.

There is no evidence to suggest that Paul saw any theological value to material poverty, but he did see concern for the poor as an important element of his apostolic calling. He made the collection for the poor of the Jerusalem Christian community a priority. But the apostle was unwilling to allow collections to be taken up for himself even though he had a right to support from the churches. Paul did not wish to live off alms. He preferred to work and was content with little in order to preserve his independence. Paul did, however, encourage people to be generous to those in need (2 Cor 9:6-9) and he regarded giving to the poor as an important virtue (1 Cor 13:3).

Other Books

"The poor" do not appear with any frequency in other books of the New Testament. When this expression does occur, these texts speak about the poor as objects of charity who are commended to the generosity of the people of means within the Christian community (see Eph 4:28; 1 Tim 6:17-19;

James 1:27; 2:14-17; 1 John 3:17). The poor in these texts are the economically poor who depend upon the charity of others to survive.

The Letter to the Colossians, one of the "deutero-Pauline" works, does not use the vocabulary of the poor. Still, the letter reflects a concern for those on the margins of both Roman society and the Christian community that is evident in the authentic letters of Paul. Colossians calls for Christian masters to treat their slaves "justly" (4:1), but more significantly, it implies that Christian slaves and masters are "brothers" (see 4:7, 9). Such an implication provides the foundation for social change, though the letter itself does not explicitly call for such a radical change (see 3:22-24). The letter expects Christian love to transcend social difference and include all believers, no matter what their socioeconomic status may be (1:4; 2:2). Finally, the condemnation of greed (3:5) serves to eliminate a significant cause of the exploitation of the poor.

First Timothy shows that the first Christians were to take responsibility for the support of widows and members of their families who were in need (5:3-13). Deacons, who ministered to the poor, were to be chosen with care (3:8-13). The letter advises those with limited means to be content with what they have so as to avoid covetousness, which threatens their commitment to the faith (6:6-10). In addressing people of means, 1 Timothy calls them to generosity (6:17-19). The word that is translated as "generous" in this passage is *koinōnikos*, which carries with it the connotation of "solidarity." The letter, then, calls for something more than liberality in almsgiving; it expects wealthy Christians to identify with the poor in their communities—to think like them, to hope like them. Such solidarity will break down the barriers that differences in economic status raise between people who are to think of themselves as brothers and sisters. While 1 Timothy appears to support a social order that countenances oppression (see 6:1-2), its emphasis on the solidarity that is to exist among Christians of every social class provides the basis for an effective transformation of an unjust world.

The book of Hebrews provides a most dramatic illustration of that solidarity when it lifts up the example of Moses, who refused to remain in the household of the pharaoh but chose "to share ill-treatment with the people of God" (11:24-26). Moses became a slave, throwing in his lot with that of the poor. Those who call for the church to make "an option for the poor" can find no better biblical example of this outside of the Incarnation than in Moses as he is depicted in Hebrews.

James 2:1-7 is a rebuke to the Christian community for keeping the poor on the margins of the community while people of means receive preferential treatment. James is astonished at such behavior since the people of means in the larger Greco-Roman society have sought to do the same to the Christian community as a whole (vv. 6-7). He argues that "the poor" are actually rich in faith (v. 5). This intangible wealth is the wealth worth having and worth respecting. He takes up this theme again in 5:1-6, in which he views wealth and poverty from an eschatological perspective. He proclaims a terrible judgment on the wealthy because of their exploitation of the poor. The intensity of his words rivals that of Amos.

The book of Revelation mentions "the poor" twice. The first time the words appear is in the letter to the church of Laodicea (Rev 3:14-22). The city prospered because of the success of its textile and banking industries. It was the richest of the seven cities addressed in the Revelation. Apparently, the Christians of the city shared in the city's wealth. The seer, however, upbraided the Christian community for its spiritual destitution. The economic prosperity of Laodicea's Christians prevented them from recognizing their true status before God. They thought that they needed nothing, but their Christian confession was tepid and lifeless and, worst of all, they did not recognize their need for conversion. They were poor indeed. Material poverty, however, offers no protection during the terrible times that the seer sees preceding the inevitable triumph of Jesus Christ. Both the rich and the poor will be marked with the sign of the beast (Rev 13:11-18). "The mark of the beast" suggests that faithful Christians will experience economic discrimination at the end of the age (see v. 17).

The eschatological perspective of James and the apocalyptic shape of Revelation imply that this age will not witness the final triumph of justice. In a sense, then, all efforts at transforming this world are provisional and incomplete. The final triumph of justice will take place when the reign of God is fully revealed. While that reign began with the coming of Christ, it will finally wrest control of this world from the powers of evil only in the age to come. Here is the most striking difference between the perspectives on the poor in the Hebrew Scriptures and in the New Testament. The Torah and the Prophets expect ancient Israel to shape its life according to the demands of justice and equity; the New Testament looks for the triumph of justice in the world to come.

Conclusion

When the New Testament speaks of "the poor," it speaks both of the "working poor" and the genuinely destitute. Members of both groups had little social status and no political power in the Roman world. They existed on the margins of society and were vulnerable to exploitation at the hands of the wealthy, both Jewish and Roman. The New Testament does not idealize poverty and does not suggest that the poor have any special access to God. But having no significant possessions, being without political power, and having no social standing eliminates one type of temptation to dismiss Jesus' call to repentance—the temptation that comes with the self-sufficiency that wealth brings. Despite the apocalyptic thrust of much of the New Testament, it does not suggest that poverty can be ignored or that its existence must be fatalistically accepted. Responding to Jesus' calls to repentance enables the disciples to hear the call for justice that comes from ancient Israel's prophetic tradition. It impels the disciples to sell what they have in order to give to the poor. Indeed, one way for the wealthy to give a tangible sign of their repentance is for them to distribute their goods to people in need.

Paul gives no evidence of any spiritualization of poverty. For the apostle, the poor are simply those in need. He showed particular concern for the church of Jerusalem because so many of the faithful were in need there. He also advised people to follow his example by supporting themselves from their work and by being happy with a less than comfortable existence. The book of James provides the single example of a New Testament author displaying the passion of the Hebrew prophets. Most often the New Testament reflects a type of solidarity that should characterize the community of faith—solidarity that makes social injustice unthinkable. Above all, the New Testament presents the life and teaching of one who was able to live without the security that comes with political power, social status, or material possessions. It challenges his followers to do the same—to be content living on the margins—because the poor are blessed: the kingdom of God belongs to them (Matt 5:3; Luke 6:20).

The apocalyptic orientation of early Christianity shaped the New Testament's most fundamental assumption about the poor and poverty: whatever believers may do to help the poor or to end poverty will be only partially successful. This world suffers under the oppression of the powers of evil, whose defeat will become complete only at the end of this age. But this apocalyptic perspective did not exempt the first Christians from the struggle against oppression and injustice, nor did it excuse them from the obligation to be generous to those in need. On the contrary, the Christian belief in the inevitable, final, and complete victory over evil that will be revealed at the end of the age gives believers the assurance that nothing they do, no sacrifice they make to end injustice and oppression, will be in vain. When Christ returns, he will join the efforts of believers to his own struggle with evil and then present a new and transformed world to God—a world of justice, peace, and love.

Questions for Reflection

1. What does Mark's story of the poor widow (12:41-44) reveal about the social, religious, and economic disparity among Jews in Jesus' day?

2. How does Jesus characterize his ministry in his answer to emissaries sent by John the Baptist (Matt 11:2-5)?

3. Why do the poor have such a prominent role in the Gospel of Luke but appear largely absent from the Acts of the Apostles?

4. What significance is there to John's assertion that Jesus and the disciples had a "common purse" (John 13:29)?

5. What is the significance of the collection that Paul took up for the poor of the Jerusalem church?

6. How does the New Testament's apocalyptic orientation influence its approach to the poor and poverty?

CHAPTER EIGHT

THE RABBINIC TRADITION

While an apocalyptic worldview affected the treatment of poverty and the poor in the New Testament, some rabbis saw poverty as a permanent part of Jewish existence even into the messianic age. In commenting on Deut 15:11 ("there will never cease to be some in need on the earth"), the Talmud states that "There is no difference between this world and the days of the Messiah except [that in the latter there will be no] bondage of foreign Powers" (*b. Ber. 34b*).[1] The existence of poverty and the opportunity for generosity toward the poor was so much a part of Jewish existence both in Palestine and the Diaspora that some rabbis simply assumed that they would continue even in the new age brought by the Messiah. On the other hand, Deut 15:4 says that there will be no poor in the land. Indeed, the rabbis did consider poverty as a great evil. They believed it was in people's power to eliminate poverty from the land. There was social and economic disparity among Jews and this gave rise to social problems. It was possible for these problems to be solved if people took their cue from the Torah and the Prophets and did their best to alleviate the economic burdens of the poor.

S.W. Baron suggested that Palestine possessed enough natural wealth to support its native population well, but most Jews who lived there in the Roman period lived in poverty.[2] But the picture is not as simple as that. While Palestine's soil was fertile enough, usually yields were low for a variety of reasons. The agricultural economy of Roman Palestine was particularly vulnerable to destabilization because of famine and war. Certainly one cause of poverty in Palestine was the almost continuous civil unrest and wars from the Maccabean revolution (167 BCE) to the Second Revolt against Rome (CE 135). Adding to these pressures brought to bear on ordinary farmers were the taxes owed to the Romans, rents owed to wealthy landowners, and loans owed to lenders.[3] The people of Roman Palestine tended to ignore the problems related to the relatively low agricultural yields and saw the existence of poverty principally as a political issue related to the Roman occupation or a religious issue related to the moral failures of the poor. Most Jews in Palestine could be classed as "working poor," in other words, people whose labor never provided the kind of return that allowed them to rise above the subsistence level. One second-century rabbi lamented: "The daughters of Israel are comely but poverty destroys their comeliness" (*m. Ned.* 9:10).[4] The situation among Jews in the Diaspora was not very different: "Ten *kabs* [measures] of poverty descended to the world: nine were taken by Babylon" (*b. Qidd.* 49b).[5] The Babylonian Talmud also notes that Jews celebrated their feasts with extraordinary joy because they provided a little relief from the burdens of poverty (*b. Shab.* 145b). Poverty, then, was the worst possible disaster: "There is nothing in the world more grievous than poverty—the most terrible of all sufferings. . . . Job [said to God]: 'Lord of the Universe! I am ready to accept all the troubles in the world, but not poverty'" (*Exod. Rab.* 31:12).[6] One rabbi put the poor in the same class as lepers and the blind (*b. Ned.* 64b). To support their contention that poverty was a curse, the rabbis often cited Prov 15:15a: "All the days of the poor are hard."

The biblical tradition, of course, presented God as both the just governor of the world and the merciful protector of the poor. Rabbinic tradition affirmed that the poor were the primary objects of God's concerns (*Exod. Rab.* 31:13). This presented the rabbis with a dilemma. One solution was to see that poverty was a virtue: "the Holy One, blessed be He, went through all the good qualities in order to give [them] to Israel, and He found only poverty" (*b. Hag.* 9b).[7] Poverty, then, was a gift of God to Israel, a gift that brought with it spiritual benefits. Poverty could lead people to repentance (*b. 'Erub.* 41b), it was a necessary step to holiness, and it kept people from experiencing the fires of hell (*b. 'Erub.* 21b). A second approach was to refocus attention away from the material and social consequences of poverty and onto spiritual qualities such as piety, meekness, and humility. Early rabbinic storytellers tried to outdo each other in describing the poverty of two famous sages, Akiva and Hillel.[8] But most rabbis were not poor. They enjoyed a special status in their communities. They were well provided for. Though the tradition usually portrays the early rabbis as poor and as having to support themselves by manual and even unskilled labor, the same tradition asserts that these same rabbis finally achieved both great learning and economic prosperity.

The prosperity of rabbis was, in part, the result of their exemption from taxation, a privilege granted by Emperor Antoninus Pius (CE 138–161) and continued even by Christian emperors. Sometimes the members of the community resented the extra burden this privilege meant for them. In the third century CE, the people of Sepphoris opposed the rabbinic ordination of a certain Hanina because he was a wealthy landowner and his property would be taken off the tax rolls because of his new status.[9]

Despite some opposition because of the social and economic status the rabbis enjoyed, they gradually gained more influence in the Jewish community. One of their principal concerns was ritual purity. For the rabbis, purity became the way to reach holiness. It required Jews to be especially concerned about matters of food, clothing, marital relations, work, and social contacts. Special laws guided people in their quest for purity. But not all Jews had the time or resources to become familiar with these laws. Not many Jews could devote themselves to study and thereby learn all the obligations that the rabbis imposed on them. Those who failed to observe the laws of purity were considered to be ignorant and negligent by the observant. Collectively they were known as ʿam haʾaretz (literally, "the people of the land"). Because the observant considered the ʿam haʾaretz to be "impure," they avoided all contact with them. Meals could not be taken in their homes, they could not serve as witnesses in a trial, and marriage between the observant and the impure was forbidden. This social differentiation led to economic neglect, leading the ʿam haʾaretz to hate the observant Jews more than their Roman oppressors (*b. Pes.* 49*b*). While identifying the ʿam haʾaretz with the poor is an oversimplification, the poor certainly made up the bulk of this group.[10] Tensions between the observant and the ʿam haʾaretz eventually led to divisions within the Jewish community. One such division was the Karaite movement, which arose in the ninth century CE. The Karaites rejected the authority of the rabbis, their interpretation of the written Torah, and their doctrine of an oral Torah. Central to Karaite belief was the glorification of the poor, with whom they identified as they reflected on texts such as Isa 29:19; 32:7; and Zeph 3:12.[11]

There were class distinctions within Jewish communities outside of Palestine, although they were not based on questions of Jewish observance. Jews in the Diaspora were integrated into local economic structures. When problems arose within specific regions, Jews tended to side with members of their economic class rather than with their fellow Jews.[12] One exception to this pattern was the responsibility that all Jews felt to ransom Jewish slaves.

The tension between the observant and the ʿam haʾaretz led to a policy of indifference toward the economically poor (see *b. Sanh.* 92*a*). To justify such actions some of the rabbis suggested a connection between poverty and sin. Sin was defined as the failure to observe rabbinic legislation concerning purity and so the poor suffered because they did not properly observe Torah. Poverty, then, was a punishment for such sin. In spite of these views, rabbinic tradition eventually displayed a genuine concern for the poor. An important dictum in that tradition declared, "By three things is the world sustained: by the Law, by the [Temple-] service, and by deeds of loving-kindness" (*m. Pirqe ʾAvot* 1:3).[13] Support for the poor became institutionalized, with specific portions allotted for the itinerant and the local poor (*m. Peʾah* 8:7). An entire tractate of the

Talmud (*Pe'ah*) is devoted to the biblical obligation of farmers to leave a por-tion of their fields to be harvested by the poor (see Lev 19:9-10; 23:22; Deut 24:19-22). The same tractate described similar agricultural gifts to those in need.

The *Tosefta Pe'ah* describes one system used for support of the poor.[14] Each town was to have two men who collected for the poor on the eve of the Sabbath. A committee of three other men was responsible for investigating the needs of the poor. In cases when the collection did not meet those needs, the members of the committee made up the difference themselves or sought a loan. Out of these funds the poor received money for a week's food. Clothing was furnished as needed. The poor from other communities were given aid if their villages were unable to help. The community was also responsible for the support of orphans. Everything was to be carried on with consideration for the feelings of the poor: "The poor man stands at your door and the Holy One, blessed be He, stands at his right. . . . If you give him something, reflect who stands at his right" (*Lev. Rab.* 34:9).[15] All members of the community were required to support these collections according to the measure of their ability, but people were not to impoverish themselves in the process of helping those in need. Therefore, limits were set on the size of donations: the minimum to be given was 2 percent of one's income and the most 20 percent.[16] Eventually care for the poor became central to rabbinic tradition: "Charity [*tzedakah*] is equivalent to all the other religious precepts combined" (*b. B. Bat.* 9a).[17]

Tzedakah is often translated as "charity," but a more accurate rendering is "doing what is right." For the rabbis, responding to the poor was not an act of charity, in other words, going beyond the call of duty. *Tzedakah* was an obligation incumbent on every Jew to ensure that there be no poor in the Jewish community. The purpose of *tzedakah* was not merely to relieve the immediate needs of the poor but to help the poor help themselves. In other words, the rabbis suggested dealing not merely with the symptoms of poverty but with its causes. To prevent poverty from becoming a permanent feature of the Jewish community, the rabbis considered an interest-free loan to be the best form of *tzedakah*. The Torah, of course, forbids the taking of interest on a loan made to a fellow Israelite (see Exod 22:25; Lev 25:35-38; Deut 23:19-20). The rabbis, then, derived the practice of charitable lending from the biblical tradition. Such charitable lending, rather than simply almsgiv-ing, was the better way to eliminate poverty from society. The goal of chari-table lending was not to ease the burdens of the needy but to make certain that there were no needy in the Jewish community. *Tzedakah* meant helping a poor person to become self-sufficient.

Rabbinic tradition does not idealize poverty. The early rabbis considered poverty an evil, though a few did make positive statements about it.

Similarly, the poor are not people who have a special relationship with God. They are people who need the charity of their fellow Jews—charity that principally takes the form of interest-free loans. God, after all, gave the people of Israel the land so that they could support themselves, though God remained the "owner" of the land. For the rabbis, poverty was a reality of economic life, but Jews ought to marshal their forces to enable the poor to rise above their poverty. This would enable the poor not only to become self-sufficient but also would make it more likely that they would become religiously observant.

Questions for Reflection

1. Who were the *'am ha'aretz*?

2. What is the goal of the duty for religious Jews to give *tzedakah*?

3. Why did some rabbis regard poverty as a punishment for sin?

CONCLUSION

Attempting a synthesis of what the biblical tradition says about the poor is risky and almost foolhardy. After all, this tradition developed over more than one thousand years. It reflects varying circumstances of time and place. It is the product of very different types of experience and exhibits an amazing variety of patterns of theological reflection. Yet there have emerged some common affirmations about poverty in the biblical tradition. The diversity that is so obvious in the Hebrew Scriptures, the intertestamental literature, the New Testament, and the rabbis is not of such a kind that drawing some conclusions about what the biblical tradition says about poverty is impossible.

First of all, the tradition is unanimous in asserting that material, economic poverty is an outrage, that it should not exist, that it is not in accord with the divine will. While the tradition is not unanimous in its explanations for the origin of poverty, that is not the most important point to be made about the scandal of poverty. What is essential is that believers recognize that poverty results from decisions that people make. Poverty does not just happen; it occurs because people make it happen. While sometimes these decisions can be laid at the feet of the poor themselves, the predominant assertion made by the tradition is that the avarice and greed of the wealthy lead them to unjustly deprive some people of their essential needs. There is no question that the biblical tradition recognizes the evil of economic oppression. In the face of this oppression, the tradition affirms that God is the protector of those who are unjustly deprived of their access to the bounty of the earth and the fruits of their labor. The challenge offered to believers is to imitate the character of God and enable the poor to overcome the oppression that they experience in their lives.

Second, the biblical tradition finds the experience of the poor to be an apt metaphor for the universal need for salvation. The poor come to depend upon God because they cannot fend for themselves; often they are powerless to change their situation. They cannot depend upon the wealthy because it is the wealthy who create and maintain their poverty. The poor have only one choice and that is to depend upon God. When people begin to recognize their need for salvation, the language of the poor becomes appropriate. After all, the wealthy stand in need before God just as the poor do. When the biblical tradition uses the language of the poor to speak about the universal experience of human poverty before God, it never denies the evil of material poverty. It never overlooks the injustice that creates oppression. It never suggests that poverty and oppression be ignored in favor of some sort of "spiritual poverty." In addition the biblical tradition does not idealize the poor as having some sort of special access to God. All people are called to repentance, and anyone—rich or poor—can resist that call. Though the Bible uses the cries of the poor to speak about the universal human need for God, it does not confer an aura of holiness around the poor, nor does it ever denigrate the need to overcome the forces that create and sustain injustice and oppression.

There are some consequences to both of these conclusions. First, if the biblical tradition regards material, economic poverty as a perversion of the divine will, believers cannot countenance its continued existence. This would be nothing less than acquiescing to the continued degradation and exploitation of the oppressed. Second, if the biblical tradition uses the language of the poor to speak about the human condition before God, then this metaphor calls for an authentic expression in the lives of believers. "Spiritual poverty" becomes authentic by incarnating itself in material poverty. "Spiritual poverty" calls for a modification of the way believers own and use economic goods. It involves more than simply acts of benevolence toward the poor; it requires a transformation of the believer's lifestyle.

Though the Bible consistently describes poverty as an evil, it can lead to liberation and redemption if it helps end the marginalization, alienation, and exploitation of the poor. Voluntary poverty can become redemptive if it leads to genuine solidarity with the economically poor and commitment to overcoming their oppression and misery. The idealization of poverty must not lead to an acceptance of an oppressive situation, but rather it ought to lead believers to oppose poverty as the evil that the Bible reveals it to be. In other words, "spiritual poverty" must lead to solidarity with the economically poor in their protest against oppression. It expresses itself through prayer to the God who takes the side of the poor against their oppressors. This is the one way that believers can justify using the language of the poor in their own prayer. For Christian believers, this solidarity with the poor is a genuine imitation of Christ, for it involves taking on the effects of human sin in order to liberate people from that sin and its terrible effects.

In today's world standing with the poor is very often a political act. Certainly there is always room for those who wish to express their solidarity with the poor through individual acts of benevolence. The poor and

oppressed certainly need people like Mother Teresa of Calcutta, whose identification with the poor was complete. The poor need those who staff shel-
ters for the homeless, food pantries for the hungry, and daycare centers for
the working poor. On the other hand, the poor today are resisting the structures of society that institutionalize poverty. In some circumstances, this
resistance is expressed through public advocacy, lobbying, protesting, and
other forms of political action. In other circumstances, such as in Latin
America, this resistance has taken the form of revolution against the
intractable forces of oppression. These circumstances require from believers
a new form of voluntary poverty that goes beyond living a "simple lifestyle."
How then can believers continue to use the language of the poor to express
their self-understanding if they are unwilling to stand with the poor in their
action against injustice? The biblical tradition will not allow believers to be
satisfied with attitudes of benevolence toward the poor. What is needed to
guarantee authenticity is action. But the church calls people to conversion,
not revolution. In other words, those who would use the language of the poor
in their prayer need to have a change of heart so that they can stand alongside the poor. More than this, they themselves can become poor. They will
thereby become instruments of justice and liberation.

The Bible can help shape an authentic response to poverty today. First of
all, it is clear that any disregard and devaluation of material poverty and con-
comitant concentration on "spiritual poverty" are contrary to biblical tradition. Similarly, radical pronouncements and scathing criticisms of injustice
and oppression that are not backed up by action do not exhibit the kind of
conversion that the gospel calls for. Finally, the biblical tradition does not
allow believers to leave social justice to political entities. The community of
faith ought to provide a model of a society that is founded on solidarity rather
than on conflict between social classes. The biblical tradition assumes that
the community of faith ought to take action on behalf of the poor. Without
such action, the community loses its reason for existence, as the people of
Israel and Judah discovered. In fact, the very existence of the poor indicates
that the community has not been living up to its responsibilities. It is even
worse if it abandons the poor to their fate.

Too often texts like Deut 15:11, "there will never cease to be some in need
on the earth" (see also Matt 26:11; Mark 14:7; John 12:8), have been read as
expressions of fatalism—as though poverty were a part of the natural order of
things. When these texts are read against the wider backdrop of the biblical
tradition, however, it is not poverty but mutual concern that is to be a normal pattern of the community's life. The Torah makes significant efforts to
ensure that justice is done for the poor. The prophets criticize the people of
ancient Israel for ignoring their responsibilities to the poor and for making

poverty to be a permanent part of ancient Israelite life. "There will never cease to be some in need on the earth" because of people's failure to end poverty. People have created poverty; they ought to be able to end it.

The last word is directed at the work of Albert Gelin, whose classic *The Poor of Yahweh* has set the tone for the discussion of poverty in the Bible. His work attempted to describe how "poverty of spirit" became the dominant pattern of ancient Israel's response to God. He described how the poor are God's clients, how poverty came to mean the ability to welcome God and be humble before God. He wished to show how the biblical tradition makes a transition from seeing poverty as a social problem to a religious metaphor. Above all he wished to demonstrate that this transition moved the center of attention away from material poverty to poverty of spirit.[1]

Much of what Gelin wrote remains just as valid and insightful today as when it was first written. The one concern of this book has been to show that the biblical tradition never minimizes or ignores material poverty and the actual poor of society. Whenever the Bible uses the vocabulary of the poor, it is calling for justice and for an end to oppression. The very metaphor "the poor of Yahweh" can have its intended effect only if people know what it means to be materially poor. The community of faith can ignore material, economic poverty only at the risk of missing its call to stand at the side of those whose cries God hears. The community of faith needs to make itself poor in order to use the language of the poor authentically. The resources of the community should be marshaled in order to bring an end to poverty. Gelin himself said as much when he wrote: "Without pretending to extract from the Bible an economic treatise, we have no right to forget the social results of its religious principles."[2] The way to ensure this is for the community of faith to stand with the poor as God does.

The Scriptures do not demand that believers adopt any one economic system whose principles are applicable to every age. What the Bible does expect of believers is that they respond with imagination, creativity, and generosity to the evils of every economic system. The Torah presents the ideals. The prophets reflect how ancient Israel failed to live out those ideals. Apocalyptic gives a vision of the future that assures believers that whatever they do to bring about the triumph of justice will not be in vain; the triumph of the poor is certain. The Gospels tell of Jesus, who called the poor "blessed" and spent his ministry reaching out to those on the margins of the Jewish community. Believers recognize that poverty is a creation of those who refuse to live according to the ideals of Torah and the gospel; they are confident that, with God's help, they can overcome human selfishness and sin so that these ideals will one day give shape to human existence and "there shall be no poor" among them.

NOTES

Introduction

1. Some Jews of the first century CE observed two tithes. The first was based on Num 18:21-24 and was to be used to support Levites and priests. The "second tithe" was based on Deut 14:22-27. This tithe of crops and herds was to be taken to Jerusalem and consumed there as part of a religious celebration. Those who lived a great distance from Jerusalem were permitted to sell their tithe and bring the money to Jerusalem to finance their celebration.

2. See J. David Pleins, "Poor, Poverty (Old Testament)," *ABD* 5:403 and Thomas D. Hanks, "Poor, Poverty (New Testament)," *ABD* 5:415.

3. For example, Pleins, "Poor, Poverty (Old Testament)," 5:410.

Chapter One: The Torah

1. See "The Form-Critical Problem of the Hexateuch," in *The Problem of the Hexateuch and Other Essays* (Edinburgh: Oliver and Boyd, Ltd., 1968), 1-78.

2. The significance of this act is not completely clear. One possibility is that possession of the household gods signified legal title to property (see E. A. Speiser, *Genesis* [AB 1; Garden City: Doubleday, 1964], 250). This hypothesis is based on the supposed parallels with second millennium BCE documents from Nuzi. Subsequent analysis of these documents, however, has cast some doubt on this suggestion. See M. J. Selman, "Comparative Customs and the Patriarchal Ages," in *Essays on the Patriarchal Narratives* (ed. A. R. Millard and D. J. Wiseman; Winona Lake, Ind.: Eisenbrauns, 1980), 115-16.

3. Joseph's comment is based on the similarity of sound between the name Ephraim and the Hebrew verb *hifranî*: "(God) made me fruitful."

4. It is not surprising that liberation theologians read the story of the Exodus as the paradigm of God's intervention on behalf of the poor. See, for example, Gustavo Gutiérrez, *A Theology of Liberation* (Maryknoll, N.Y.: Orbis Books, 1973), 155, 157.

5. This conclusion assumes that the present form of the Torah was completed early in the Persian period, but the books of Ezra and Nehemiah do not explicitly identify the law book as the Pentateuch, so that some interpreters do not accept this identification; for example, Rolf Rentdorff assumes that the law book promulgated by Ezra was lost and the author of the book of Ezra mistakenly identified that book with the Pentateuch. See his "Ezra und das 'Gesetz,'" *ZAW* 96 (1984): 165-84. Rentdorff's speculative assertions are not persuasive.

6. A. Brucq, *Le Livre des Proverbes* (Paris: Gabalda, 1964), 33-34.

7. F. Charles Fensham, "Widow, Orphan and the Poor in Ancient Near Eastern Legal and Wisdom Literature," *JNES* 21 (1962): 129-39.

8. B. Z. Wacholder, "Sabbatical Year," *IDBSup*: 762-63.

9. Christopher J. H. Wright, "Sabbatical Year," *ABD* 5:859.

10. Daniel L. Smith-Christopher maintains that Deuteronomy's use of "brother" reflects the need for a stronger sense of community identity during the postexilic period. See his *A Biblical Theology of Exile* (OBT; Minneapolis: Fortress, 2002), 138-42. While the catastrophe of the exile may have made a heightened sense of group solidarity necessary, Deuteronomy is probably also responding to the baneful consequences of the social stratification and the economic inequities that came with the monarchy.

11. See his *Ancient Israel* (New York: McGraw-Hill, 1961), 175-77.

12. See his *Exodus* (OTL; Philadelphia: Westminster, 1962), 189.

13. See also 3:18, 20; 10:9; 15:3, 7, 9, 11; 17:15; 18:2.

14. See his *Deuteronomy* (OTL; Philadelphia: Westminster, 1966), 152.

15. In commenting on this transformation of tithing, von Rad asserts: "From the standpoint of old conceptions of a sacrifice this is an astonishing rationalization of cultic usage!" See his *Deuteronomy*, 103.

Chapter Two: The Former Prophets

1. Although nineteenth-century students of the Hebrew Bible noticed that phraseology reminiscent of Deuteronomy appears throughout the books from Joshua to 2 Kings, Martin Noth was the first to suggest that these books were actually components of a unified literary composition, which he called the Deuteronomistic Historical Work. See his *Deuteronomistic History* (JSOTSup 15; Sheffield: University of Sheffield, 1981). This is a translation of Noth's 1943 monograph entitled *Überlieferungsgeschichtliche Studien.* Though several modifications of Noth's hypothesis have been suggested since it first appeared, the current trend is to return to Noth's view that the Deuteronomistic History is a unified literary composition from the sixth century BCE.

2. See J. David Pleins, "Poor, Poverty (Old Testament)," *ABD* 5:404, 408, 413.

3. George Mendenhall, "The Hebrew Conquest of Palestine," *BA* 25 (1962): 66-87; Norman K. Gottwald, *The Tribes of Yahweh* (Maryknoll, N.Y.: Orbis Books, 1979); Gottwald, "Rethinking the Origins of Ancient Israel," in *"Imagining" Biblical Worlds* (ed. D. M. Gunn and P. McNutt; JSOTSup 359; Sheffield: Sheffield Academic Press, 2002), 190-201; and Robert B. Coote, *Early Israel: A New Horizon* (Minneapolis: Fortress Press, 1990).

4. The corvée was labor on state projects by citizens who were not compensated for their work.

5. Baruch Halpern, "Gibeon: Israelite Diplomacy in the Conquest Era," *CBQ* 37 (1975): 303-16.

6. The kingdom of Israel endured six dynastic changes. Of its kings, seven were assassinated and one committed suicide. The kingdom of Judah was ruled by the same dynasty, except for seven years when Athaliah, a member of the northern Omride dynasty, ruled following the death of her son Amaziah and her purge of the males of the Davidic dynasty (see 2 Kgs 11). Despite the apparent stability of the Davidic dynasty, there was significant social and political unrest in Judah as well. Five monarchs, including Athaliah, were assassinated and three were deposed. While the Deuteronomist asserts that the root of this instability was the worship of gods other than Yahweh, it is more than likely that there were political, social, and economic causes as well. These will be profiled below.

7. For an analysis of the literary features of this story, see Robert Alter, *The Art of Biblical Narrative* (New York: Basic Books, 1981), 37-41.

8. Judges 4:2 gives Jabin the title "king of Canaan." Canaan was a geographical name with no political significance. Before the rise of national states in the region, the city-state was the principal political entity in Canaan. The text implies that Jabin ruled the city-state of Hazor.

9. The RSV translates Judg 6:6: "And Israel was brought very *low* because of Midian." The NAB translation reads: "Thus Israel was reduced to *misery* by Midian" (my emphasis). The Hebrew verb that these English translations are rendering is *dll*, whose semantic field includes "poverty, weakness, lack." Forms of this word appear forty-eight times in the Hebrew Bible and, in most cases, they refer to the suffering caused by the circumstances in which the oppressed find themselves. While the RSV and NAB translations are accurate, the Deuteronomist makes it clear that the misery of the Israelites was the result of their impoverishment following Midianite raids.

10. The Deuteronomist makes use of an adjective (*dāl*) derived from the root discussed in the previous note. The RSV renders it as "weakest" and the NAB as "meanest." But the implication is that the state of Gideon's clan was caused by the Midianite raids that destroyed the Israelite economy. Gideon asserts that his clan thus does not have the resources to mount an effective resistance to Midianite demands.

11. Hannah eventually had six children: Samuel plus three other sons and two daughters (see 1 Sam 2:21).

12. The words of verse 8a are virtually identical with those of Ps 113:7-8. Perhaps both texts reflect a slight variation of a standard formula with which Israelite poets acclaimed God's care for the poor.

13. See Ralph W. Klein, *1 Samuel* (WBC 10; Waco, Tex.: Word Books, 1983). On page 78, Klein makes a distinction between a secular and theological critique of the monarchy in 1 Sam 8. The theological critique supposedly begins in verse 18 while the secular critique runs from verses 10-17. What Klein takes to be a "secular" critique is quite theological because it involves giving what had previously been the prerogatives of God to a human being.

14. The bride-price apparently was paid by the groom to the bride's father. It is mentioned only here and two other places in the Hebrew Bible. In Gen 34:12, Shechem asks Jacob to state the bride-price for Dinah. Exodus 22:16-17 requires a man to pay the bride-price to the father of a virgin he has seduced. The Genesis text implies that the father could set any price he chooses while the Exodus text assumes a specific price. In the Deuteronomic parallel, the man must pay the woman's father fifty silver shekels, though the text does not use the term "bride-price" for this payment (Deut 22:28-29). These few texts make it difficult to appreciate the role of the bride-price in ancient Israel culture and so it would be rash to suggest that these texts support the notion that women were fundamentally chattel in ancient Israelite society. See C. J. H. Wright, "Family," ABD 2:766.

15. This is reminiscent of Josh 15:16, which has Caleb offer his daughter to the man who would attack and capture Kiriath-sepher. In Gen 29:15-20, Jacob does not perform any military exploit but works fourteen years for Laban. His labor satisfied the requirement of the bride-price for Rachel.

16. This, of course, assumes that David knew exactly what he was doing when he began his affair with Bathsheba. Bathsheba's father was Eliam, a member of a politically influential family in Judah (2 Sam 23:34). The Deuteronomist wants to show David as someone who took what he saw as necessary steps to ensure political support for his rule.

17. The Hebrew word here is *rāš* which is used to speak of a person who is economically poor or at least of modest means. It also carries with it the connotation of someone who, as a consequence of his economic position, has an inferior social status. This is clear from the word *niqleh* ("lightly esteemed"), which is linked with *rāš* in 1 Sam 18:23. By marrying Michal, David enjoyed a vastly improved social status.

18. See R. C. Bailey, *David in Love and War: The Pursuit of Power in 2 Samuel 10–12* (JSOTSup 75; Sheffield: Sheffield Academic Press, 1989). Bailey regards David and Bathsheba as coconspirators in a plot to effect a political marriage. Jon D. Levenson and Baruch Halpern, in "The Political Import of David's Marriages," *JBL* 99 (1980): 507-18, describe a pattern in David's marriages that suggests that the affair with Bathsheba happened by chance.

19. See U. Simon, "The Poor Man's Ewe-Lamb: An Example of a Juridical Parable," *Bib* 48 (1967): 208, who describes a juridical parable as a story that disguises a violation of the law in a parable in order to lead the guilty party to pass judgment on himself. For another view, see George W. Coats, "Parable, Fable, and Anecdote: Storytelling in the Succession Narrative," *Int* 35 (1986): 170-75.

20. Organized systems of taxation supported the monarchies throughout the ancient Near East. For example, see D. B. Redford, "Studies in Relations between Palestine and Egypt during the First Millennium B.C.: I The Taxation System of Solomon," in *Studies in the Ancient Palestinian World* (ed. J. W. Wevers and D. B. Redford; Toronto: University of Toronto, 1972), 141-56.

21. The difficulties that drought brought to the poor is well illustrated by the story of Elijah and the widow of Zarephath (1 Kgs 17:8-12). For the widow and her son the long drought meant starvation. There is no reason to consider that her situation was unique.

22. Nahman Avigad, "Samaria (City)," *NEAEHL* 4:1300-10.

23. The dominant scholarly view also identifies "the book of the law" with Deuteronomy—or some form of it—although there have been some suggestions otherwise. See A. D. H. Mayes, *Deuteronomy* (NCB; Grand Rapids: Eerdmans, 1981), 85-103.

Chapter Three: The Latter Prophets

1. A. S. Kapelrud, "New Ideas in Amos" (VTSup 15; 1966), 203-4.

2. Robert B. Coote, *Amos among the Prophets: Composition and Theology* (Philadelphia: Fortress, 1981), 32-35.

3. Most commentators hold that Amos 9:11-15, which speaks about a restoration for Israel, is a later addition to the book; see, for example, Hans Walter Wolff, *Joel and Amos* (Hermeneia; Philadelphia: Fortress, 1977), 352-53. But Francis I. Anderson and David Noel Freedman assert that except for the reference to "the fallen booth of David" (v. 11), the rest of the oracle "could have come from almost any period from the middle of the eighth century on." See their *Amos* (AB 24A; New York: Doubleday, 1989), 893.

4. Richard H. Hiers, "Day of the Lord," *ABD* 2:82.

5. Thomas L. Leclerc suggests that Isaiah followed the lead set by Amos, though Isaiah spells out a practical program by calling Judah to "seek justice." See his *Yahweh Is Exalted in Justice: Solidarity and Conflict in Isaiah* (Minneapolis: Fortress, 2001), 37-38.

6. Magen Broshi, "The Expansion of Jerusalem in the Reigns of Hezekiah and Manasseh," *IEJ* 24 (1974): 21.

7. Micah was not the only biblical author to use such a metaphor. See Ezek 34:2-3;

Ps 14:4; 53:4; Hab 3:14. This underscores the biblical tradition's aversion to the injustice of ancient Israel's social and economic system under the monarchy.

8. Yigal Shiloh, "Jerusalem," *NEAEHL* 2:704-8.

9. For example, James Luther Mays, *Micah* (OTL; Philadelphia: Westminster, 1976), 95.

10. The reference to Babylon in verse 10 is anachronistic since the power that threatened Jerusalem in Micah's day was Assyria. Yehezkel Kaufmann suggests that the original text likely mentioned Assyria but was revised when Babylon became the dominant power a century and a half later. See his *The Religion of Israel* (abr. ed.; Chicago: University of Chicago Press, 1960), 352.

11. F. C. Fensham, "Zephaniah," *IDBSup*: 984. Many scholars do, however, regard Zephaniah as an exilic or postexilic work on the basis of a few passages added at the end of the book. The core of the book, however, does not presuppose the exile. See Norbert F. Lohfink, S.J., *Option for the Poor: The Basic Principle of Liberation Theology in the Light of the Bible* (Berkeley: BIBAL, 1987), 59.

12. For this reason, the RSV translates these words as "humble" and "lowly."

13. See his *The Poor of Yahweh* (Collegeville, Minn.: Liturgical Press, 1964), 31.

14. Lohfink, *Option for the Poor*, 60, also considers Gelin's spiritualizing interpretation as incorrect.

15. Jeremiah's reaction to the corruption of Jerusalem was similar to that of Micah, who also came from a village of Judah and was shocked by what he observed in the capital. Jeremiah, however, had another reason for his criticism of Jerusalem. Anathoth was a city to which Solomon sent the priest Abiathar into internal exile following Abiathar's actions in support of Adonijah in the struggle for succession (see 1 Kgs 2:26-27). Jeremiah was one of the "priests of Anathoth" (Jer 1:1) and so he had little sympathy for Jerusalem's upper classes.

16. There are no texts in the Hebrew Bible that describe the actual observance of a Jubilee or Sabbatical Year in ancient Israel. The economy that developed with the rise of the Israelite national states made the Jubilee Year irrelevant since land distribution was no longer patrimonial but prebendal. Ownership of the land was in the hands of the king. Still, this ancient law appealed to prophets, who saw the justice of restoring ownership of ancestral lands to the families that once held them. Similarly, there is no direct evidence of the observance of the Sabbatical Year. Jeremiah 34 reflects an emergency situation and not an actual Sabbatical Year. Nehemiah 10:31b, however, does require the postexilic community to observe such a year. In modern Israel, religious Jews do observe this ancient custom.

17. These are the confessions or laments of Jeremiah: 11:18–12:17; 15:10-21; 17:14-18; 18:18-23; 20:7-18. In most other prophetic books, the person of the prophet is hidden behind the message he proclaims.

18. The topography of the Jerusalem area made attack from the north of the city the only possibility. Steep approaches on the south, west, and east made attacking from these sides suicidal for any invader.

19. For example, Jer 39:1-10 summarizes 2 Kgs 25:1-12 and Jer 52:1-34 repeats much of what is found in 2 Kgs 24:18–25:30. The passages from Jeremiah do, however, contain some additional information that complements what is found in 2 Kings.

20. J. J. M. Roberts, *Nahum, Habakkuk, and Zephaniah* (OTL; Louisville: Westminster/John Knox, 1991), 84.

21. The Chaldeans were an Aramean tribal group that migrated to the southern part of

Mesopotamia around 900 BCE. They were the dominant group in the Neo-Babylonian kingdom founded by Nabopolassar (626–605 BCE), the father of Nebuchadnezzar.

22. See Martin Noth, *The History of Israel* (London: Adam & Charles Black, 1960), 289-99. The extent of the return from Babylon is still a matter of some discussion among historians. C. C. Torrey asserted that there is no evidence that many exiles returned. See his *Ezra Studies* (Chicago: University of Chicago, 1910), 288. More recently L. Grabbe made a similar point in his *Leading Captivity Captive: "The Exile" as History and Ideology* (JSOTSup 278; Sheffield: Sheffield Academic Press, 2000), 62-79.

23. Zechariah 4:10 calls this period "the day of small things."

24. This situation was complicated by the Persian policy that granted local autonomy to Judah. The transition to limited self-rule likely was marked by problems of law and order. See C. Meyers and E. M. Meyers, *Haggai, Zechariah 1–8* (AB 25B; New York: Doubleday, 1987), 423-24.

25. There is just one explicit reference to the poor in the oracles of these two prophets of the early restoration period. An inquiry about fasting leads to Zechariah's version of the central message of the prophets: justice for the poor. See Zech 7, especially verses 8-10.

26. For example, see A. George, S.M., "Poverty in the Old Testament," in *Gospel Poverty* (ed. M.D. Guinan, O.F.M.; Chicago: Franciscan Herald Press, 1977), 17.

Chapter Four: Wisdom Literature

1. R. B. Y. Scott suggests that "the wise" in Jer 18:18 were royal counselors. See his "Priesthood, Prophecy, Wisdom and the Knowledge of God," *JBL* 80 (1961): 3. Though this conclusion appears to enjoy wide scholarly support, R. N. Whybray demurs. See his *The Intellectual Tradition in the Old Testament* (Berlin: Walter de Gruyter, 1974), 24-31.

2. For example, H. D. Preuss, "Erwägungen zum theologischen Ort alttestamentlicher Weisheitsliteratur," *EvT* 30 (1970): 393-417. In Preuss's view, wisdom literature is not divinely inspired and therefore should not be used by the Christian preacher.

3. See J. D. Pleins, "Poverty in the Social World of the Wise," *JSOT* 37 (1987): 61.

4. F. C. Fensham, "Widows, Orphans and the Poor in Ancient Near Eastern Legal and Wisdom Literature," *JNES* 21 (1962): 129-39.

5. Thomas McCreesh, O.P., "Proverbs," *NJBC* 28:65.

6. This chapter has a number of parallels with the negative confession described in chapter 125 of the Egyptian Book of the Dead. In that text the deceased are required to assert that they have avoided all forms of immoral behavior. If the deceased are judged to be speaking the truth, they are permitted to continue their journey to the otherworld.

7. Elias Bickerman, "Koheleth (Ecclesiastes) or the Philosophy of an Acquisitive Society," in *Four Strange Books of the Bible* (New York: Schocken, 1967), 158-67. The tone of the book of Ecclesiastes makes it probable that it reflects the experience of someone reasonably well-to-do. For example, words such as "profit" and "gain" recur in the book with frequency.

8. F. Crüsemann, "The Unchangeable World: The 'Crisis of Wisdom' in Koheleth," in *God of the Lowly: Socio-Historical Interpretations of the Bible* (ed. W. Schottroff and W. Stegemann; Maryknoll, N.Y.: Orbis Books, 1984), 59-64.

9. Crüsemann, "The Unchangeable World," 62-63.

10. The author witnessed this firsthand since he was certainly from the upper class himself. He implies that he enjoyed a high status in society as a teacher (Sir 39:4a; 51:23-24),

that he traveled abroad frequently (Sir 34:12, 39:4*b*), and that he studied the Scriptures (Sir 39:1-3). Sirach was among the elite of Judean society.

11. H. G. Kippenberg, *Religion und Klassenbildung im antiken Judäa* (Göttingen: Vandenhoeck und Ruprecht, 1978), 36-37, 78-79.

12. The stories about Daniel and his friends in Dan 1–6 come from the Hellenistic period and describe the kind of temptations that existed for influential Jews to compromise their ancestral religious traditions in order to win the favor of their foreign masters.

13. M. Hengel, *Judaism and Hellenism* (2 vols.; Philadelphia: Fortress, 1974), I:48. See also note 381 in II:38.

14. See Patrick W. Skehan and Alexander A. DiLella, *The Wisdom of Ben Sira* (AB 39; New York: Doubleday, 1987), 255. DiLella notes that the dog and hyena were natural enemies and that the latter was numerous in Sirach's time.

15. Though Sirach is speaking about the behavior of individuals, his insights capture the way that wealthy nations deal with developing nations, using them for economic, political, and military advantage.

16. D. Winston, *The Wisdom of Solomon* (AB 43; Garden City, N.Y.: Doubleday, 1979), 100.

17. The author sees the ancient Egyptians and Canaanites as symbols of the hated Alexandrians and Romans of his day, and is convinced that God will vindicate the "honest poor" (= the Jews) once again.

18. The *Testaments* had their origin in the middle of the second century BCE, when memory of this persecution was still fresh. See H. C. Kee, "The Testaments of the Twelve Patriarchs," in *The Old Testament Pseudepigrapha* (ed. J.H. Charlesworth; 2 vols.; Garden City, N.Y.: Doubleday, 1983), 2:778.

19. The manuscripts of this text include 4Q415-418, 418a, 423, 1Q26. See John Strugnell and Daniel J. Harrington, *Qumran Cave 4 XXIV* (DJD 34; Oxford: Clarendon, 1999).

20. *Qumran Cave 4*, 3. The Hebrew word that the text uses for the recipient of the instruction is *mbyn*, which they transliterate as *mēvîn* and translate as "maven," in other words, an "expert" or "expert in the making."

Chapter Five: The Psalms

1. See *The Psalms* (OTL; Philadelphia, Pa.: Westminster, 1962), 93.

2. See *The Poor of Yahweh*, 36-37. There has been some criticism of Gelin's hypothesis. See E. Brammel, "*ptōchos, ptōchei, ptōcheuo*," TDNT 6:892, and Leander E. Keck, "Poor," *IDBSup*: 673.

3. See *Asylie und Schutzorakel am Zionheiligtum: Eine Untersuchung zu den privaten Feindpsalmen* (Leiden: Brill, 1967).

4. This pattern appears in the prayer that Deuteronomy requires be said by the Israelite peasant who brings firstfruits to the temple (Deut 26): distress (v. 6), cry for help (v. 7*a*), God hears (v. 7*b*), God delivers (vv. 8-9), Israel celebrates (vv. 10-11).

5. See Norbert Lohfink, S.J., "Von der 'Anawim-Partie' zur 'Kirche der Armen,'" *Bib* 67 (1986): 153-76. He describes German biblical scholarship of the late nineteenth and early twentieth centuries using these psalms to describe a "party" or a "movement" of the poor in ancient Israel. French biblical scholarship tended to spiritualize this movement. Lohfink sees these theories that reflected nineteenth-century European intellectual movements as precursors of the contemporary liberation theologies.

6. Psalm 37:11 promises that the 'ănāwîm "shall inherit the land." Perhaps Jesus had this text in mind when he promised that the meek will inherit the earth (Matt 5:5).

7. Gelin, *The Poor of Yahweh*, 54. In the Septuagint, Pss 9 and 10 appear as a single psalm. There is a similarity and sometimes an identity of expression in both psalms. In addition, the Hebrew text shows traces of an acrostic scheme that embraces both psalms. Psalm 10 lacks a title.

8. Gelin, *The Poor of Yahweh*, 33.

Chapter Six: Apocalyptic Literature

1. W. A. Beardslee, "New Testament Apocalyptic in Recent Interpretation," *Int* 25/4 (1971): 424.

2. John J. Collins, "Introduction: Towards the Morphology of a Genre," *Semeia* 14 (1979): 9.

3. It is likely that the *maśkîlîm* were among the Jewish elite. They were well-educated and served as civil servants in the Diaspora. Though they were not revolutionaries, they were completely loyal to their ancestral religious traditions. See J. J. Collins, "Daniel and His Social World," *Int* 39/2 (1985): 136-37. The *maśkîlîm* attempted to straddle the two worlds in which they found themselves: traditional Judaism and civil service. The stories of Dan 1–6 show that living in both worlds, though difficult, was not impossible.

4. The book of Daniel asserts that the Jewish revolutionaries provided only "a little help" to the community suffering because of Antiochus's persecution. See Dan 11:34.

5. See Peter Schäfer, "The Hellenistic and Maccabean Periods," in *Israelite and Judean History* (ed. J. H. Hayes and J. M. Miller; OTL; Philadelphia, Pa.: Westminster, 1977), 576-95.

6. See Leslie J. Hoppe, "Religion and Politics: Paradigms from Early Judaism," in *Biblical and Theological Reflection on the Challenge of Peace* (ed. J. T. Pawlikowski and D. Senior; Wilmington, Del.: Michael Glazier, 1984), 45-54.

7. The text is taken from John J. Collins, "Sibylline Oracles," in *The Old Testament Pseudepigrapha* (ed. James H. Charlesworth; 2 vols.; Garden City, N.Y.: Doubleday, 1983, 1985), 1:370.

8. Some interpreters hold that the letter of Enoch begins in chapter 91 and concludes with chapter 107. For example, see J. C. VanderKam, *Enoch: A Man for All Generations* (Columbia: University of South Carolina, 1995), 89.

9. The translation of texts from *1 Enoch* taken from that of E. Isaac, "1 (Ethiopic Apocalypse) of Enoch," *OTP* 1:5-89.

10. Geza Vermes, *The Dead Sea Scrolls in English* (Baltimore, Md.: Penguin Books, 1962), 156.

11. *DSSE*, 166. The phrase "well-loved poor" probably reflects the belief of the Qumran people that their lifestyle was a mark that they were God's elect. While they were not destitute, their life in the Judean wilderness contrasted dramatically with the usual manner of life that people lived in the cities of Judah.

12. *DSSE*, 199-200.

13. For example, Bammel, *TDNT* 6:897. K. Schubert, *The Dead Sea Community* (London: Adam and Charles Black, 1959), suggests that the members of the Qumran community practiced voluntary poverty.

14. See Leander E. Keck, "The Poor among the Saints in Jewish Christianity," *ZNW* 56 (1965), 76-77. David Flusser suggests that the use of the term "poor" in the scrolls is fig-

urative. See his "Blessed Are the Poor in Spirit," *IEJ* 10 (1960): 1-13.

15. Denise Dombkowski Hopkins, "The Qumran Community and 1QHodayot: A Reassessment," *RQ* 10 (1981): 363-64.

16. Leslie J. Hoppe, "Prayer and Mission: The *Hodayot* of Qumran," in *Scripture and Prayer* (ed. C. Osiek and D. Senior; Wilmington, Del.: Michael Glazier, 1988), 76-87.

17. The translation is taken from R.B. Wright, "Psalms of Solomon," *OTP* 2:661.

Chapter Seven: The New Testament

1. See F. Hauck, "*ptōchos*," *TDNT* 6:886-87.

2. Glanville Downey, "Who's My Neighbor? The Greek and Roman Answer," *ATR* (1965): 3-15.

3. D. E. Nineham, *St. Mark* (Baltimore, Md.: Penguin, 1963), 334.

4. "The Poor Widow in Mark and Her Poor Rich Readers," in *A Feminist Companion to Mark* (ed. Amy-Jill Levine; Sheffield: Sheffield Academic Press, 2001), 122.

5. There is no consensus about what "in spirit" means. See Leander E. Keck, "Poor," *IDBSup*: 674. The expression is found in the War Rule of Qumran (1QM 14:7). Though membership in the Qumran community involved the acceptance of voluntary poverty, at Qumran the expression likely reflected the community's claim of inclusion among the righteous.

6. Henry J. Cadbury suggests that Luke-Acts appeals to the conscience of people of means. See *The Making of Luke-Acts* (New York: Macmillan, 1927), 263. He is followed by Robert Karris, who admits that Luke's community is made up of both the rich and the poor, but that the Third Gospel is concerned with the problems and concerns of the rich. See "Poor and Rich: The Lukan Sitz im Leben," in *Perspectives on Luke-Acts* (ed. C. H. Talbert; Danville, Va.: Association of Baptist Professors of Religion, 1978), 112-25.

7. Texts unique to Luke: 4:18; 14:13, 21; 16:20, 22; 19:8. Texts from Q: 6:20; 7:22. Texts from Mark: 18:22; 21:3.

8. Paul S. Minear, "Luke's Use of the Birth Stories," in *Studies in Luke-Acts* (ed. L. E. Keck and J.L. Martyn; Nashville: Abingdon Press, 1966), 115.

9. W. D. Davies, *Invitation to the New Testament* (Garden City, N.Y.: Doubleday, 1966), 156.

10. The text of Mary's Song alludes to Judg 5:24; 2 Sam 6:16; 1 Sam 2:1-10; Isa 35:6; 40:9-10, 29-31; 41:8-10, 17-20; 42:1-4, 7; 49:1-7; 50:4-9; 52:13; 53:12; 61:1-3; Mal 3:12; Zeph 3:17; Ps 111:9; and Jdt 13:18.

11. Similar stories are found in Egyptian and rabbinic texts. See Joachim Jeremias, *The Parables of Jesus* (New York: Charles Scribner's Sons, 1963), 183.

12. John E. Stambaugh and David L. Balch, *The New Testament in Its Social Environment* (Philadelphia, Pa.: Westminster, 1986), 71.

13. Addison G. Wright suggests that Jesus could not be pleased when he observed the widow contributing all she had to the temple. Indeed, Jesus' comments on the ultimate destiny of the temple imply that the widow's sacrifice was a waste. See "The Widow's Mites: Praise or Lament?—A Matter of Context," *CBQ* 44 (1982): 261-63.

14. Joseph A. Fitzmyer, S.J., *The Gospel According to Luke I-IX* (AB 28; Garden City, N.Y.: Doubleday, 1981), 250.

15. See Jacques Dupont, O.S.B., "Community of Good in the Early Church," in his *The Salvation of the Gentiles* (New York: Paulist, 1979), 87-91.

16. Joachim Jeremias, *The Eucharistic Words of Jesus* (rev. ed.; New York: Scribner's, 1966), 54.

17. See Robert J. Karris, O.F.M., *Jesus and the Marginalized in St. John's Gospel* (Collegeville, Minn.: Liturgical Press, 1990), 9-12.

18. Karris, *Jesus and the Marginalized*, 42-45.

19. A problem with the Greek syntax of 1 Cor 7:21 has led to the suggestion that a slave need not refuse manumission because of the principle that Paul states. See S. Scott Bartchy, *Mallon Chrēsai: First-Century Slavery and the Interpretation of 1 Corinthians 7:21* (SBLDS 11; Missoula, Mont.: SBL, 1973).

20. Gildas Hamel suggests that the poor of Jerusalem were not necessarily defined by their economic needs. These "poor" spent much time in the temple at prayer and simply entrusted their welfare to designated overseers. Supporting these people was a form of tithing. See *Poverty and Charity in Roman Palestine, First Three Centuries C.E.* (Berkeley: University of California, 1989), 188-89. This suggestion is speculative.

21. See Martin Hengel's discussion of "self-sufficiency" in Greco-Roman culture in *Property and Riches in the Early Church* (Philadelphia, Pa.: Fortress, 1974), 54-59.

Chapter Eight: The Rabbinic Tradition

1. Maurice Simon, trans., *Berakoth* (Hebrew-English Edition of the Babylonian Talmud; ed. I. Epstein; London: The Soncino Press, 1965).

2. Salo W. Baron, *A Social and Religious History of the Jews* (2nd ed.; 18 vols.; New York: Columbia University Press, 1952), 2:164.

3. See Hamel, *Poverty and Charity in Roman Palestine*, 94-163.

4. Herbert Danby, trans., *The Mishnah* (Oxford: Oxford University Press, 1933), 277.

5. H. Freedman, trans., *Kiddushin* (Hebrew-English Edition of the Babylonian Talmud; ed. I. Epstein; London: The Soncino Press, 1966).

6. S. M. Lehrman, trans., *Midrash Rabbah: Exodus* (ed. H. Freedman and Maurice Simon; London: The Soncino Press, 1939), 391.

7. I. Abrahams, trans., *Hagigah* (Hebrew-English Edition of the Babylonian Talmud; ed. I. Epstein; London: The Soncino Press, 1984).

8. See Samuel Safrai, "Tales of the Sages in the Palestinian Tradition and the Babylonian Talmud," in ScrHier 22 (ed. Joseph Heinemann and Dov Noy; Jerusalem: Magnes, 1971), 220-25.

9. Baron, *A Social and Religious History*, 2:241.

10. Hamel, *Poverty and Charity in Roman Palestine*, 205-6.

11. N. Wieder, "The Qumran Sectaries and the Karaites," *JQR* 47 (1956-57): 283-89.

12. Baron, *A Social and Religious History*, 1:281.

13. Danby, *The Mishnah*, 446.

14. See George Foot Moore, *Judaism in the First Centuries of the Christian Era* (3 vols.; New York: Schocken, 1971), 2:174-76.

15. J. Israelstam and Judah J. Slotki, trans., *Midrash Rabbah: Leviticus* (ed. H. Freedman and Maurice Simon; London: The Soncino Press, 1939), 435-36.

16. Martin Hengel, *Property and Riches in the Early Church: Aspects of a Social History of Early Christianity* (Philadelphia, Pa.: Fortress, 1974), 20.

17. Maurice Simon and Israel W. Slotki, trans., *Baba Bathra* (Hebrew-English Edition of the Babylonian Talmud; ed. I. Epstein; London: The Soncino Press, 1976).

Conclusion

1. Gelin, *The Poor of Yahweh*, 26.

2. Gelin, *The Poor of Yahweh*, 113.

SELECT BIBLIOGRAPHY

Amit, Yairah. "The Jubilee Law: An Attempt at Instituting Social Justice." Pages 47-59 in *Justice and Righteousness: Biblical Themes and Their Influence*. JSOTSup 137. Edited by H.G. Revenlow and Y. Hoffman. Sheffield: JSOT Press, 1992.

Barton, John. "Ethics in Isaiah of Jerusalem." *Journal of Theological Studies* 32 (1981): 1-18.

———. "Ethics in the Book of Isaiah." Pages 67-77 in *Writing and Reading the Scroll of Isaiah*. Supplements to Vetus Testamentum 70. Edited by C.C. Boyles and C.A. Evans. Leiden: Brill, 1997.

Berquist, James A. " 'Good News to the Poor': Why Does this Lucan Motif Appear to Run Dry in the Book of Acts?" *Trinity Seminary Review* (Spring 1987): 18-27.

Boerma, Conrad. *The Rich, the Poor and the Bible*. Philadelphia, Pa.: Westminster, 1979.

Coggins, Richard J. "The Old Testament and the Poor." *Expository Times* 99 (1987): 11-14.

Epzstein, Léon. *Social Justice in the Ancient Near East and the People of the Bible*. London: SCM, 1986.

Fensham, F. Charles. "Widow, Orphan and the Poor in Ancient Near Eastern Legal and Wisdom Literature." *Journal of Near Eastern Studies* 21 (1962): 129-39.

Gelin, Albert. *The Poor of Yahweh*. Collegeville, Minn.: Liturgical Press, 1964.

Georgi, Dieter. *Remembering the Poor: The History of Paul's Collection for Jerusalem*. Nashville: Abingdon Press, 1991.

Gillingham, S. "The Poor in the Psalms." *Expository Times* 100 (1988-89): 15-19.

Gillman, John. *Possessions and the Life of Faith: A Reading of Luke-Acts*. Collegeville, Minn.: Liturgical Press, 1991.

Gottwald, Norman. *The Tribes of Yahweh*. Maryknoll, N.Y.: Orbis Books, 1979.

Guinan, Michael D., ed. *Gospel Poverty: Essays in Biblical Theology*. Chicago: Franciscan Herald Press, 1977.

Gutiérrez, Gustavo. *A Theology of Liberation*. Maryknoll, N.Y.: Orbis Books, 1973.

Hamel, Gildas. *Poverty and Charity in Roman Palestine, First Three Centuries C.E.* Berkeley: University of California, 1989.

Hanks, Thomas D. "Poor, Poverty (New Testament)." Pages 414-24 in vol. 5 of *The Anchor Bible Dictionary*. Edited by David Noel Freedman. 6 vols. New York: Doubleday, 1992.

Hengel, Martin. *Property and Riches in the Early Church*. Philadelphia, Pa.: Fortress Press, 1974.

Hobbs T. R. "Reflections on 'the Poor' and the Old Testament." *Expository Times* 100 (1989): 291-94.

Houston, Walter. "The King's Preferential Option for the Poor: Rhetoric, Ideology and Ethics in Psalm 72." *Biblical Interpretation* 7 (1999): 341-67.

Karris, Robert J. *Jesus and the Marginalized in St. John's Gospel*. Collegeville, Minn.: Liturgical Press, 1990.

————. "Poor and Rich: the Lukan Sitz im Leben." Pages 112-25 in *Perspectives on Luke-Acts*. Edited by Charles H. Talbert. Danville, Va.: Association of Baptist Professors of Religion, 1978.

Keck, Leander E. "Poor." Pages 672-75 in *The Interpreter's Dictionary of the Bible: Supplementary Volume*. Edited by K. Crim. Nashville: Abingdon Press, 1976.

Leclerc, Thomas L. *Yahweh Is Exalted in Justice: Solidarity and Conflict in Isaiah*. Minneapolis, Minn.: Fortress, 2001.

Lohfink, Norbert. *Option for the Poor: The Basic Principle of Liberation Theology in Light of the Bible*. Berkeley: BIBAL, 1987.

————. "Von der 'Anawim-Partie' zur 'Kirche der Armen.' " *Biblica* 67 (1986): 153-76.

Malbon, Elizabeth Struthers. "The Poor Widow in Mark and Her Poor Rich Readers." Pages 111-27 in *A Feminist Companion to Mark*. Edited by Amy-Jill Levine. Sheffield: Sheffield Academic Press, 2001.

Malina, Bruce J. "Wealth and Poverty in the New Testament and Its World." *Interpretation* 41 (1987): 354-67.

Maynard-Reid, Pedrito U. *Poverty and Wealth in James*. Maryknoll, N.Y.: Orbis Books, 1987.

Mays, James Luther. "Justice: Perspectives from the Prophetic Tradition." *Interpretation* 37 (1983): 5-17.

Pilgrim, Walter E. *Good News to the Poor: Wealth and Poverty in Luke-Acts*. Minneapolis, Minn.: Augsburg, 1981.

Pixley, Jorge V., and Clodovis Boff. *The Bible, the Church, and the Poor*. Maryknoll, N.Y.: Orbis Books, 1989.

————. "Qoheleth: A Teacher for Our Times." *Currents in Theology and Mission* 26 (1999): 123-35.

Pleins, J. David."Poor, Poverty (Old Testament)." Pages 402-14 in vol. 5 of *The Anchor Bible Dictionary*. Edited by David Noel Freedman. 6 vols. New York: Doubleday, 1992.

————. "Poverty in the Social World of the Wise." *Journal for the Study of the Old Testament* 37 (1987): 61-78.

Redford, D. B. "Studies in Relations between Palestine and Egypt during the First Millennium B.C.: I The Taxation System of Solomon." Pages 141-56 in *Studies in the Ancient Palestinian World*. Edited by J.W. Wevers and D.B. Redford. Toronto: University of Toronto, 1972.

Schottroff, W., and Wolfgang Stegemann. *Jesus and the Hope of the Poor*. Maryknoll, N.Y.: Orbis Books, 1986.

Simon, U. "The Poor Man's Ewe-Lamb: An Example of a Juridical Parable." *Biblica* 48 (1967): 207-42.

Stegemann, Wolfgang. *The Gospel and the Poor*. Philadelphia: Fortress Press, 1984.

Tamez, Elsa. *Faith without Works Is Dead: The Scandalous Message of James*. Bloomington, Ind.: University of Indiana, 1989.

Waldow, H. Eberhard von. "Social Responsibility and Social Structure in Early Israel." *Catholic Biblical Quarterly* 32 (1970): 182-204.

Weinfeld, Moshe. *Social Justice in Ancient Israel and in the Ancient Near East*. Minneapolis, Minn.: Fortress Press, 1995.

Whybray, R. N. *Wealth and Poverty in the Book of Proverbs*. Sheffield: JSOT Press, 1990.

Wright, Addison G. "The Widow's Mites: Praise or Lament?—A Matter of Context." *Catholic Biblical Quarterly* 44 (1982): 261-63.

Scripture Index

DATE DUE